3-28

PUBLIC POLICY STUDIES IN AMERICAN GOVERNMENT

Edgar Litt, General Editor

PUBLIC
HOUSING
The Politics
of Poverty

PUBLIC HOUSING
The Politics of Poverty

LEONARD FREEDMAN
University of California at Los Angeles

HOLT, RINEHART AND WINSTON, INC.

New York   Chicago   San Francisco   Atlanta
Dallas   Montreal   Toronto   London   Sydney

Foreword to the Series

A series denoted to the consequences of American public policy ought, at the outset, to indicate why it came into being. What has been lacking in the scholarly literature is overt analysis of the political consequences of policy on human institutions and the life style of human beings themselves. A review of the literature convinced the editor, and his colleagues who are to contribute to the series, that the vast analytical skills of political scientists have for too long been directed at the "input" side of politics, the ways in which policy is fashioned or administered out of the mélange of groups competing for public favor. Scholars have studied the behavior of organized interest groups, the calculations of administrative and policy experts, and the meaning of concrete policies for the totality of the political system itself. Yet, in an era where federal policies themselves are major sources of impact and of innovations on society, it is crucial that the scope of our inquiries not be restricted.

The scholar's responsibility extends to an evaluation of policy forming agencies in terms of clear and realistic values and to an evaluation of the impact of policy "outputs" on the social system. Such responsibility has been asserted by one critical voice in the present epoch in this way:

> Of basic importance is the modern redefinition of "politics." No longer does the term refer to the promotion of justice or the search for the best organization of social life. The term now refers to "who gets what, when, how" or to some similar concept, which focuses not on justice but on power. This focus makes political science more quantifiable and political scientists more pliable and useful for the powers that be. At the same time it severs the study of politics from any direct bearing on the task of developing institutions and organizations in the service of human needs.[1]

The volumes in this series will raise this issue for the distribution of power in the American society, the civil liberties of the individual in times of immense governmental control, the quality of personal and political education received by black and white Americans, and the distribution of housing and other social goods in our urban centers. In our view, this perspective best accounts for the processes and quality of our political life. Moreover, these studies build on the intellectual tradition of public policy exploration that has importantly contributed to the maturation of the field of political science itself.

Storrs, Connecticut   E. L.

---

[1]Christian Bay, "The Cheerful Science of Dismal Politics," in Theodore Roszak (ed.), *The Dissenting Academy* (New York: Pantheon, 1967), p. 3.

jected in several other cities as well. Moreover, there was persistent opposition at the national level, too. Congress, after passing a major housing act in 1949 which called for a substantial expansion of public housing, made drastic reductions in appropriations for the program after 1951. Consequently, a housing program that was scheduled for completion by 1955 or 1956 has still not been fully implemented to this day.

These facts led me to undertake a broad study of the reasons why the public housing program has had such a difficult time in America. This study became my doctoral dissertation, which was completed in 1959 at UCLA under the title "Group Opposition to Public Housing."

Since 1959 the situation has changed in a direction favorable to public housing, and the housing programs have been given a considerable boost by the housing legislation of 1968. Yet, the public housing program is still generally unloved. It has grown, but the pace has been slow, and alternative programs have had to be developed to provide the full response to the low-income housing problem, which could no longer be entrusted to public housing alone. And these programs have had to be carefully constructed to overcome the basic difficulty that undermined public housing—the profound weakness of the poor in the American system of government and politics.

The present book takes this last concept as its major concern. The legislative process and the interest-group struggle over public housing receive due attention in this study, for there is no better example than the public housing case of obstructionism by legislatures and harrassment by interest groups. But even more serious problems facing the housing program are to be found in certain attributes of our political culture—attitudes on poverty, on race, and on public ownership. In examining how these attitudes were articulated in the public housing conflict from the inception of the programs to the present time, we may glean some significant insights for a number of areas of contemporary public policy.

As this book was going to press a decision was announced that makes it likely that the controversy over public housing, which had been relatively subdued during most of the 1960s, may again become heated during the 1970s. On July 1, 1969, Federal District Judge Richard B. Austin ordered the Chicago Housing Authority to build 75 percent of all new public housing projects in predominately white communities and at least one mile from the edge of the nearest black ghetto; to limit future projects to no more than three stories, and to avoid clearing project sites with the aldermen of the wards involved. The problem to which this decision was addressed—the existence of enormous, high-rise projects, confined within the ghettos, housing only black families—is discussed in Chapter 4 of this volume. It will be clear from what is said there that the court decision alone will not dispose of the problem, and that difficulties will presist even if there are similar decisions in other cities and if all these are fully backed by the federal government. The outraged reactions to the decision by white homeowners and their political representatives were depressingly reminiscent of the attacks on public housing during the 1950s, and where evidence of the prospect that public housing will again be caught up in the deep antagonisms of the American city.

The sources for this study include government publications, correspondence from organizational files, articles from the popular press, scholarly works, and literature from groups on both sides of the public housing issue. For the inquiring reader who may wish to pursue a personal investigation, the bibliography at the end of the book should prove to be a useful list of sources for ideas examined herein. Personal interviews were also conducted by the author with congressmen and their staffs, with representatives of the various interest groups involved in the issue in Washington, and with people engaged for and against public housing in major cities, such as Los Angeles, Chicago, New York, Seattle, Birmingham, and Newark, as well as smaller communities in all regions of the country. The interviews were supplemented with a considerable amount of personal correspondence.

I am indebted to many people for help given me in preparing this study. I am particularly grateful to the editor of this Public Policy series, Edgar Litt, whose suggestions and criticisms were enormously helpful, not only in detail, but also in basic conceptualization; to Bruce Ricks of the UCLA Graduate School of Business Administration, who read the manuscript and made a number of important suggestions and corrections; to Anne Bodenheimer and Anthony Imada for research assistance; and to Magdalen Suzuki, who skillfully executed the tasks of checking references and typing the manuscript.

Los Angeles, California   L. F.
July 1969

Contents

PUBLIC HOUSING

The Politics of Poverty

Introduction

In July of 1949 the 81st Congress passed, and President Truman signed, a major housing act.[1] This act declared as an objective of public policy "the realization as soon as feasible of the goal of a decent home and a suitable living environment for every American family." To achieve this ambitious purpose, several kinds of programs were included in the provisions of the act.[2] Among

[1] Public Law 171, 63 Stat. 413 (1949).

[2] The main provisions of the act were:

Title I   slum clearance, community development and redevelopment. This empowered local public agencies, after a public hearing, to acquire a blighted area, clear the land and make it available for public or private redevelopment. The Housing and Home Finance Agency was authorized to make loans or grants—$1 billion in loans and $500 million in capital grants—to meet losses involved in slum clearance. Families displaced must be properly relocated.

Title II   amendments relating to the Federal Housing Administration.

these was a program of low-rent public housing—government-owned housing for the poor. Authorization was given to complete 810,000 public housing units within six years. That schedule was soon abandoned. After six years barely 200,000 units were completed and the total had not reached 300,000 by 1960.[3] Twenty years later the six-year goal set in 1949 has still not quite been reached. True, the program is still alive and, spurred by fresh authorizations in the 1965 and 1968 housing acts, is growing significantly. But this should not obscure the fact that for several years public housing was the object of bitter dissension both in Washington and in communities around the country. Yet, on the face of it, the existence of so much controversy is surprising. For one thing, there was hardly anything new or innovative about the 1949 legislation. The history of public housing goes back to the New Deal's Public Works Administration, whose housing division constructed over 21,000 units by November 1937.[4] Then came the Wagner-Steagall Act of 1937, which established the United States Housing Authority, empowered to make construction loans

---

Title III　low-rent public housing (amendments to the 1937 housing act).

Title IV　housing research by HHFA to promote cost reductions and increased production; incentives to localities to do their own studies for redevelopment, etc.

Title V　farm housing—special loans for home or building improvements.

Title VI　(a) a national housing census to be taken in 1950 and every ten years thereafter; (b) banking provisions; (c) provision for public housing in Washington, D.C.

[3]Completion figures from *The Housing Yearbook, 1963* [Washington, D.C.: The National Housing Conference, 1963], p. 71, were as follows:

1948	1202	1953	58,214	1958	15,472
1949	267	1954	44,293	1959	21,832
1950	1023	1955	20,899	1960	16,401
1951	9994	1956	11,993		
1952	58,258	1957	10,513		

Not until the late 1960s did the figures surpass those of 1952 and 1953. Production from September 1967 to September 1968 was almost 75,000, double the previous year's rate. However, this was not all new public housing; some of the units were leased from private landlords, others rehabilitated, under provisions of the 1965 housing act.

[4]U.S. Housing and Home Finance Agency, *17th Annual Report* (Washington, D.C.: Government Printing Office, 1963), p. 275.

to specially created local housing authorities and to provide subsidies ("annual contributions") to the housing authorities to keep the rents at levels the poor could afford. Under the 1937 housing act, 114,000 units of low-rent public housing were built in 361 projects.[5] World War II brought a massive program of government housing construction for war workers. Much of this was temporary housing, but there were also more than 170,000 new permanent units, some of which were absorbed into the regular public housing program after the war.[6]

Thus, there was nothing remarkable about the plan to build low-rent public housing under the 1949 act. The scale was larger than before: There was to be a revolving fund of $1.5 billion, from which local housing-authority construction loans could be made and guaranteed by the Public Housing Administration,[7] and annual contributions of up to $336,000,000 were authorized. Yet, even with the additional 810,000 units this would finance, the public housing program in the United States would still be quite small in comparison with similar programs elsewhere. The governments of most industrialized nations have provided housing for large numbers of the working class for several decades. In the United Kingdom, approximately one out of every five households occupies a rental unit owned by local government agencies and subsidized by the national government. The programs in France, Holland, and Scandinavia are also much larger proportionately than our own.[8] Each of these countries has been responding to the fact that the private housing industry has been unable to provide a decent living environment for the poor. The same fact is true of the United States. A great many low-income people live in deplorable housing conditions. The Census figures provide abundant evidence of this, and even the most cursory inspection of the dismaying blight at the center of so many of our cities confirms the statistical data. What the Census calls "substandard" housing includes homes that, at best, lack the amenities that

[5] Housing and Home Finance Agency, *15th Annual Report*, 1961, p. 210.

[6] Housing and Home Finance Agency, *15th Annual Report*, 1961, p. 210.

[7] The successor to the United States Housing Authority and the wartime Federal Public Housing Authority.

[8] Glenn H. Beyer, *Housing and Society* (New York: Crowell-Collier and Macmillan, Inc., 1965), pp. 517–524.

Americans regard as indispensable and, at worst, are damp, decaying, crowded, and verminous. Millions of people lived in such conditions in 1949, and millions still do today.

This is why the 1949 public housing proposals attracted powerful conservative as well as liberal support. Indeed, the legislation is known as the Taft-Ellender-Wagner Act, for its sponsorship brought together in the Senate Robert A. Taft, the perennial candidate of the conservative Republicans against the men of the Eastern Establishment; Allen J. Ellender, Southern segregationist, but New Deal supporter; and Robert F. Wagner, one of the great names of big-city liberalism. Here, then, it might be thought, was a clear consensus in favor of action to remedy a pressing social evil. The action proposed was merely an extension of a well-established program, and one in which America was far behind most other countries of the Western world.

Yet the passing of the 1949 act proved to be the signal for the eruption of an intense and punishing conflict over the implementation of its public housing sections. Conflict is not unusual in American legislative politics, but this was dissension of an unusually furious and persistent nature. Why was this so? Why has public housing, despite the auspicious characteristics mentioned, become enmeshed in such controversy and been developed so haltingly in the United States?

As the answers to these questions are explored in the course of this book, it will become apparent that no single explanation of the troubles of public housing is adequate. The housing program has faced a combination of unfavorable political and social factors. These factors have been divided into two categories, the first relating to the governmental and political system; the second, to the general climate of opinion.

THE GOVERNMENTAL AND POLITICAL SYSTEM

Obstructions in the Legislative Process

The impediments strewn throughout the American legislative process have been described many times. Perhaps no system in the world is as richly endowed as our own with barriers to the advancement of new proposals. While some kinds of needs—spending on rivers and harbors, for example—are able to take the hurdles easily in stride, innovation in federally supported welfare programs is notoriously difficult.

The public housing case offers an exceptionally comprehensive example of vulnerability to legislative harassment. If one were to undertake a simulation exercise designed to uncover all the possible points at which a program might encounter opposition, something very much like the public housing struggle would emerge. The program was faced by hostile forces at well-nigh every stage in the legislative system, national and local, where decisions have to be made.

It is true that there are other cases in which the initial legislative struggle has lasted longer. Federal aid to education and Medicare each took about twenty years to get on the statute books as against five years for the Taft-Ellender-Wagner Act. But the housing act's travails were worse in two important respects: First, while the battle to pass the public housing clauses of the act was hard-fought, the real struggle did not begin until *after* the act was passed. It was then that the program came up against what Robert Bendiner has called the "obstacle course on Capitol Hill,"[9] made up in this case of the Appropriations, Rules, and standing committees of the House of Representatives, the membership of the House as a whole, and conference committees with the Senate. Year after year the conflict continued in Washington, inflicting fearful damage on the program. Moreover, congressional resistance bought time until a change in the presidency undermined a vital source of support for public housing. The election of Eisenhower confirmed irretrievably the program's lost momentum. There was some expansion again under Kennedy and Johnson, together with important improvements in the quality of the program. But it was too late ever to recapture the vision of 1949.

Even this does not convey the full scope of the conflict that engulfed public housing. The 1949 legislation required that housing projects must be operated locally; legislative and administrative action must be taken in each community requesting public housing allocations. As a result, bitter campaigns, sometimes dominating the local political scene for a considerable period, were fought in Los Angeles and Chicago, Seattle and Akron, Houston and Miami, Portland and St. Petersburg, as well as in

Robert Bendiner, *Obstacle Course on Capitol Hill* (New York: McGraw-Hill, Inc., 1964).

many other cities. The campaigns were initiated at one or more of a series of stages in the local legislative and administrative process; and if the program survived challenges at various points in city-council procedures, it might still have to face a full-scale confrontation in a referendum. Public housing did not lose all these battles at all these stages, of course, but it suffered enough defeats not only to limit or kill the program in particular cities, but also to undermine the position of its advocates in Washington.

Hence, the campaign against public housing was the more effective for being conducted both nationally and locally at the same time. Setbacks in the communities could be used to reinforce the resistance in Washington; and drastic congressional cutbacks assured that the public housing forces in the communities would not be left with very much to fight for.

The Effectiveness of Hostile Interest Groups

Arrayed against public housing was a coalition of groups peculiarly well equipped to take advantage of the opportunities for obstruction provided by the legislative process. The private housing organizations, particularly the realtors, the home builders, and the savings and loan leagues, were singled out by a congressional committee investigating lobbying practices in 1950 as being especially skillful and resourceful in their pressure tactics.[10] For one thing, they employed able, experienced staffs in Washington who knew how to move around in the labyrinthine windings of the legislative process. With party leadership relatively weak, congressional power is fragmented; determined, nationally organized groups who know what they want and persist in trying to get it are in a good position to benefit from the diffusion of legislative authority. Facing a system that contains innumerable "points of access,"[11] the private housing groups have known at what points and at what times they must apply their pressure.

Even more important, the structure of the private housing organizations enabled them to seize upon the most characteristic

---

[10]U.S. Congress, House of Representatives, *General Interim Report of the House Select Committee on Lobbying Activities*, H.R. Rept. 3138, 81st Cong., 2d sess., 1950, p. 24.

[11]See David B. Truman, *The Governmental Process* (New York: Alfred A. Knopf, 1951).

feature of the congressman's behavior—his tendency to respond to influences from his home district. It happened to be the case that each of the private housing organizations, while maintaining a national structure, was made up of local units that wielded considerable influence in most of the communities where new public housing projects were proposed. This made it possible for the anti-public housing groups both to coordinate local pressures on Congress and to play an important supporting role in many of the local campaigns.

Of course, there were groups on the pro-housing side, and the coalition of forces defending public housing used many of the same techniques as their opponents, often with considerable success. Obviously, the opposition forces did not have everything their own way, for a good deal of public housing legislation has been passed. Even so, the preponderance of organizational skill, money, and zeal was clearly on the opposition side during the critical years of the struggle, and this was an important factor in the ordeal to which public housing was subjected.

THE CLIMATE OF IDEAS AND ATTITUDES

The general political and cultural climate in the country is always a critically important factor for social welfare legislation. In the case of public housing the prevailing climate was usually uncongenial, for the program ran counter to widely held views about the poor, about the black American, and about the role of government.

Public Housing Is for the Poor Only

The fact that the majority in America are relatively affluent represents an extraordinary achievement that is true of no other major industrial state. But the consequence of this for the minority who are still poor is to reduce them to a state of political weakness and isolation. The general attitude of the majority appears to be somewhat impatient toward those who have been left behind economically. Some obligation to the poor is recognized; but legislation to carry out this obligation has not been enthusiastically welcomed, except where the majority, too, have some stake in the legislation.

This broad consideration has been reinforced in the housing context by two factors. First, the majority by and large are not badly housed. Despite many obvious inadequacies, the fact is that "the people of the United States have more housing space per person and better equipped housing than do the people of other countries."[12] Since the majority have managed—ostensibly by their own efforts[13]—to obtain good housing for their families, they have displayed little sympathy with those who must turn to government to provide it for them.

Second, the majority have preferred to live at a comfortable distance from the poor. As soon as they could, they have moved to the suburbs, leaving the city centers to the low-income groups. But after the enactment of the Taft-Ellender-Wagner Act, the program's administrators in some cities began looking for sites outside of the poverty areas, adjacent to or even within more prosperous neighborhoods. This aroused deep resentments, for it threatened to nullify the success of the middle or lower-middle class in escaping from the poor. It would bring close to them large numbers of people afflicted with the culture of poverty and concentrated into large, unattractive blocks of apartments. The reaction, not surprisingly, was often fearful and angry, replete with anxious forebodings about damage to the quality of school systems, to property values, and to personal status.

Public Housing Includes a High Proportion of Black Tenants

The resentments and anxieties that public housing aroused in the hearts of many suburbanites stemmed not only from class and income differentiation. Race exacerbated the problem. The poor include a considerably disproportionate number of blacks and other ethnic minorities. Moreover, even when blacks earn enough money to be able to afford better housing, they are often denied the opportunity through discrimination. Inevitably, then, public housing tenants included a large and growing number of blacks. As their numbers increased, the housing projects became less attractive to low-income whites, many of whom moved out to be replaced by more blacks. So public housing projects, already

[12]Martin Meyerson, Barbara Terrett, and William L. C. Wheaton, *Housing, People, and Cities* (New York: McGraw-Hill, Inc., 1962), p. 3.

[13]Most people are able conveniently to ignore the massive federal role in middle-income housing. See Chapter 5.

segregated by class, became citadels of segregation by race. And as this happened, the attitudes of the white, affluent majority grew even less sympathetic to the program and even more resistant to allowing new projects into their neighborhoods.

Thus, racial tensions and prejudices have played a major role in the public housing controversy, and the public housing program continues to illustrate all too well the dilemmas contained in the growing racial confrontation in our cities.

Public Housing Runs Counter to Persisting Strands of Ideology

It has been argued that in our economic affairs we are close to "the end of ideology."[14] But if ideology is dying, its death throes in the case of public housing have been prolonged and convulsive. Most of the overt charges against the program were cast in ideological language. Public housing, it was alleged, was socialism and, as such, antithetical to the American way. The argument has a certain salience. Even though government regulation and subsidization are an integral part of the economy, there is not a great deal of direct government ownership; and public housing *is* owned by government. While this was probably not the primary factor in shaping the general public attitude toward public housing, it served to inspire the remarkable fervor with which the private housing groups attacked the program.

Of greater significance was another aspect of the American creed—the deep attachment to the notion of home ownership. A very high proportion of families in the United States own their own homes, and this has become the root of a whole range of attitudes with important ideological overtones. It has particular relevance to public housing, for it ties in directly with the prevailing opinions about the poor. Most of the poor, in urban areas at least, do not own their homes. And this again has been seen as part of their failure. Because of their inability to become property owners, they are viewed as tenants of the state, whose rents must be subsidized out of the taxes of the solid, thrifty, homeowning majority. Consequently, several of the recent proposals for rehousing the poor have placed heavy emphasis on ways of helping low-income people to become home owners.

[14]Daniel Bell, *The End of Ideology,* new rev. ed. (New York: Collier Books, 1962).

The factors included above under the governmental and political system will be elaborated in Part I of this book; those that make up the climate of opinion are the subject of Part II. It will be suggested that, while Part I contains some extremely important considerations, the central thesis of this study is contained in Part II. This thesis is that the American governmental and political system has been weighted heavily *against* the interests of the poor.

It is true that the unique characteristics of the American governmental structure would in themselves have been sufficient to present serious problems for public housing. Few proposals can emerge unscathed from the process of congressional scrutiny. Similarly, the program would have suffered less havoc if hostile interest groups had not enjoyed such ready access to the decision points proliferated throughout the system.

Just the same, if these had been the only difficulties, the program might well have surmounted the inevitable delays and harassments and eventually have achieved impressive stature. This has been the case with Medicare legislation, for example, despite the long and tortuous road it had to travel. More than most other programs, however, public housing suffers from the fact that it serves only the poor. This has magnified each of the obstructions defined in Part I into an immensely formidable barrier. For among the poor, there is a low incidence of voting and political activism, and, as previously indicated, the poor tend to be viewed with some disfavor by the majority. Consequently, a program whose clientele consists exclusively of the poor is likely to be treated with little enthusiasm by Congress and to be an easy prey for well-organized hostile interest groups.

Moreover, in treating the public housing program harshly, congressmen and lobbyists could claim that they were simply expressing the wishes of the majority of the people. This runs counter to some journalistic commentaries which have contended that the will of the people, as declared in the 1949 housing act, was subverted by special interests conspiring to bend the system to their private purposes.[15] As is made clear in Part I of this book, there were indeed powerful special interests, and they did succeed to a considerable extent in thwarting the policies of the

---

[15]See, for example, Karl Schriftgiesser, *The Lobbyists* (Boston: Little, Brown & Company, 1951), chap. 14.

Taft-Ellender-Wagner Act. But the elements analyzed in Part II indicate that this outcome was probably not inconsistent with the wishes of the majority. This cannot be proved conclusively, but available evidence suggests strongly that, while most people did not care deeply one way or the other, the general inclination was toward a scaling down of the proposals of 1949. Of course, this interpretation is even more baneful to the interests of the poor than the muckraker's view. If the majority will has been denied, sooner or later it might reassert itself. But if the issue was handled in a way that was broadly responsive to the wishes of the majority, then the prospects for the poor would seem to be especially dismal.

While the public housing case reveals the weakness of the poor in the American system, it does not follow from this that their cause is hopeless. There are redeeming features even in the public housing conflict. The program, after all, has survived and even continues to expand. If the bruising struggle held back its growth, it also led to some sorely needed improvements in its quality and flexibility. Moreover, the program is but one among many devices now being tried or introduced which could considerably ameliorate the housing plight of the low-income groups.

If the new legislation is fully implemented (and this is by no means assured), it could be symptomatic of a significant shift in the prevailing attitudes toward the poor and of their status in the political system.

There is still a long way to go in this direction, however, and the major events in the public housing controversy described in this book constitute a study in the political powerlessness of the poor in America.

PART I
THE GOVERNMENTAL AND POLITICAL SYSTEM

Chapter 1
The Legislative Process: Protracted Conflict

We have in this country, says James MacGregor Burns, "government by fits and starts,"[1] a system characterized by occasional spurts of energy interrupting long periods of torpor. Whether or not this view has general validity, the public housing case would seem to provide a perfect illustration of Burns's thesis.

In contrast with the housing program's steady growth in other countries, its advancement here has been frequently disrupted, proceeding apace only when a whole series of special circumstances came into play simultaneously. In the absence of any of these exceptional circumstances, support for the program receded, leaving it stranded in a limbo between life and death, until a new conjunction of factors brought another infusion of vitality.

[1]James MacGregor Burns, *The Deadlock of Democracy* (Englewood Cliffs, N.J.: Prentice-Hall, Inc., 1963), p. 2.

Some of the prerequisites for the growth of the program wi
be considered later. In this chapter the focus will be on tho
elements intrinsic to the mechanics of the legislative proces
Specifically, two circumstances proved to be essential. First, the
must be a large Democratic majority in the House of Representa
tives. Even a slight Democratic margin would be usually sufficie
in the Senate—long inclined to be more liberal and more respor
sive to urban interests than the House.[2] But in the House, th
Democratic majority must be large enough to allow for a consid
erable number of defections on the issue.

Second, there must be strong support from the White Hous
On this issue, as on so many others, the vital legislative role of th
modern presidency was fully revealed. This was exemplified fror
the beginnings of the program. Its establishment under WPA wa
an executive branch initiative. Then, when it was proposed i
1935 to provide public housing with a more secure legislativ
framework, the fact that there were more than three times a
many Democrats as Republicans in the House was in itself r
guarantee that the change could be accomplished. Representativ
Henry Steagall of Alabama was chairman of the Banking an
Currency Committee, and he had no use for public housing. So h
prevented any vote on the issue in 1935 or 1936;[3] and in Ju
1937, as the pressure for action in his committee mounted, he le
town to go fishing. Only when the President, defeated on th
Supreme Court battle and seeking a congressional victory, at la
applied pressure to Steagall did the legislation begin to move. Th
1937 housing act carried the names of Wagner and Steagall, i
congressional sponsors, but it would not have reached the statut
books without the application of presidential leadership at ever
major stage of its development.[4] The same considerations wer

[2]"Senators represent whole states, most of which contain at least one majc
urban center. They must therefore be concerned with urban interests, pa
ticularly the activist minorities—labor unions, racial minorities, religou
ethnic groups—that can have a crucial bearing on elections" (John Bibby an
Roger Davidson, *On Capitol Hill* [New York: Holt, Rinehart and Winsto
Inc., 1967], p. 18).

[3]Timothy L. McDonnell, *The Wagner Housing Act* (Chicago: Loyola Un
versity Press, 1957), pp. 113, 210–214.

[4]McDonnell, *The Wagner Housing Act*, pp. 171, 342–343, 359.

to apply in the later battles over the program. Only when strong presidential leadership was exercised and only when the House was Democratic by a very substantial margin would public housing be able to make its way safely through the innumerable hazards which bestrew the legislative arena. And even then success would be achieved tenuously and with the utmost difficulty.

THE NATIONAL SCENE

Precarious Victory: 1945–1949

Toward the end of World War II, the White House had some studies made of postwar housing requirements. These led to Administration support for expansion of the public housing program. Bills were introduced in the House and Senate, and hearings were held in 1945 and 1946. According to one study, the "Wagner-Ellender-Taft Bill might have been adopted almost without controversy in the fall of 1945 or in early 1946";[5] and in fact it did pass the Senate by voice vote in 1946. Whether the House, with a Democratic margin of only 243 to 190, would have acted favorably on the bill so quickly seems questionable. In any case, it did not get out of the House Banking and Currency Committee that year.

Whatever chance there might have been for the legislation in the 79th Congress was, of course, gone when the election returns establishing the 80th Congress came in. Jesse Wolcott, a long-time friend of the private housing groups, became chairman of the House Banking and Currency Committee, and he made it clear that the House would not have time to get to the bill in 1947. Even in the Senate, despite a 7 to 6 favorable vote in the Banking and Currency Committee, the bill did not reach the floor. In 1948 the Taft-Ellender-Wagner Bill did reach the Senate floor and passed by voice vote, but Wolcott—though his own committee turned against him—secured the help of the Rules Committee to

---

[5]Martin Meyerson, Barbara Terrett, and William L. C. Wheaton, *Housing, People, and Cities* (New York: McGraw-Hill, Inc., 1962), pp. 283–284.

bring about the passage of a housing act that made no mention of public housing.[6]

The scene was transformed by the 1948 election. A President who believed in public housing and had used it as a campaign issue was reelected.[7] There were now 263 Democrats to 171 Republicans in the House, and the margin was 54 to 42 in the Senate. All of the key committee chairmen[8] were sympathetically disposed to public housing. Congress had before it the recommendations of three of its committees which had held hearings over a period of four years expressed in 9000 pages of testimony. Each of these committees had endorsed public housing—including a joint committee of the 80th Congress (which Wolcott had proposed as a delaying tactic). In addition, there was the persistent sponsorship, since 1945, by Robert A. Taft and Allen J. Ellender, as well as Robert F. Wagner. It is hardly surprising, then, that the bill in 1949 passed both Banking and Currency Committees easily, and the Senate gave a large majority to the bill on the floor.[9] One obstinate hurdle did intervene in the House, for the Rules Committee voted 7 to 5 against giving clearance to the bill.

[6]Public Law 832, 62 Stat. 1268 (1948). Wolcott's success in defeating President Truman's housing proposals was one of the reasons given by the President for recalling Congress into special session on July 26, 1948. This helped him dramatize his charge that the 80th Congress was a "do-nothing" Congress. Congress' response on housing was to do something—but not very much. Senator Joseph McCarthy introduced a bill similar to Wolcott's, without any public housing, and this was the bill the President signed.

[7]Richard O. Davies, *Housing Reform During the Truman Administration* (Columbia, Mo.: University of Missouri Press, 1966), pp. 95–97. Both the Democratic and Republican party platforms endorsed public housing in 1948, although the Republican statement was lukewarm. (See Kirk H. Porter and Donald Bruce Johnson, *National Party Platforms 1840–1956* [Urbana, Ill.: University of Illinois Press, 1956], pp. 432, 452.)

[8]Maybank in the Senate Banking and Currency Committee, Spence in the House Banking and Currency Committee, and Sabath in the House Rules Committee.

[9]The Senate Banking and Currency Committee reported the bill (*S. 1070*) by a vote of 9 to 3; and on the floor their report was approved with only one insignificant amendment by 57 to 13. Ten of the Senators who voted for the bill in 1949 had been against it in 1948 (only Senator Knowland moved in the opposite direction). (See *Congressional Quarterly Almanac,* V [1949], 278; and *Congressional Record,* XCV, Pt. 4, 81st Cong., 1st sess., April 21, 1949, 4903.)

However, this was no more than a brief nuisance, for the House had passed on its opening day a "21-day rule," enabling the leadership to bypass the Rules Committee. A threat to do precisely this forced the release of the bill to the floor, where it was sustained by 227 to 186.[10] The conference committee reached agreement, their report was approved by both houses by voice vote, and the President signed the Taft-Ellender-Wagner Act triumphantly.

Yet, even in victory there were premonitions of disaster. The Taft-Ellender-Wagner Act was not just a public housing statute. It called for "housing production and related community development sufficient to remedy the serious housing shortage" and to eliminate "substandard and other inadequate housing through the clearance of slums and blighted areas"; and the greater part of these objectives was to be met by aids of various kinds to the private housing industry. These were the provisions which received the most widespread support. Public housing was much less enthusiastically received, as was made clear by the voting on the public housing sections. On three motions to delete public housing entirely, one was defeated by five votes, one by only one vote, and one actually carried by three votes.[11] Thus, it could not be claimed that the will of the majority in the House was being thwarted by an obscurantist and negativist committee structure. On this issue, the Rules Committee was more in tune with the House majority than the Banking and Currency Committee. As the public housing forces celebrated their victory in July of 1949, they could not free themselves of an undertone of anxiety, for their 810,000 units had been approved with reluctance and only by the narrowest of margins.

Still, if some of them suspected that their victory might not be final, they could hardly have predicted the magnitude of the

[10]*Congressional Record*, XCV, Pt. 7, 81st Cong., 1st sess., June 29, 1949, 8677–8678. The House Banking and Currency Committee approved a bill (*H.R. 4009*) that included a figure recommended by President Truman of 1,050,000 units over a seven-year period in place of the earlier Taft-Ellender-Wagner proposal for 500,000 units in five years. The National Public Housing Conference and the American Federation of Labor had asked for 1,000,000 units spread over four years, the Congress of Industrial Organizations for 2,000,000 in four years.

[11]*Congressional Record*, XCV, Pt. 7, 81st Cong., 1st sess., June 29, 1949, 8644, 8667–8668.

trouble that lay ahead. Since 1945 they had fought a prolonged and bitter battle. They had produced their own generation of veterans who could wearily add their experience to the legends of congressional resistance to innovation. But, having at last attained their goal, they still would not be able to rest. On the contrary, the most arduous tribulations must yet be faced, and the battles which had been won must be refought under much less propitious circumstances than had prevailed in 1949.

Roadblock: The House Appropriations Committee

The 1950 congressional election results warned of impending difficulties. The Democratic margin in the House fell to thirty-five, in the Senate to only two. Clearly, "the Truman–Fair Deal influence on Congress had been virtually nullified."[12] Immediately, the 21-day rule was revoked, and in the new House, eight out of the twelve members of the Rules Committee were hostile to public housing.[13]

Still, the opposition had to find an opening. The Taft-Ellender-Wagner Act was already on the books. To repeal the act with its public housing provisions would be well-nigh impossible, for Congress was still organized by Democrats, and Harry Truman was still in the White House.

In such circumstances, the obvious place to attack an enacted program was the Appropriations Committee. As most federal agencies know all too well, authorization by Congress is one thing, appropriation another. This was, in fact, the basis of the opposition strategy. As the London *Economist* explained: "Since the programme requires an annual appropriation, its opponents have since had repeated opportunities of replaying the match."[14] Yet the obvious was not actually so self-evident. The *Economist*'s interpretation overlooks the fact that the 1949 housing act did not, at the time it was passed, appear to place any significant

[12]Congressional Quarterly *Congress and the Nation* (Washington, D.C.: Congressional Quarterly Service, 1965), p. 11.

[13]Even in 1949 the Rules Committee had been hostile to public housing by 7 to 5. By 1951 Representative Lyle of Texas had changed his mind, so the margin was now 8 to 4 against the program.

[14]The London *Economist* (October 29, 1955), p. 391.

power over public housing in the hands of the Appropriations Committees.[15]

A great deal of money was needed, of course, to pay for 135,000 units a year for six years. Yet there were two points at which the arrangements for funding had to be made, and at neither of these did the legislation appear to give more than a perfunctory role to the Appropriations Committees. First, the Public Housing Administration had to secure the short-term financing during project construction, for which it used its power of Treasury borrowing as back-up security for private loans to local housing authorities. This required relatively small sums and no congressional action.[16]

The more substantial need for federal funds resulted from subsidizing the rents of housing project tenants. To keep the rents down, the legislation authorized the Public Housing Administration to make firm and binding commitments to the local housing authorities over periods of not more than forty years. Annual authorizations for this purpose were not to exceed $85,000,000 at first, rising eventually to $336,000,000. This was the basis for long-term contracts between the federal government and the housing authorities. Certainly the Appropriations Committees of Congress would be asked to provide the funds as the demand for them became due annually under the contracts. Yet no discretion seemed to be left to Congress or its committees by the language of the act, which declared that:

> The faith of the United States is solemnly pledged to the payment of all annual contributions contracted for pursuant to this section, and there is hereby authorized to be appropriated in each fiscal year, out of any money in the Treasury not otherwise appropriated, the amounts necessary to provide for such payments.[17]

[15]Warren Jay Vinton, "Representative Smith's Roadblock," *The Housing Yearbook, 1959* (Washington, D.C.: The National Housing Conference, 1959), pp. 13–16.

[16]For long-term financing, the local housing authorities sell their own bonds secured by a pledge of the annual contributions from the federal government.

[17]Section 305(a), amending Section 10(e), United States Housing Act of 1937.

To fiscal conservatives this kind of arrangement represents "back-door financing," which they believe to be inimical to sound budgetary practice and to effective control by Congress. Still, the language was unequivocal, and the Appropriations Committees, when called upon to approve the allocation of funds to subsidize the housing-project rents, could not renege on the solemnly pledged word of the United States.

There was general agreement in 1949 that this was the intent of the act. A statement to realtors from their Washington headquarters conceded the point:

> These amounts, once authorized, are *not* subject to effective annual Congressional review as would be the usual appropriation. (PHA can bypass Congress and demand the money directly from the Treasury.)[18]

It is true that the act allowed for the possibility of variations in the rate of construction and federal subsidization. The annual figure could go up to 200,000 units and down to 50,000 units. But this decision was not supposed to be within the purview of Congress. Only the President, after consultation with the Council of Economic Advisors, had the right to approve such fluctuations; and the target of 810,000 units in six years was to be unaffected by the year-to-year variations.

Despite all this, the House Appropriations Committee succeeded in seizing jurisdiction of the matter in 1951. Once it had done so, the figure of 50,000, which was to be the temporary minimum under the 1949 act, became the maximum; and this maximum was approved in 1951 and never attained again before the late 1960s.

It was the Korean conflict that provided the opening for the Appropriations Committee. On July 8, 1950, President Truman asked the Housing and Home Finance Agency to limit public housing to not more than 30,000 units for July to December, 1950, pending reexamination of the program in the light of the international situation. This was to conserve materials in short

---

[18]Realtors' Washington Committee, "Federal Expenditures and Commitments Under Public Housing Act," Washington, D.C., July 20, 1949 (Mimeographed).

supply and to hold down inflationary pressures.[19] The rate was allowed to pick up again in the first half of 1951, when nearly 60,000 units were started. But with the war dominating national economic decisions, this pace could not be maintained. Again the President imposed a limit: No more than 75,000 units could be put under contract in 1952.

The House Appropriations Committee decided that this was too much. Since there was a war on, since materials were scarce, since inflation was a danger, why not cut still further a program which, by the President's own admission, did not have top priority? So the committee recommended a program of only 50,000 units for fiscal 1951. No significant challenge emerged to the committee's right to become involved.[20] Moreover, when the Independent Offices Appropriations Bill reached the floor, it quickly became apparent that the Appropriations Committee, far from thwarting the will of the congressional majority, was merely providing the membership of the House with an opportunity to express its hostility to public housing. The House voted by a large margin to cut even below the Appropriations Committee's recommendation of 50,000 units to a contemptuous 5000,[21] and it reluctantly accepted the higher figure only after the Senate refused to go below 50,000 in two conference committees.[22]

There was no ambiguity in the Independent Offices Appropriations Act of 1951 concerning its contravention of the previous public housing legislation. The act declared:

[19]The limit was to be imposed not on planning, site acquisition, slum demolition, or architect's work, but at the point where a project was about to be bid. It was estimated that this would result in a 25 percent cutback, since otherwise approximately 40,000 units might have reached the construction stage by the end of the year. (See *Journal of Housing*, VII, no. 8 [1950], 263.)

[20]There were some murmurings from the House Banking and Currency Committee. There (by the test of votes on the floor) the members stood 16 to 11 in favor of public housing in 1951. However, the sixteen in favor were on record only as supporting 50,000 units against proposals to cut still further.

[21]This was on the motion of Representative Gossett of Texas and approved by a vote of 181 to 113. Fourteen of the thirty members of the Appropriations Committee voted for this cut, despite the committee's recommendation of 50,000 units.

[22]The first conference report was rejected by the House, 188 to 186.

> Notwithstanding the provisions of the United States Housing
> Act of 1937, as amended, the Public Housing Authority
> shall not, with respect to projects initiated after March 1,
> 1949, authorize during the fiscal year 1952 the commence-
> ment of construction of in excess of fifty thousand dwelling
> units.[23]

While there was no limitation on future years (the House tried to
set one, but the Senate prevailed in conference), there was no
suggestion that the figure authorized was a temporary recognition
of the national emergency to be compensated for in future years.
The basic housing statute had been altered, and this had been
accomplished by the Appropriations Committee, which is not
ostensibly concerned with substantive legislation. The program
was back in the hands of Congress, contrary to the intention of
the Wagner-Steagall and Taft-Ellender-Wagner Acts.

Yet, the 1951 act was hailed by Raymond Foley, the HHFA
Administrator, as a demonstration that "in two years we have
made immense progress toward thorough acceptance of the doctrine uttered in 1949."[24] And the National Housing Conference,
which had fought over the years for public housing, claimed the
outcome as "one of public housing's greatest victories!"[25] Nothing
could illustrate more vividly the dire straits in which the public
housing cause had so quickly fallen than these triumphant en-
comiums for 50,000 units in place of 135,000.

In retrospect, however, a case can be made for the enthusiasm of 1951. The next year, the Appropriations Committee
moved to cut the program further. The pattern of 1951 was
repeated in 1952, but on an even further diminished scale. To
President Truman's proposal of 75,000 units "as part of the
restrictive policy followed on non-defense housing,"[26] the House
Appropriations Committee countered with a recommendation for
25,000. On the floor, the House approved only 5000 again and

[23]Public Law 137, 65 Stat. 277 (1951).

[24]Speech to the National Housing Conference annual meeting, Washington,
D.C., June 25, 1951; quoted in *Journal of Housing,* VIII, no. 7 (1951), 230.

[25]*Journal of Housing,* VIII, no. 9 (1951), 297.

[26]Annual Budget Message. *Congressional Record,* XCVIII, Pt. 1, 82d Cong.,
2d sess., January 21, 1952, 345.

gave way before the Senate's insistence in conference to a compromise figure of 35,000.[27]

Two more years were to pass before Congress acted on the feeling expressed by Senator Maybank that the Banking and Currency Committees ought to "reassert its jurisdiction over housing [matters]."[28] In those two years, the House Appropriations Committee was to become even more virulently hostile to public housing than it had been in 1951 and 1952. But 1951 and 1952 were the crucial years of its intervention, for they provided time for other factors to come into play, factors which—operating from a different direction—would bring about a further deterioration in the health of the public housing program.

The Eisenhower Years

Whatever the travails of public housing before November 1952, there was always the hope that presidential power, however reduced, might provide some protection against the ravages of its foes in Congress. This thin hope was gone with the election of Dwight D. Eisenhower. While he had said nothing specifically on the issue during the campaign, public housing supporters scanned his past statements and anxiously noted such comments as: "If all Americans want is security, then they can go to prison. They'll have enough to eat, a bed and a roof over their heads."[29]

Very quickly there was more concrete reason for apprehension than vague surmises based on past statements of general philosophy. The new President appointed Albert M. Cole as the new Housing and Home Finance Agency Administrator. Cole, from Kansas, had served four terms in the House since 1944 and was a member of the Banking and Currency Committee when he was defeated in 1952. In Congress, not only had Cole voted consistently against public housing, he was one of its most aggressive opponents. During the 1949 floor debate, he had offered two amendments to limit the program, propounded several of the

[27]The Senate had asked for 45,000 units.

[28]*New York Times* (April 5, 1954), pp. L–1, L–16.

[29]"The Next President—Where He Stands on Public Housing," *Architectural Forum*, XCVI, no. 6 (1952), 137. The 1952 Republican platform said nothing about public housing.

standard anti-public housing arguments, and had declared that "government control of the individual family life, the individual home, the individual—this threat may become so strong as to strangle the people of America."[30] So he cast his vote against the program in 1949, and in 1951 and 1952 he supported the moves to reduce it to only 5000 units.

The appointment of Cole caused consternation in the pro-public housing camp. The poacher had become gamekeeper. The bitterest opponents of public housing in Congress had sent one of their number to capture the command post of the program. At the same time, they had become the dominant force in Congress itself, for both houses of the 83d Congress were organized by the Republicans,[31] and to defeat public housing, it was no longer even necessary to rely on the conservative Republican–Southern Democratic coalition which had dealt so harshly with the program in the 82d Congress.[32] Now, all the centers of power in the House were controlled by declared enemies of public housing, and each of the key committees had clear majorities hostile to the program.[33] The result was that in 1953 there would have been no appropriation for public housing at all had not the Senate, after a

[30]*Congressional Record*, XCV, Pt. 6, 81st Cong., 1st sess., June 22, 1949, 8151–8152.

[31]In the House the lineup was 221 Republicans to 213 Democrats; in the Senate, 48 Republicans to 47 Democrats.

[32]In 1949 a key vote on a June 29 motion to delete public housing showed 184 Democrats and twenty-four Republicans for the program, sixty-four Democrats and 140 Republicans against it. In 1951, a test vote on May 4 revealed ninety-six Democrats and seventeen Republicans supporting 50,000 units of public housing, fifty-eight Democrats and 123 Republicans voting to reduce the program to 5000 units. The anti-public housing alliance in the 82d Congress was made up essentially of conservative (but non-Taftian) Republicans (there were almost monolithic blocks of nay votes from Iowa, Kansas, Maine, and Nebraska), and Southern Democrats (especially from Mississippi, South Carolina, Virginia, and Texas—less so from Alabama, Georgia, and Tennessee).

[33]The House leadership was again that of the 80th Congress—Joseph W. Martin as Speaker; Charles A. Halleck, Majority Leader; Jesse P. Wolcott, chairman of Banking and Currency; Leo E. Allen, Rules chairman; John Taber, Appropriations chairman. Anti-public housing majorities in the committees were 15 to 12 in Banking and Currency, 10 to 2 in Rules, 36 to 14 in Appropriations.

long deadlock, wrung approval for 20,000 units from the House;[34] and in 1954, the House Appropriations Committee succeeded in causing such a hopelessly snarled procedural tangle that no new starts were included in the appropriations bill.[35]

Nonetheless, the program was not quite dead. It survived because it existed, because it is very difficult to eliminate completely any instrumentality which is part of the structure of government and which continues to have a constituency, however attenuated that constituency's power may be. Even Albert Cole could not—and indeed, would not—kill it. He had become gamekeeper, not executioner. He was no longer a congressional critic, but head of the agency that was responsible for the administration of public housing. Thus, soon after his appointment, he set to work to bring a measure of reassurance to the program's officials and supporters. In an energetic series of regional "shirt-sleeve conferences," he met with people working in the housing field, both public and private. He approached these meetings, he said, with "certain ideas and beliefs" but with "an open mind." He explained that he had voted against the Taft-Ellender-Wagner Bill in 1949 because it was "defective in some respects and could not satisfactorily accomplish all the purposes ascribed to it"; but while he still had a number of reservations, "under the present demands on local resources, I do not see how in most cities housing for such families can be provided in sufficient quantities

[34]President Eisenhower proposed 35,000 units. The House Appropriations Committee recommended no public housing at all, and its position was upheld on the floor by 245 to 157. Only the Senate's fight for 35,000 units and the holding of two conferences produced the compromise of 20,000.

[35]The Administration proposed a four-year program of 35,000 units a year. This was endorsed by the Senate after its Banking and Currency Committee (Republican leadership and all) had called for a resumption of the full program legislated in 1949. But then the House Banking and Currency Committee, entering the field for the first time since 1949, recommended no public housing. This was upheld on the floor, and only vigorous pressure by the Senate spokesmen in the conference committee produced a final authorization of 35,000 units for *one* year. Next, the House Appropriations Committee, obstinately insisting on its right to intervene, called for a still lower figure. This caused the profound confusion which resulted in no new starts being included in the 1954 appropriations act. (See Congressional Quarterly, *Housing a Nation* [Washington, D.C.: Congressional Quarterly Service, 1966], p. 30.)

without some subsidy from the federal government."[36] Low-income housing, he said, if fitted into a total program of redevelopment and if commanding citizen approval, was an essential part of the Eisenhower administration's program.

It was difficult for Mr. Cole's old allies in the fight against public housing to believe that he had to such a degree succumbed to the Establishment line. Representative Curtis of Missouri explained it away as a temporary aberration:

> The reason Mr. Cole testified as he did—he naturally is the head of the organization which is the public housing organization—he testified as the people in his office put the matter before him, and that is the reason he was acting, I would say, in his titular capacity. After Mr. Cole gets an opportunity to dig into this program and get rid of some of these advisors, he will be able to come up with his own ideas and his own program.[37]

Cole did come up with his own ideas. They did not embrace anything like the full Taft-Ellender-Wagner program, but they were not as antipathetic to public housing as Representative Curtis hoped. Cole responded somewhat sheepishly to the taunts of Democrats on the Banking and Currency Committee on his change of heart.[38] He insisted that basically he had not changed his views: "I am not in favor of socialized housing, I mean I am not in favor of the Government building and subsidizing housing for people who can afford to own their houses and to rent their houses. . . ."[39] His argument, in essence, was that public housing was necessary and acceptable—and, therefore, not "socialized housing"—so long as it was on a small enough scale and within carefully circumscribed conditions. In this approach Cole was

[36]*Journal of Housing,* X, no. 3 (1953), 77; and X, no. 10 (1953), 367–369. See also National Housing Conference, *Newsletter* (July 15, 1953) (Mimeographed).

[37]*Congressional Record,* XCIX, Pt. 3, 83d Cong., 1st sess., April 21, 1953, 3513.

[38]"I do not know whether you are enjoying the probing of my mind and conscience or not . . . but I think it is a proper question" (U.S. Congress, House of Representatives, Banking and Currency Committee, *Housing Act of 1954, Hearings* on H.R. 7839, 83d Cong., 2d sess., 1954, p. 135; hereinafter referred to as: House, *Hearings, Housing Act of 1954*).

[39]House, *Hearings, Housing Act of 1954,* p. 135.

supported on the one hand by the President and on the other by the new Public Housing Administration Commissioner, Charles E. Slusser.

Slusser, too, had to face allegations that he was hostile to public housing. By profession he was a realtor. He had been mayor of Akron, where public housing had lost in a referendum. But he denied any antagonism to the program. He favored some changes, he said, but he had not been recommended for the job by Senator Taft "for the purpose of liquidating the low-rent public housing program. I am going to fight for it."[40] Actually, Taft had been unhappy about the appointment of Cole; but he felt that, from the public housing point of view, the important appointment was that of Commissioner of Public Housing, and that Slusser would work to strengthen the program.

The first tangible indication of the Administration's support for the program was a recommendation by the President for 35,000 units for 1953. This was to be on a "marking-time basis," pending a new high-level study of all federal housing programs. That study was undertaken in 1953 by a President's Advisory Committee on Housing Policies and Programs. When the report of the committee appeared in December, it included the statement: "We recommend continuation of the public housing program for low-income families as contained in the Housing Act of 1949,"[41] the number of units to be determined by the Administration and Congress.

---

[40]Quoted in *Journal of Housing*, X, no. 10 (1953), 388. See also "Who's Who in U.S. Housing Agencies," *The Housing Yearbook, 1954* (Washington, D. C.: The National Housing Conference, 1954), p. 58: "I believe that public housing is the best tool we have for rehabilitating the slums of America and the people who live there."

[41]President's Advisory Committee on Government Housing Policies and Programs, *Recommendations on Government Housing Policies and Programs* (Washington, D.C.: Government Printing Office, 1953), p. 261. Membership in the committee was fairly heavily weighted in favor of private building, financing, and real estate interests. However, there was a public housing subcommittee in which the interests of both sides were well represented. The committee's recommendations included the use of existing structures, with rehabilitation if necessary, for public housing; lower densities and scattered sites; designs conforming to local patterns; and more attention to the low-income aged. Except for the emphasis on the aged, not much was done about these recommendations during the Eisenhower years; but all were pursued by the Kennedy and Johnson administrations.

The Administration's response was another proposal for 35,-000 units for 1954. When the Appropriations Committee's intervention cut off the supply of funds for that year, the President came back the next year with a recommendation for 35,000 units a year for two years. This faced difficulties again in Congress, despite the fact that the Democrats were once again in control,[42] and despite the Senate's vote for a return to the full schedule of 135,000 a year proposed in 1949. Wolcott, though no longer a committee chairman, fought a delaying action through the Rules Committee, receiving the cooperation of its new chairman, Judge Howard W. Smith. When Wolcott proposed an amendment on the floor to delete public housing, the House supported him against the recommendation of the Banking and Currency Committee. Only the Senate's obduracy produced an agreement finally on 45,000 units for one year.

This was a significant gain, but it was for one year only. And the single-year appropriations presented an acute problem for the Public Housing Administration. They had to work out contracts and help arrange short-term and long-term financing with a large number of local government authorities all over the country. These arrangements were subject to local political pressures and to modification or even cancellation if a city council or the electorate turned against the program. Sites had to be purchased, community facilities provided, zoning laws changed, building permits approved, construction contracted for and pursued through its many stages. The process was long and intricate. It called for predictability; but from 1951 through 1954 the House Appropriations Committee had made everything unpredictable. It required an even flow of negotiation and administration; and this was ruled out by the annual reconsideration of the program in Congress and by PHA staff cuts imposed by slashes in appropriations. The program moved along spasmodically. Few congressmen were clear as to precisely how many units of public housing were at what stages of development. Every congressional hearing was characterized by bemused questions to the PHA staff concerning how much public housing was "in the pipeline"; and if the figure was substantial, critics would demand to know why, with so many

[42]At the beginning of the 84th Congress, there were 232 Democrats and 203 Republicans in the House; forty-eight Democrats and forty-seven Republicans in the Senate.

dwellings authorized but not yet completed, any additional number need be approved by Congress.

This recurrent administrative agony was at last eased by the 1956 housing act, which provided for 35,000 units a year for two years. Inevitably this did not come easily. After the Senate had again called for a return to the full 1949 act, and the House Banking and Currency Committee had urged the construction of 50,000 units a year for three years, Wolcott again talked with Judge Smith and the Rules Committee voted to table the bill. Only intense pressure from the Administration succeeded finally in persuading the Rules Committee to relinquish its hold on the bill, and the Eisenhower two-year program was accepted by both houses.

Thus, the worst fears of the public housing forces that the Eisenhower administration would destroy the program completely were not realized, and there was even a clear improvement in the status of the program after 1954. It could be argued that Eisenhower, simply by administering the program and recommending funds for it, had given it a bipartisan legitimacy, so that it would never again be viewed as merely a New Deal, Fair Deal measure.

Nonetheless, the Eisenhower years gave the public housing supporters little enough cause for rejoicing. For one thing, the program's growth was on a scale drastically reduced from the Taft-Ellender-Wagner proposals. The Administration success in 1956 was in behalf of a program of 100,000 fewer units a year than the original schedule. Then it transpired that the 1956 act, far from establishing a new plateau from which further advances might be made, became a peak from which President Eisenhower preferred to descend. By the middle of his second term, he was "displaying his increasing judgment that the Federal government should recede from activity in many fields,"[43] and it became clear that public housing was one of those fields. His 1959 housing proposals contained no provision whatever for public housing. It is true that this position was strongly challenged by a new Congress in which the Democrats again had a majority even larger than that which had prevailed in 1949.[44] But this established only

---

[43] Congressional Quarterly, *Congress and the Nation*, p. 490.

[44] The 1958 elections sent to the House 283 Democrats and 154 Republicans; and in the Senate, Democrats outnumbered Republicans by 66 to 34.

one of the two conditions necessary for strong legislative action or public housing. Without Administration support, even the most enthusiastic congressional backing could not do a great deal for the program. Congress did succeed in forcing the Administration to accept 37,000 units in 1959,[45] but the Administration, helped by the House Rules Committee, prevented any further authorization for 1960.[46] So by 1960, less than one-quarter of the program proposed in 1949 had been completed; from 1955 through 1960 there was no year in which public housing units completed exceeded 22,000; and, since building costs had risen sharply, it would now be impossible to complete anything like the 810,000 units with the funds authorized in 1949.

Moreover, the Eisenhower approach was to make public housing a minor appendage of other government housing programs. Thus, the President picked up a recommendation of the 1953 advisory committee that public housing be utilized as "relocation housing for families displaced through urban redevelopment, rehabilitation, and law-enforcement programs."[47] This was only one of the advisory committee's suggestions on public housing, but to the Eisenhower administration it became the fundamental tenet. Hence, in 1954 the Administration proposed that public housing be built only in communities where it was needed to relocate families displaced by slum clearance, urban renewal or other governmental programs. Of course, public housing advocates had always argued that the program should be an integral part of total community plans for slum clearance and redevelopment. But in the form in which the idea was expressed in the 1954 act, it proved to be another roadblock. Under the 1954 bill

---

[45]The President exercised two vetoes of the 1959 housing bill, complaining that it would authorize 190,000 more units, though 100,000 already authorized units had not been completed.

[46]The Senate, after rejecting a proposal for another 37,000 units, supported by 42 to 39 a proposal for 25,000 units. The House Banking and Currency Committee included no provision for public housing; but fear that the Senate's proposal might prevail in conference prompted the Rules Committee to hold up the housing bill in its entirety. The "stop-gap" bill that emerged in the session following the national party conventions of 1960 was devoid of references to public housing.

[47]President's Advisory Committee on Government Housing Policies and Programs, p. 261.

complained Senator Herbert Lehman, "you cannot have public housing unless you have slum clearance. Chances are you cannot get a slum clearance project in much less than two years, whereas the authority for public housing runs out in one year."[48] More latitude was provided in the 1955 Administration proposals, and the requirement criticized by Senator Lehman was expunged by Congress in the 1955 act. Still, the Administration's attitude that public housing was a necessary evil, acceptable only in small doses as a consequence of the dislocation caused by other programs, persisted throughout the Eisenhower years.

Finally, the Administration's attitude toward public housing from 1953 through 1960 was rigid and unimaginative. Several of the proposals of the 1953 advisory committee pointed toward a more flexible, variegated program. None of these was picked up by the Administration. Under the direction of Cole and Slusser the operational watchwords for public housing were "economy" and "efficiency." There must be no frills, and embellishments in the form of social services must be kept to a minimum. There were indications of change when Bruce Savage succeeded Slusser as Public Housing Commissioner. Savage, though a realtor by background, brought to the PHA interesting and lively ideas on design, management, and welfare policies.[49] However, his tenure did not begin until early in 1960, so he proved to be a lame duck appointee. When Eisenhower left the White House, the public housing program was alive but small, sterile, and widely unpopular.

Modest Revival: The Kennedy Program

Efforts to revitalize the enfeebled program were undertaken after the inauguration of John F. Kennedy. The President was sympathetic to the program, and while the new Congress contained fewer Democrats than its predecessor,[50] the margin in the House was almost the same as that of the vintage year of 1949. Thus, the conditions were present for a new advance for public housing. The President proposed 100,000 additional units of pub-

[48]*Congressional Record,* C, Pt. 9, 83d Cong., 2d sess., July 28, 1954, 12373.

[49]*Journal of Housing,* XIX, no. 8 (1962), 431, 443.

[50]The Democratic majority in the 87th Congress was 263 to 174 in the House and 64 to 36 in the Senate.

lic housing.[51] On the floor of the House, a proposal to delete public housing was defeated by 168 to 141, so there was still considerable opposition to public housing within Congress. However, by this time public housing was a secondary issue in the debates on housing policy.[52] Altogether, in fact, the passage of the 1961 act took only thirteen weeks, a far cry from the marathon struggles of the 1940s and 1950s.

Nor was the Kennedy contribution to public housing limited to the surge of new construction. The 1961 legislation made some useful changes in the program. For example, the elderly could qualify more easily, and a small amount of money was made available for experimentation with new methods for providing housing for low-income families. More important, President Kennedy appointed to the top administrative posts governing the program people whose record included a long association with public housing. This was true of Robert C. Weaver, the new HHFA Administrator.[53] And if public housing was no longer Weaver's primary interest, it emphatically was the central concern of the incoming Public Housing Commissioner, Marie C. McGuire. Mrs. McGuire had had nineteen years of experience in public housing, many of them as Executive Director of the Housing Authority of San Antonio, Texas. Under Mrs. McGuire the word went out from Washington within days of the passing of the 1961 act that the old ways were to be reexamined—and sometimes abandoned. Innovations were proposed and carried through in such areas as housing project design, the acquisition of rehabilitated housing, the leasing of rooming houses, and cooperation

[51]The Kennedy proposal as approved authorized construction of enough public housing units to bring annual federal contributions up to the full $336 million approved in the 1949 act—an amount never achieved because Congress had not authorized enough units since 1949. The new expenditures would add an estimated 100,000 units. It would use up the funds authorized in 1949—but rising costs had long ruled out the possibility of constructing 810,000 units with the 1949 authorization.

[52]Most of the controversy over the 1961 act revolved around section 221(d)(3), a proposal for no-down-payment sales and rental housing for moderate- to low-income families.

[53]Weaver had been a consultant to the Public Works Administration Housing Division, special assistant to United States Housing Authority Administrator Nathan Straus; and a member of the New York City Housing and Redevelopment Board.

with private builders; and services were expanded through collaboration with other federal agencies.

New Approaches: The Johnson Program

The newly favorable atmosphere for public housing did not end with the death of President Kennedy. Lyndon Johnson had always been a champion of better housing for the poor. Indeed, one of the first public housing projects built under the 1937 housing act was located in his congressional district.[54]

By 1964 all of the 100,000 units authorized in 1961 were under contract, and there was need for new legislation. Though the "bare-bones" legislation of 1964 merely contained interim provision for 37,500 additional units of public housing,[55] by 1965 the President was ready to move beyond this. His 1965 message on housing was placed in the larger contexts of full-scale urban development[56] and of the War on Poverty. "We hope to achieve," said the President, "a large increase of homes for low- and moderate-income families—those in greatest need of assistance—through an array of old and new instruments designed to work together toward a single goal."[57] This "array of old and new instruments" proved to be an assemblage of the ideas put forward by President Eisenhower's 1953 advisory committee; by a variety of friendly (and unfriendly) critics of public housing from the

[54]Johnson, then Congressman from Texas, was photographed visiting the forty-unit Santa Rita Court in Austin, which opened on June 24, 1939. He "was instrumental in bringing into being" this project. (See *Journal of Housing,* XIX, no. 8 [1962], 444.)

[55]Public Law 88–635. There was also an authorization of $5 million for low-cost housing demonstration projects, and $1,250,000 appropriated for 1965. Other provisions called for relocation payments for those displaced by public housing projects; a special annual subsidy of $120 to displaced families and the elderly who could not afford public housing rents; and making single low-income displacees eligible for public housing and for the special subsidy.

[56]The President's proposal to establish a Department of Housing and Urban Development was accepted by the 89th Congress.

[57]The President's housing and urban development message to Congress, "Message on the Cities," March 2, 1965. (See *Public Papers of the Presidents of the United States* [Washington, D.C.: Office of the *Federal Register,* National Archives and Records Service, 1966], Lyndon B. Johnson, 1965, p. 231.)

late 1950s; by a report by Ernest M. Fisher of Columbia University on housing policy, commissioned by the Eisenhower administration and delivered to HHFA in 1960;[58] and by the new leadership at HHFA and PHA.

Public housing was to receive a sizable boost: an additional 60,000 units a year for four years. Of these, 35,000 were to be new units and 25,000 were to be existing units purchased from private owners and, if necessary, rehabilitated to meet the standards of the low-rent public program. The four-year program was designed to bypass the hazard of the Appropriations Committee, and has succeeded in so doing.[59] Furthermore, a number of provisions of the legislation served to make the public housing program into a much more flexible, imaginative tool for rehousing the poor than it had ever been before.

The acceptance of this program by Congress could hardly be in question: The President had been elected by an overwhelming majority, the Democratic margins in both House and Senate had not been matched since 1936,[60] and almost everything the President was proposing was being accepted by Congress. The request for 60,000 units a year for four years was endorsed—35,000 new units, 15,000 units to be purchased from private owners, and 10,000 units to be leased from owners for low-rent use. The leasing provision represented the only significant amendment to the Administration's proposals. It came from Representative Widnall and the Republican minority on the Banking and Currency Committee, and its acceptance smoothed the path of the public housing proposals generally.[61] In the Senate Banking and Curren-

[58]Ernest M. Fisher, *A Study of Housing Programs and Policies* (Washington, D.C.: Housing and Home Finance Agency, January 1960). Dr. Fisher's recommendations included a "balanced inventory" of publicly assisted housing—balanced and varied by age, size, height, family size, and ownership.

[59]There was a little grumbling about this in committee, but without effect. (U.S. Congress, House of Representatives, Banking and Currency sub-committee, *Housing and Urban Development Act of 1965, Hearings on H. R. 5840 and Related Bills,* 89th Cong., 1st sess., 1965, Pt. 1, p. 267; hereinafter referred to as: House, *Hearings, Housing and Urban Development Act of 1965.*)

[60]The Democratic majority in the 89th Congress was 295 to 140 in the House, and 68 to 32 in the Senate.

[61]Similarly, the Public Housing Administration did not resist Senator Tower's amendment to permit tenants to purchase public housing units.

cy Committee, Chairman A. Willis Robertson filed a statement opposing the public housing provisions. But even Senator Tower of Texas would not support him, and spoke of public housing as one of "several meritorious programs" in the bill.[62]

Applications for the new units came flooding in from all around the country, as they had after the passage of the 1949 and 1961 acts. 1966 proved to be the second biggest year in public housing history, and within two years of the passage of the 1965 bill all of the 240,000 units were applied for. Moreover, the old problems about the blockages in the pipeline had been largely resolved. The long-range planning made possible by the 1961 and 1965 housing acts, and the vigorous administration of the PHA since 1961, at last produced a steady flow of activity. The series of legislative convulsions over public housing at last appeared to be over, and the administrators could get on with their job.

There was still more favorable action from Congress in 1968. Despite the reduction of the Democratic margin in the House to 248 to 187, the recurrent outbreaks of violence in the cities and the growing militance of the poverty movement produced a remarkable degree of congressional receptivity to the President's new low-income housing proposals. The 1968 Housing and Urban Development Act went considerably farther than the 1965 legislation in providing for the expansion of established programs and the introduction of new concepts for housing the poor. Included in the authorizations was $400 million for public housing, enough for 395,000 units in three years—75,000 in fiscal 1969, 130,000 in 1970, and 190,000 in 1971.

Moreover, after 1966 the administrators of public housing were working within a framework more supportive of their purposes than ever before. They were part not of an agency but of a full-fledged Cabinet Department of Housing and Urban Development. Replacing the Public Housing Administration was a more

---

[62] U.S. Congress, Senate, Banking and Currency Committee, *Housing and Urban Development Act of 1965,* S. Rept. 378, 89th Cong., 1st sess., 1965, p. 99. However, this has to be seen in the context of Senator Tower's hostility to rent supplements (see this book, Chapter 3). Tower also proposed an amendment that would instruct the Housing Administrator to undertake a study of the public housing program with a view to strengthening it or establishing an alternative approach giving an increased role to private enterprise. The amendment was accepted by the Senate but did not survive the conference committee.

broadly based Housing Assistance Administration, which would be in a better position than its predecessor to coordinate the various elements involved in rehousing the poor.[63]

THE LOCAL SCENE

The torment inflicted on the public housing forces in Washington was an ordeal over a long period of time, with the Appropriation and Rules Committees taking the lead in the attack on the program until a new, less sympathetic regime controlled the White House. Surcease came eventually only when, twelve years after the enactment of the Taft-Ellender-Wagner Act, an administration once again favorably disposed to public housing came to office.

But this account tells only part of the story of public housing's tribulations. There was a spatial as well as a temporal dimension. The crucial decisions on the program must be made not only in Washington but also in every community in which it might be located. This was pointed out by the opposition groups as soon as they had lost in 1949. "We are bloody but unbowed," wrote Calvin Snyder of the National Association of Real Estate Boards to the local units of the organization. "The fight has just begun. The authorization of this gigantic multibillion dollar program has been issued by the Congress. The completion of the program is another thing."[64] And the first points of contact for the renewed struggle must be in the communities. "The scene of battle will now shift from the national level to the local and State level. . . . Hell," Snyder concluded, "we haven't begun to fight."

The Shift from Federal Control

The basis for the new opportunities for opposition was to be found in the provisions of the 1937 Wagner-Steagall Act, which

[63]Robert C. Wood and Dwight A. Ink, "Organization of the Department of Housing and Urban Development," *Journal of Housing,* XXIV, no. (1967), 145–150.

[64]U.S. Congress, House of Representatives, House Select Committee on Lobbying Activities, *Housing Lobby, Hearings Pursuant to H.R. 298,* 81st Cong. 2d sess., 1950, Exhibit 349, p. 947; hereinafter referred to as: House, *Hearings, Housing Lobby.*

were carried forward into the 1949 act. Before the 1937 act the program, established under the Public Works Administration Housing Division, had been more or less free from local control. The decisions came from Washington, and they were made personally by the administrator of PWA, Harold Ickes.[65] This was one of the reasons why the public housing forces moved to establish a new framework in the 1937 act in which there would be less dominance from Washington. A long-range, large-scale program, operating in many different communities, could not hope to survive the Ickes style, effective though it was in directing the PWA crash projects. It would be stultifying administratively and damaging politically, for the programs would need a degree of community support that was unlikely to be forthcoming for projects that would be viewed as federal installations, their tenants in the position of wards of the national government.

In addition, the power of the PWA Housing Division to use eminent domain was challenged in the courts and the rulings went against PWA.[66] This caused PWA to encourage the formation of local housing authorities which could handle land acquisition under authorization from the state. After 1937 this became the standard approach.

Under the new dispensation, the federal government would still control the funds, and thus the right by contract to approve site selections, rentals, plans, and costs, and to establish the broad principles under which the housing projects would operate. However, the 1937 and 1949 acts vested the planning, construction, administration, and ownership in local housing authorities. Nothing could happen until state laws were passed allowing such local

---

[65]It was said of Ickes that "no project was approved, no contract let unless his sign appeared on the approving document. Never was this sign a mere rubber stamp. . . . With full responsibility for all the complex and exacting affairs of one of the largest regular Government departments, and the tremendous pressure of conducting the PWA program, the Administrator still found time to scrutinize with minute care every detail of the Housing Division's operations" (Michael W. Strauss and Talbot Wegg, *Housing Comes of Age* [New York: Oxford University Press, 1938], p. 122).

[66]U.S. v. Certain Lands in City of Louisville, Jefferson County, Ky. *et al.*, 78 F. 2d 64 (1935); U.S. v. Certain Lands in City of Detroit *et al.*, 12 F. Supp. 345 (1935); In the Matter of the Acquisition of All Privately Owned Land in the City of Washington, District of Columbia, 63 Wash. Law Rep. 822 (1935).

agencies to be established and until a formal request for funds was submitted to Washington by the local housing authorities. Nor could a program get under way without the signing of a "cooperation agreement" between the local housing authority and the municipal government exempting the housing authority from local taxes, and insuring the availability to public housing projects of necessary public services and facilities.

It was this requirement of initiation and then operation by community agencies, demanded and achieved by the public housing forces, that was to open the way for the local attacks on the program. Had the administration of the program continued to be controlled solely from Washington, it could have been attacked only in Washington. However, this could hardly have been foreseen in the 1930s, and even if it had, the administrative, political, and legal arguments for decentralization could not have been resisted.

In the aftermath of the 1937 act, the opportunities for local resistance were used only in a few, scattered cases and then in desultory fashion. The determined effort to beat the program in the cities followed the Taft-Ellender-Wagner Act. If this were to be successful, the opposition would have to move quickly, for the passage of the 1949 act triggered eager responses from many parts of the country.

The States

It was too late in most cases to do very much about stopping the program at the first of the stages which controlled local action—state legislation. This was a source of considerable chagrin to the opposition. The states must be involved in passing the enabling legislation governing the creation of local housing authorities, as well as in providing the tax exemption required under the act. And the state legislatures, dominated in so many cases by rural interests and susceptible to the blandishments of skilled lobbyists, might have seemed a particularly suitable arena in which to launch a counterattack against a program that appealed largely (though by no means entirely)[67] to urban areas.

[67]"More than 80 percent of all localities for which active reservations have been approved under the Housing Act of 1949 have populations of less than 25,000" (Housing and Home Finance Agency, *17th Annual Report* [Washington, D.C.: Government Printing Office, 1963], p. 277).

As the pro-public housing National Housing Conference pointed out to its members:

> In many legislatures, urban populations are grossly underrepresented. So far, rural public housing is not widely enough known to impress legislators where rural interests predominate.[68]

Attempts were indeed made to stop the program at the state level. There was a hard-fought battle in the Maine Senate, for example, and only the casting vote of the President of the Senate brought approval for the program.[69] However, Maine was the forty-second state to pass the enabling legislation. The problem for the opposition was that most of the states had already taken action while the 1937 program was relatively noncontroversial. Thus, it was the opposition forces which had to take the initiative and overcome the obstacles of the legislative process. Sometimes these can be as formidable at the state level as in Congress, and it was the defenders of public housing who could use the complex parliamentary machinery to ward off threats to their cause. The National Housing Conference advised its members:

> Right now, your job is to get those booby-trap bills smothered in committees, before they get out on the floor for a vote. In some cases, we are told, the only hope is to defeat them in committee.[70]

If the bills survived the committees of one house, there was another house with its committees to work on. And if this, too, endorsed the opposition's bills undoing state public housing legislation, a governor might be ready with his veto.

Consequently, the private housing groups did not push very hard in most places for repeal of the state laws which made possible local action on public housing. They did try one other

[68]National Housing Conference, *Newsletter* (February 19, 1951) (Mimeographed).

[69]"State News" *Journal of Housing,* VI, no. 6 (1949), 183.

[70]National Housing Conference, *Newsletter* (February 19, 1951) (Mimeographed).

tactic at the state level, however. This was to promote further legislation that would make harassment of the program easier at the community level. Thus, it would serve the opposition's purposes well if local referenda could be required by state law before a program could be implemented in a community. Such proposals were accepted by the Legislatures of Nebraska and Texas.[71] A similar idea was put to the voters of California in a statewide referendum in 1950, and it was approved by a narrow margin. These victories were to have considerable significance later, leading to a large number of referendum battles, in many of which public housing lost. However, no other state accepted this proposal. It was rejected in Pennsylvania and New Jersey; and though bills requiring local housing referenda passed the Illinois Legislature in 1951, Governor Adlai Stevenson vetoed them.

It quickly became clear to the opposition forces that they must concentrate at the local, not the state, level. The states had already acted; and by March 1950, 473 applications for new public housing programs had been sent to Washington by housing authorities in thirty-eight states, the District of Columbia, Puerto Rico, and the Virgin Islands. By the same date, 123 cooperation agreements had been entered into between municipalities and local housing authorities, and these encompassed a total of over 100,000 units.

It is true that under the cautious leadership of Raymond M. Foley, the Housing and Home Finance Agency and the Public Housing Administration were moving very slowly in their handling of local applications.[72] Nonetheless, the momentum was gathering, and if it were not to become irreversible, the opposition must attack immediately at the sources of the demand—the local communities.

[71]Results of votes in state legislatures, city councils, and referenda referred to in this chapter are listed in the *Journal of Housing* for the periods in question; in the *Congressional Record*, XCVIII, Pt. 2, 82d Cong., 2d sess. March 20, 1952, 2632; and in "Some Examples of Successful Opposition to Socialized Public Housing" by the National Association of Real Estate Boards, 1965 (Mimeographed).

[72]"His general attitude is reflected in the fact that the PHA did not even have ready the forms necessary for the local authorities to make application for public housing funds until December of 1949" (Davies, *Housing Reform During the Truman Administration*, p. 130).

The Cities

The first efforts to defeat public housing locally were applied n the city councils, and at that point several successes were rapidly chieved by the opposition. By 1951 more than thirty municipalies had voted against the program, the greater number being in California, Texas, Arizona, Illinois, Michigan, and New Jersey.[73] Here and there, too, a mayor vetoed favorable city-council acion.[74]

Where the city councils would not reject public housing utright, challenges could still be made at each of the specific teps which must be taken to implement the program. Beyond the nitial decision for or against public housing, the program needed .pproval by the municipality at each of a number of legislative .nd administrative steps. These were drawn to the attention of its nembers by the National Association of Home Builders:

> There are several strategic points at which you can drag public housing out into the open and rally public support against it. These points are the very steps through which every public housing project must go. If you know these steps—if you watch for them—if you take action when they are about to occur—you will have an excellent chance to stop socialized public housing projects in their inception. . . Hit the public housing program in your city at each of these steps.[75]

However, there were no large cities among these. South Bend, Tucson, Amarillo, and Portland, Maine, were the largest communities in which city ouncils rejected public housing during this period. And challenges to the rogram were turned back in the city councils of Dallas, Jacksonville, Milvaukee, and Little Rock, among other cities.

In Detroit, Mayor Cobo's dislike of public housing and especially of rojects on vacant sites, led to the abandonment of several of the sites recommended by the Detroit Housing Commission. In Bay City, Michigan, he mayor vetoed the city commission's 7 to 2 approval of a cooperation greement on public housing, then persuaded two commissioners to switch, o that the resulting 5 to 4 vote was not enough to override his veto. (See *Journal of Housing,* VII, no. 3 [1950], 80, and VIII, no. 6 [1951], 195.)

National Association of Home Builders, "The Ten Basic Steps of Public Housing," Washington, D.C., 1949 (Mimeographed), p. 1.

The required procedures included applying to the Public Housing Administration for a preliminary loan to cover the cost of project planning; signing a cooperation agreement between housing authority and city council, which entailed the waiving of taxes on the projects; selecting sites; approving building and zoning permits and the vacating of streets; arranging construction loans and permanent financing; selecting the tenants; setting the rents; demolishing an equivalent number of slum units.

Not all of these actually provided useful occasions to harass the programs. The 1949 law allowed five years for equivalent slum demolition, so the construction of projects could not be delayed on this account. The Home Builders Association expressed the hope that the program could be slowed down "if banks, institutions and individuals would refuse to buy these bonds" on the grounds that "such participation is not in the interest of private enterprise."[76] But, of course, few private investors are swayed by such ideological pleas, and the housing issues were judged, like municipal bonds in general, by the criteria of the financial market.

Other points in the procedure were more useful to the opposition. There were court tests of preliminary loan applications and of cooperation agreements. While the cases were all settled in favor of the program,[77] they enabled the opposition to force delays in construction. Even questions which appeared to be within the administrative discretion of the housing authorities, such as tenant selection and the setting of rents, were made matters of public debate as the opposition used them in their efforts to influence the city councils. Then, more formidable than any of these as a hurdle in the path of the program was the stage of site selection. Once this point was reached the debate moved away from generalities and turned to matters directly affecting the character of communities and neighborhoods. The potency of this factor was demonstrated in Chicago. There was no difficulty in getting Chicago's aldermen to accept the need for public housing in general terms. But they became locked in conflict for more

[76]National Association of Home Builders, "The Ten Basic Steps of Public Housing," p. 3.

[77]See, for example, Pontiac Tax Payers Association and Donaldson, a Taxpayer v. City of Pontiac et al., Circ. Ct. Co. Oakland, Mich., no. 25316 (October 4, 1949); Blumenschein v. Housing Authority of the City of Pittsburgh, 379 Pa. 566 (1954).

than two years over the question of where the housing projects were to be located. Similarly, Detroit, Philadelphia, and other major cities endorsed the principle of public housing, then ran into difficulties in selecting suitable sites.

Where, at every stage of action by local government officials the opposition failed to stop public housing, one final recourse might still remain. In a number of cities the referendum made it possible to go over the heads of the elected representatives to the people themselves.

The usefulness of this device was demonstrated soon after the enactment of the Taft-Ellender-Wagner Act, for public housing was successfully challenged by referendum in Grand Rapids and St. Petersburg in 1949. Then, in 1950, came a major setback for the program in a referendum in Seattle. There, the city council took favorable action on the program on a 7 to 2 vote, and resisted the opposition's request for the matter to be submitted to the electorate at the next election. So petitions were circulated to place the issue on the ballot, and in the ensuing referendum public housing was defeated by a margin approaching 2 to 1. Next, the city council of Portland, Oregon, at the urging of an overconfident housing authority, sought to head off opposition by themselves setting up a referendum—which they lost. In St. Joseph, Missouri, the mayor vetoed the council's approval of public housing; the council overrode the mayor's veto; a referendum was forced, and the program was beaten. During 1950 and 1951, public housing received other referendum setbacks in Racine, Madison, Flint, Kenosha, Houston, Lubbock, Tucson, East Orange, and a number of smaller communities. In 1952 the program was rejected in Akron and, the biggest blow of all, in Los Angeles.

The Los Angeles struggle calls for special comment here not only because it was the biggest city in which public housing was repudiated by direct vote of the people, but also because it presents the most remarkable illustration of the manner in which the American legislative process offers innumerable points for the making and remaking of decisions, until the original decision is either countermanded or seriously diluted.

Los Angeles

Almost every point at which public policy is made in the American system was involved at some stage of the conflict over public housing in Los Angeles. Briefly stated these were as follows:

The City Council   In August 1949 the city council *unanimously* approved a cooperation agreement with the city housing authority for an application for 10,000 units of public housing on sites to be selected by the housing authority. Then, as the opposition campaign developed and intensified, council support for the program began to slip. In June 1951 some proposed sites were approved, but only by 10 to 5. Municipal elections (though not fought on the public housing issue) cost the program one more vote, so only two more switches were needed to provide an anti-public housing majority. One came in November 1951 in the person of a councilman who, in June, had been an enthusiastic backer of the program. On December 3, 1951, the determining shift came. The councilman in question, long a friend of labor and a supporter of public housing for many years, had changed his mind, he explained, only after a long night "considering the situation."[78] Henceforth there was a majority of 8 to 7 on the council against public housing. The council then asked the city attorney how it could break the contract it had signed with the Public Housing Administration. The attorney's suggestion was that the city cancel the contracts, and either negotiate a settlement with the city housing authority or leave it to the courts to decide. The council followed this advice and instructed city department heads to cease processing street openings and other steps essential to the advancement of the program.

The Courts   Ever since 1937 the courts had endorsed the legal standing of the program throughout the country. The same was true of the Los Angeles program. The city housing authority, joined by the seven minority members of the city council, filed suit with the California Supreme Court against the cancellation of the contracts, and in April 1952 the court declared:

> It was obviously never assumed, and certainly it was not authorized by law, that after the City Council had declared the need, had given requisite approvals of a project under

---

[78]*Los Angeles Times* (December 4, 1951), Pt. I. pp. 1–2.

State and Federal law, and had undertaken binding commitments, it would or could repudiate them.[79]

It was the court's unanimous decision that the city must comply with the provisions of the cooperation agreement entered into in 1949. In June, the California Supreme Court issued a writ of mandamus ordering the council to get on with the job. When the council procrastinated, holding up necessary action on streets, building and zoning, and other administrative requirements, the housing authority filed contempt proceedings, and the United States Supreme Court refused the city council's petition for a writ of certiorari.

The Referendum   Seeking the broadest possible base of support for its position, the anti-public housing majority on the council ordered that the issue be placed on the ballot for the June 1952 municipal elections. In 1950 there had already been a statewide referendum (Proposition 10) requiring that a local referendum be held before the signing of any future public housing contracts. Proposition 10 had applied only to projects not already authorized, and the Los Angeles City Council, then almost solidly in favor of public housing, had taken action to authorize twelve sites before the proposition could go into effect. Nonetheless, the Los Angeles voters had given a margin of 150,000 to the proposition, without which it would not have carried. Clearly another referendum in 1952 would help anti-public housing in Los Angeles.

By June 1952, however, the procedure contained a serious flaw. The court decision in April meant that the referendum could have no legal effect. The state attorney general declared, and the Los Angeles city attorney conceded, that even if the proposition passed, it would not override the court's decision.

However, the ballots had already been printed, and the State Supreme Court refused to stop the referendum. The dubious legal status of the proposition did not inhibit either side in the conduct of its campaign. Everyone knew that the court had not finally disposed of the matter. On such a crucial question, with the stakes so high, politicians would not abdicate to judges. The issue was certain to appear again in the political arena, and the

[79]City of Los Angeles v. Housing Authority of the City of Los Angeles, 38 Cal. 2d 853 L.A. No. 22211 (1952).

results of an appeal directly to the people would carry great weight in the final political settlement.

The outcome was a resounding defeat for public housing by 379,000 to 258,000. The vote went against public housing in twelve out of the fifteen councilmanic districts. The position of all eight of the councilmen who had voted against the program was endorsed in their districts. Four of the seven public housing supporters found that their constituencies did not agree with their position—in one case by a 2 to 1 margin.

The Mayor Los Angeles has a weak-mayor system of government. On most issues the council has greater influence than the chief executive. Nonetheless, considerable importance attached to the mayor's office in the public housing case. The mayor made the appointments of the housing authority commissioners; he could exercise the power of veto, which could only be overridden by the votes of ten councilmen; he was the city's chief negotiator with Washington when political considerations entered, as they certainly did in the public housing context; and as chief official spokesman for the city, the mayor could have an important influence in the shaping of public opinion.

Until the summer of 1953 the Los Angeles mayor was Fletcher Bowron, who became an ardent protagonist of the program during the late 1940s.[80] When the council went over to the opposition cause, the mayor countered by eliciting a demand from the Public Housing Administration Commissioner for the enforcement of the contract;[81] then Bowron challenged the council's efforts to bypass his veto power by abrogating the contracts by resolution rather than by ordinance.[82] During the referendum

---

[80]Bowron had been unenthusiastic about public housing before the war but became a convert in the postwar period.

[81]If the city tried, said Commissioner Egan, "deliberate and willful abandonment . . . of the projects . . ." it would be sued for the recovery of net expenditures to date of $12,679,952. (See *Los Angeles Times* [December 15, 1951], Pt. I, p. 3.)

[82]The city attorney had given an opinion that the council could cancel the contracts by resolution, and that an ordinance was not necessary. An ordinance was subject to the mayor's veto, and this would take ten council votes to override. But there were only eight votes in the council against public housing. Bowron, therefore, insisted that only an ordinance would suffice; and if the resolution were really an ordinance, then he was vetoing

campaign he was the leading spokesman for the public housing side, holding a television conference every day for a full week to project his position.

From the opposition's point of view, the city's weak-mayor system had produced an uncomfortably strong mayor. So they moved to get rid of him and replace him in 1953 with a man who could be relied upon to oppose public housing. They chose Representative Norris Poulson, a conservative who had voted consistently against the program in Congress since 1948. In the campaign,[83] Bowron, mindful of the 1952 referendum result, tried to keep public attention away from the public housing issue as such. But Poulson kept talking about the issue, and won by 287,000 to 252,000.

Less than a week before leaving office, Bowron, in the face of Poulson's outraged expostulations, filled three vacancies on the housing authority with a prominent Democrat, a labor attorney, and the president of the Greater Los Angeles CIO Council. But this was the last device at his disposal, and henceforth the way was clear for Poulson to conduct the negotiations with Washington that would lead finally to a settlement.

The State Legislature   The California state legislation empowering local government to institute public housing had been passed well before the Los Angeles troubles had started. Still, the statewide referendum in 1950 started the chain of reaction against the program in Los Angeles. And there were ways in which the California Legislature could be brought into the picture to harass the local housing authority. After the Los Angeles referendum defeat in 1952 a committee of the State Assembly came into the city to hold hearings obviously calculated to embarrass the program. Then the State Senate Committee on Un-American Activities began an investigation of alleged Communist party activity in

---

it. Bowron's statement was part of a message to the council, which was reprinted as a pamphlet and widely distributed. (See *Honorable Fletcher Bowron, Mayor of the City of Los Angeles, to the City Council, on the Resolution Rescinding the 10,000 Unit Program of Slum Clearance and Low Rent Housing Passed by the Council December 26, 1951.* [Los Angeles: Citizens' Housing Council of Los Angeles, n.d.].)

[83] In the primary, Poulson led Bowron by more than 30,000 votes, but a run-off was necessary.

the housing authority. Following the mayoralty campaign, bills were introduced in the Legislature to help Los Angeles abandon the uncompleted projects and to give the incoming city administration the power of dismissal without cause over the housing commissioners. The bills passed the Assembly and then a Senate committee. However, they were strenuously resisted and finally beaten on the Senate floor.[84]

Congress   While the struggle was going on in Los Angeles, the House Appropriations Committee and the House of Representatives as a whole were cutting the program back sharply. Thus, it may well be that in any case there would not have been enough money available from Washington to build the full 10,000 units on schedule. Republican congressmen from Los Angeles were among the leaders of the moves to hold the program's appropriations down.

Nor was this the full extent of congressional intervention. During the Bowron-Poulson campaign, the Los Angeles City Council invited Representative Clare Hoffman's Government Operations Committee to come to town to hold televised hearings following up the charges of Communist infiltration into the program which had been introduced by the committees of the state Legislature.

Finally, the Congress was involved in preparing the ground for the final settlement. The 1951 appropriations act had included a provision that would allow a community to break a contract it had signed with PHA, so long as the community settled all the expenses incurred under the contract.[85] The next year, Los Angeles Congressmen Poulson and McDonough tried to insert provisions into the legislation that would let Los Angeles off more lightly, but the 1952 appropriations act said exactly the same thing on the question as the 1951 act. Work on the program continued and the costs mounted. However, after Poulson's election, the House voted for a proposal which Poulson hailed as a

---

[84] The defense in the Senate was led by the AFL and the San Francisco Housing Authority. The opposition was finally able to salvage only two relatively innocuous bills, worked out with the Los Angeles Housing Authority's attorneys. (Interviews by author with staff of Los Angeles City Housing Authority; see also *Journal of Housing*, X, no. 7 [1953], 235.)

[85] Public Law 137, 65 Stat. 277 (1951).

move that "should pave the way for us to get rid of this program
New Deal hangers-on are trying to ram down our throats."[86]
Then Senator Knowland persuaded the Senate to accept a suggestion of his own that committed Congress further to a solution that
would help the opponents of the program in Los Angeles.[87]
Subsequently, Congress readily endorsed the settlement worked
out between the city's representatives and the Administration,
which would charge only a portion of the full costs to the Los
Angeles taxpayers.

The Administration   The PHA tried to hold the city to its
contract as long as it was politically feasible to do so. When public
housing first lost its majority in the council, Public Housing Commissioner Egan threatened that if the contract were broken, the
city would have to pay the net expenditures to date of well over
$12 million. Then when the courts ordered the work to continue
in 1952, PHA advanced an additional $8 million.

In the light of the referendum defeat, however, it was obvious that there must be some reduction of the program, and Mayor
Bowron went to Washington and brought back a compromise
proposal.[88] But, at this point the council was in no mood for
anything short of the end of the program, and the proposal was
rejected.

Compromise became acceptable to the council, paradoxical-
ly, only after the election of Poulson. In large part, this was
because the same election that had made Poulson mayor had also
changed the composition of the city council, and actually had
shifted the majority to 8 to 7 in favor of public housing.[89] Thus,
Poulson had to seek a settlement that would not be totally unacceptable to the housing authority.

[86]Quoted in the *Los Angeles Times* (April 23, 1953), Pt. I, p. 11.

[87]This would allow a grace period of 180 days for the working out of an
agreement between Los Angeles and the federal government. (See *Congressional Record,* XCIX, Pt. 3, 83d Cong., 1st sess., April 22, 1953, 3595.)

[88]This compromise proposal would have reduced the total number of units
from 10,000 to 7000 and would have cut down the size of the hotly disputed Rose Hills project.

[89]The *Los Angeles Times* endorsement was successful in only one of three
districts, (see this book, Chapter 2).

So the new mayor went to Washington and talked there with Albert Cole. There were discussions, too, with Sherman Adams at the White House. The outcome of these and later negotiations was that the two largest, and most controversial, projects were abandoned;[90] and, instead of 10,000 units in eleven projects, there would be 4357 units in nine projects. The Los Angeles City Council approved, 13 to 1.

Settlement "Do you mean to say," asked one councilman incredulously, "that this is the last vote we'll have to make on this public housing issue?"[91] It was not surprising that he found it hard to believe. The battle had dragged on for years, devouring the time and energies of city councilmen, two mayors, the electorate, investigating committees, state and national legislatures, the local housing authority, the PHA, and the HHFA; even the White House had been involved at the end. Moreover, the participation of each of these agencies of government had not followed an orderly sequence. For simplicity of presentation each agency has been treated separately here. In actual fact, a number of them were frequently involved concurrently, each going off in a different direction, causing an almost farcically confused clamor of lawyers, politicians, administrators, and spokesmen for the many interested groups. Rarely can the American political system have enveloped a public issue with such an incredible chaos of arguments and maneuvers.

Nonetheless, eventually the matter was resolved. The *Los Angeles Times,* a major critic of the program, still disliked the very existence of the housing authority, and indicated that "one day, to be sure that we will never be in jeopardy again, we must renew the fight in Sacramento to change the State Housing Code under which the Housing Authority anomaly exists."[92] But this never happened. By the close of 1955 all nine projects containing

---

[90]The Rose Hills and Chavez Ravine sites were eliminated. The federal government agreed to take over the costs already incurred and sell the land to the city. This would result in a deficit of between $5 and $6 million to the federal government.

[91]*Los Angeles Times* (August 7, 1953), Pt. II, p. 4.

[92]*Los Angeles Times* (July 30, 1953), Pt. II, p. 4.

357 units were completed. For Los Angeles, it was the end of the affair.[93]

Summing Up the Local Battles

The rejection of public housing by the Los Angeles electorate was the climax of a series of referendum defeats beginning in 1949. By the end of 1952, the program had been defeated by direct vote of the people in some forty communities. Offsetting this, the supporters of the program could point to only twenty referendum victories.

This record falls considerably short of constituting a clear nationwide rejection of public housing. For one thing, after 1952 the program was upheld in referenda more often than not. From 1953 through 1955 there were but five tests of public housing at the polls, and the opposition won only one of these. There were more challenges in 1956, and subsequently there were periodic bursts of referendum activity, which resulted in important victories for the opposition in Dallas, San Antonio, Stockton, California, and Des Moines. However, public housing was endorsed in more than two out of three of the approximately 150 referenda between 1956 and 1964 (most of them occurring in California, Texas, and Nebraska, the three states requiring a referendum on every public housing proposal).

Then (for reasons to be explored later) the defeats were concentrated on the western seaboard, in Texas, and in the Midwest, with only a handful in the East and the South.

Finally, most of the referendum rejections came in small-[94] or medium-sized cities. In the East and the Southeast, all were of under 100,000 population. In the Midwest, only Akron, Grand Rapids, and Flint comprised communities of over 100,000. Only in the West and Southwest did defeats occur in cities whose population exceeded a third of a million. These were Portland, Seattle, Houston, and Los Angeles. None of the great urban centers of the East and Midwest vetoed public housing by vote of

---

But see Chapter 2 for following discussion of the later controversy over the Chavez Ravine site.

Some were very small indeed. The vote in Southampton, Connecticut, was 2 to 71; and in East Nicolaus, 20 to 26.

the people. In Chicago, efforts to place the issue on the ballot failed and nowhere near the required number of signatures was obtained. In New York City,[95] Pittsburgh,[96] Washington, Baltimore, and Cleveland, public housing was not a source of deep contention.

Thus, the setbacks for public housing at the polls were limited by region and, with few exceptions, by size. It is true that there were actions hostile to the program in several city councils as well as in referenda. However, the city councils of Dallas, Jacksonville, Milwaukee, and Little Rock, among many others, refused to respond to the arguments of the opposition. Also, there were many other communities in which public housing was accepted without any significant challenge. For despite the conflict that raged in Washington and in a considerable number of cities, there were still many places in which these alarms were heard as distant and meaningless murmurings, and the procedures for approving and constructing public housing projects were fulfilled without interference. As time has gone by, more and more communities have come to accept the program as useful and noncontroversial. Since 1961, over five hundred new local housing authorities have been created, bringing the total to over 1500, serving more than two thousand localities. So the storm surrounding public housing in the communities waxed and waned roughly in conjunction with the conflict in Washington; and as the program emerged into a condition of serene acceptance in Congress, so the local attacks dwindled.

When all this is said, however, there is no escaping the national significance of the votes against public housing at the ballot box. There were about 250 referendum challenges from 1949 through 1965, and of these about 40 percent were successful. The larger number of the defeats occurred in the years when the debate in Congress was at its height. The returns from Lo

[95]However, support in the city for state-subsidized public housing declined in the late 1950s, as evidenced by the returns on statewide referendums. In 1949, 84 percent of the city's voters voted affirmatively on the issue. By 1964 the proportion was down to 57 percent with the result that a strongly negative vote upstate took the proposal down to defeat. It was the first defeat on a referendum on the financing of low-rent housing out of the sixteen held since 1938 (*New York Times* [November 5, 1964], p. 1–33).

[96]See Robert K. Brown, *Public Housing in Action: The Record of Pittsburgh* (Ann Arbor, Mich.: University of Pittsburgh Press, 1959).

Angeles, Seattle, Portland, Akron, and other communities were frequently referred to by congressmen hostile to the program.[97] And to the extent that these could be dismissed as localized phenomena, and thus not relevant to the problems of the big Eastern and Midwestern cities, the conflicts over site selection in Chicago, Detroit, and elsewhere pointed in the opposite direction. The referenda and the site battles made it inevitable that some congressmen, not initially hostile to the program, would begin to back away from it. Public housing, it appeared, was all too often a source of trouble and contention. It could split communities in two. There could hardly be many votes to be gained in championing the cause—and perhaps a great many to be lost.

So the local controversies were a significant, if not indispensable, factor in changing the tide of opinion in Congress against public housing. And, as Congress cut back the program's appropriations, the damage this caused was greater than that inflicted by all the local defeats. The 5500 units turned back by Los Angeles, the 1200 by Seattle, the smaller numbers by other communities that cast their vote negatively, could easily have been absorbed by New York City alone. But the drastic scaling down of the program by Congress and the Eisenhower administration meant that projects spurned by one community would be available to no other—not, at least, until the revival of the program in the 1960s.

THE LEGISLATIVE PROCESS—AN INTERIM ASSESSMENT

A final assessment of these events as a test of the capacity of the American system to handle public policy questions must await

[97]Congressman Fisher of Texas cited the defeats of public housing in support of his move to cut the program sharply (*Congressional Record,* XCVIII, Pt. 2, 82d Cong., 2d sess., March 20, 1952, 2631). Representatives McDonough and Hiestand of California drove home the lesson of Los Angeles repeatedly in the House (*Congressional Record,* XCVIII, Pt. 6, 82d Cong., 2d sess., June 27, 1952, 8354; *Congressional Record,* XCIX, Pt. 3, 83d Cong., 1st sess., April 21, 1953, 3504). See also House, *Hearings, Housing Act of 1954,* pp. 104, 169–179. Congressman Cederberg of Michigan, former mayor of Bay City which had upheld public housing in a referendum by the narrowest of margins, declared in 1953 that "one of the easiest ways to effect a great relief to some of the mayors . . . is to kill [public housing]" (*Congressional Record,* XCIX, Pt. 3, 83d Cong., 1st sess., April 21, 1953, 3502).

consideration of other factors in the rest of this book. Still, purely in terms of the processes of government, the public housing issue was handled in a remarkably chaotic and frenetic fashion.

It is true that tidiness, both legislative and administrative, should not be the prime value in a democratic system. It is also reasonable to assure ample time for consideration, and even for reconsideration leading to the possible repudiation of established policies.

But the Taft-Ellender-Wagner Act, after all, had been given the most thorough scrutiny before it was accepted. Under most other systems of representative government, the public housing program would surely have been implemented in considerable measure at least, and then would have undergone an orderly process of modification and adjustment as defects showed up. Its fate under the American system was very different. No sooner was the program given legislative authorization than it was set upon from all directions and belabored unmercifully. At stage after stage in Washington, in community after community in the nation, it had to present itself for decision as though no prior verdict in its favor had ever been rendered. It is one thing to provide opportunities for reconsideration; it is another to present them in such profusion that the burden of proof is always placed on the proponents of a program, no matter how many times their proposals are endorsed. Sooner or later in such circumstances doubts about a policy are bound to grow. This would be especially so in the case of public housing, for there were widespread doubts about the program to begin with. The system gave a strong advantage to opposition groups which were adept at building upon these doubts. And these opposition groups were able to bring about important defeats for the program in several communities by constant reiteration of themes expressive of status and racial hostilities.

The incessant harassment of the program both nationally and locally took a heavy toll administratively. Large bureaucracies in any event tend to timidity and rigidity. But the administrators of public housing faced incredible insecurities. They could not plan from year to year, even month to month, without the fear that their prospects would be undermined from some as yet undetermined source. It is hardly surprising that eventually the pervasive anxiety of its organizers helped to fix the program in a sterile and inflexible mold.

Slowly in the 1960s the situation changed. The Kennedy administration brought some fresh ideas into the program; the 1965 housing act improved the program further, expanded its size, and established a new consensus in place of the divisiveness of the 1950s. The 1968 Johnson proposals opened up the prospect of a further surge of activity and eventually the restoration of the pace proposed in 1949. But even if, by the 1970s, this prospect is achieved, it will have taken a full generation to bring about. Of that generation, a large number of people will have grown up in abominable conditions who might, with the help of a more coherent process of public policy making, have known decent surroundings. Moreover, the program is only now recovering from the psychic damage inflicted upon it by so much hostility in so many places over so long a period of time. Despite the renewed stature bestowed by the 1965 and 1968 legislation, public housing is unlikely to regain the high expectations which it evoked before the legislative and administrative turmoil which enveloped the program during the 1950s.

Chapter 2
Group Pressures

Each of the innumerable stages in the making of decisions governing the public housing program provided a "point of access" for a wide array of private and public housing groups. These groups used the abundant opportunities the system offered to influence the outcome significantly.

The extent of this influence was not as great as claimed by some critics. Public policy, after all, is rarely the simple resultant of group pressures. Legislators respond not only to special interests, but also to presidential leadership, party loyalties, other legislators, their own consciences, and the tides of opinion in their constituencies. Nonetheless, in the public housing case there was an extraordinary amount of activity by interest groups. There is no way to calculate precisely the impact of their pressure on the decisions that were made. Yet, it is unlikely that public housing would have suffered such severe punishment had it not been for the sustained and furious attack on the program by national and local organizations.

THE OPPOSITION GROUPS

National Groups

Both nationally and locally, opposition groups included most of the trade associations directly and indirectly engaged in the building, selling, or financing of housing. At the national level, three of these associations carried the major part of the campaign:

The National Association of Real Estate Boards (NAREB) is a trade association of "realtors"—real estate brokers who are accepted into membership on local real estate boards. When the Taft-Ellender-Wagner program was enacted in 1949, the association included approximately 44,000 realtors in over 1100 real estate boards in communities encompassing most of the nation's urban areas. By the time the 1965 housing act was law, the membership was approaching 75,000 individuals in nearly 1500 local boards. The association describes itself as "a trade and professional organization, to improve the real estate business, to exchange information, and, incidentally, to seek to protect the commodity in which we deal, which is real property, and to make home ownership and the ownership of property both desirable and secure."[1] The headquarters of NAREB is in Chicago, but the association maintains a Washington office, which houses the Realtors' Washington Committee, the organization's legislative arm. Executive vice-president of the association for thirty-two years until his retirement in 1955 was Herbert U. Nelson, a well-known figure on Capitol Hill for most of those years.

The National Association of Home Builders (NAHB) grew out of one of the specialized institutes of NAREB—the Home Builders Institute—and became an autonomous organization in 1943. In 1949 there were 16,500 member home-building companies, mostly small-scale operations typically constructing about fifteen houses a year.[2] By 1965 membership had grown to 40,-

---

[1]U.S. Congress, House of Representatives, Select Committee on Lobbying Activities, *Housing Lobby, Hearings Pursuant to H.Res. 298,* 81st Cong., 2d sess., 1950, Exhibit 349, p. 11; hereinafter referred to as: House, *Hearings, Housing Lobby.*

[2]House, *Hearings, Housing Lobby,* p. 234.

000, close to 80 percent of the total number of house builders in the country. During the period of the struggle against public housing, the organization's executive vice-president was Frank W. Cortwright, whose offices were in the impressive Washington headquarters of the association.

The United States Savings and Loan League (USSLL) had close to 3700 members in 1949, including most of the savings and loan associations in every state in the country. The number had reached 5000 by 1965. The primary business of the league is to make long-term loans for the purchase and construction of homes, originally for lower-income groups, but in recent years mainly for those of middle and upper incomes. The league's headquarters is in Chicago, and there is a Washington office. The chairman of the executive committee for many years, Morton Bodfish, lived in Chicago, but he was active and influential in Washington.

These three groups and their leaders—Nelson, Cortwright, and Bodfish—were the major spokesmen for the opposition to public housing in the decisive years after 1949. They were closely backed by other powerful organizations. The United States Chamber of Commerce, with 2600 local chambers in 1949 (2900 in 1965), worked against public housing through its construction division. Then there were the Mortgage Bankers Association of America, the American Bankers Association, the National Apartment Owners Association, the Producers' Council, and a number of specialized associations of building-material manufacturers and subcontractors, including the National Association of Retail Lumber Dealers, the National Association of Lumber Manufacturers, the Associated General Contractors of America, and the Building Products Institute.[3]

Each week in Washington, twenty-three of the private housing organizations met for lunch as the "National Homes Foundation," for which NAREB provided the secretariat. The foundation did not constitute a close-knit general staff, and there were many issues on which the component organizations disagreed fundamentally. But during the period of greatest controversy over public housing, they were united in their dislike of the proposed

---

[3] See *Congressional Quarterly Almanac,* V (1949), 286; House, *Hearings, Housing Lobby,* pp. 181–183.

program. It was, they declared, a threat by government to the well-being and integrity of the private industry that they represented.

Their efforts to counter this threat from the late 1940s through the mid-1950s were brilliantly executed. Most of the private housing groups had able and experienced representatives in Washington, professionals at their craft of lobbying. In their campaigns against public housing, they neglected none of the techniques described in many case studies of pressure-group operations.

Working in the approved tradition, they helped to write speeches for congressmen; provided them with searching questions to fire at administration officials;[4] and drafted bills and amendments, either at the request of a legislator or for submission to any one of several legislators known to agree with their policies.[5] They advised congressmen as to which legislative procedures would best obstruct public housing proposals.[6] They stood ready, as the lobbyist always does, to "give the facts" to congressional committees. While the entertainment they offered members of Congress was rarely on the lavish scale of an earlier and cruder era, they did discuss business with them over lunch and dinner. Sometimes handsomely paid speaking engagements were arranged for friendly legislators, and the private housing leaders sought ways to be of personal service to congressmen and their families.[7]

There was also the fact that a number of key legislators had been employed in some branch of the housing industry before

---

[4]House, *Hearings, Housing Lobby,* p. 400, and Exhibit 306, p. 868.

[5]U.S. Congress, House of Representatives, Select Committee on Lobbying Activities, *United States Savings and Loan League, H.R. Rept.* 3139, Pursuant to H. Res. 298, 81st Cong., 2d sess., 1950, Exhibit 82, p. 92. (Hereinafter referred to as: House, *H.R. Rept. 3139, United States Savings and Loan League.*) This is an interoffice memorandum by Morton Bodfish in which he says: "I wonder if Monroney has seen the lobbying amendments that we developed in connection with Dirksen?"

[6]See memorandum "To Harry" [Cain] headed: "Suggested Procedure for Action by the Senate Banking and Currency Committee on *S. 1459* and *H.R. 3492,*" from the Realtors' Washington Committee, in House, *Hearings, Housing Lobby,* Exhibit 305-B, pp. 864–865.

[7]House, *H.R. Rept. 3139, United States Savings and Loan League,* Exhibit 255, p. 213, and Exhibit 166, p. 150; House, *Hearings, Housing Lobby,* p. 54.

being elected. Others were still so employed or had entered into a business relationship with the industry after being elected to Congress. Thus, many congressmen had been made counsel to or directors of building and loan associations, while others had been connected with realty organizations.[8]

It is not surprising, then, that there were many spokesmen for the housing industry's interests in Congress and, more particularly, in key congressional committees dealing with housing matters. However, eager supporters for the private housing industry were to be found even among those who had never been on its payroll. The housing industry is made up primarily of small businessmen. The House of Representatives includes a high proportion of men with a background in small business or whose friends are mostly small businessmen—often, in fact, realtors, or home builders or savings and loan officials. These legislators come from the same kind of background as the businessmen, and have common values and experiences. During the housing controversy, such congressmen did not have to be "bought" or even persuaded by the housing industry.

At the same time, it was necessary for the industry to cultivate a favorable climate of opinion in the country at large. Toward this end the national staffs worked assiduously, through news releases, pamphlets, articles, and speeches. They aimed not only at the diffuse target of mass opinion, but also at specific organizations that might be able to exert influence on the lawmakers. Thus, an adverse report on public housing came out of the 1946 American Legion Convention; this resulted from the presence on the Legion's housing committee of a number of real estate men.[9]

[8]In the 80th Congress two of the members of the House Banking and Currency Committee who helped Chairman Wolcott prevent action on the Taft-Ellender-Wagner Bill were described as having "spent most of their lives in the real-estate business, and both still list themselves as executives of savings and loan associations." (Nathan Straus, "Why You Can't Get That New Home," *The American Magazine* [December 1947], p. 133).
Senator John W. Bricker, a consistent foe of public housing, was a building and loan association director. Senator Harry P. Cain had been in banking for ten years and was to become vice-president of a savings and loan association after leaving the Senate. (See also, *Wall Street Journal* [April 3, 1959], pp. 1, 18.)

[9]See Straus, *The American Magazine,* p. 133. See also Harry Conn, "Housing: A Vanishing Vision," *The New Republic* (July 23, 1951), p. 12.

All of these tactics have been used at one time or another by every effective lobby in Washington. The private housing groups practiced them with at least as much skill as any other congerie of lobbyists. But there was another technique deployed by the housing groups more effectively than by almost anyone else: This was the application of grass-roots pressure from all around the country at strategic times and places in the Washington legislative process. The use of this device is a natural consequence of the fact that most of the power sources of the American national legislature are back home in the states and districts. The private housing organizations were especially well equipped to take advantage of this condition. Savings and loan leagues and units of the NAHB were widely distributed throughout the country and were frequently important forces in their communities. To an even greater extent, the NAREB had its roots in the local situation, for there was a real estate board in almost every sizeable community. It is not surprising that the Buchanan Committee's investigation of lobbying in 1950 should have found that "the National Association of Real Estate Boards . . . has systematized all means of direct contact between its members and legislators more completely than any other group appearing before this committee."[10] Perhaps the American Medical Association has an even greater advantage in this respect, since every member of Congress has his own doctor, and doctors are even more widely distributed (and have much greater prestige) than realtors. Nonetheless, during the struggle over public housing, NAREB developed a machinery for the application of local pressures on the national scene which no other organization could match.

The fulcrum of their effort was the Enlarged Realtors' Washington Committee. Joining the fifty core members of the Realtors' Washington Committee in the enlarged committee were the president and secretary of each of the local real estate boards, the board of directors of the national association, and "800 additional persons who have volunteered their services."[11] When any of these came to Washington, they themselves or their local boards paid their expenses. As Herbert Nelson explained, the purpose of

---

[10]U.S. Congress, House of Representatives, *General Interim Report of the House Select Committee on Lobbying Activities*, H.R. Rept. 3138, 81st Cong., 2d sess., 1950, p. 24.

[11]House, *Hearings, Housing Lobby*, p. 9.

the committee was "to write or wire their Senators or Representatives regarding any crucial matters which may arise from time to time that seriously affect the real estate industry and where quick action is required." The essential prerequisite for those who were invited to join was that they be "closely acquainted or have personal contact with members of Congress."[12] This requirement was even more rigorously adhered to in the case of the core Realtors' Washington Committee. Prospective members were recommended on the basis of their being "our best contact with Senator Buck" or having close personal contact with Senator Taft and members of his campaign committee or being a "former classmate of House Majority Leader Charles Halleck, member of same fraternity and close personal friend."[13] "I will be glad to serve on the RWC," said one Californian. "As a matter of fact, I had lunch last Saturday with Congressman-elect Donald L. Jackson and I have every reason to feel that Jackson would like to see things our way. . . . Confidentially, a newspaper in which I am interested was probably the deciding factor in securing the primary nomination for Jackson. . . . Let me know when I can be of help."[14]

Membership in the core RWC entailed regular meetings in Washington. With the enlarged RWC, the emphasis was on contact with the individual members of Congress by letters, telegrams, phone calls, and sometimes personal visits. Letters were sent out from Washington asking local real estate boards to get together with other local organizations hostile to public housing and to wire, write, or phone their representatives in Congress. The response was voluminous. More important, it came when and where it was needed. For the essence of pressure politics is timing. A bill entering the American legislative process winds sluggishly along, subterranean much of the time, coming into sight with little warning. Yet, when its progress can be charted and anticipated, it is vulnerable, since there are so many points in the system at which it is open to attack. The lobbyist out to defeat a bill must learn precisely at what time and at what place to deploy his forces and upon which members of which committee, at what stage, using what procedural device.

[12]House, *Hearings, Housing Lobby,* Exhibit 270, p. 840.

[13]House, *Hearings, Housing Lobby,* Exhibit 263, p. 118.

[14]House, *Hearings, Housing Lobby,* Exhibit 274, p. 842.

The realtors' representatives were skilled at this task. Their knowledge of legislation and legislators, and their information on what was happening to any bill was generally sound. And they had a national communication network that could be activated with great speed. The secretaries of local real estate boards stood ready to act on urgent requests from Washington. Lists were maintained in Washington of general congressional contacts for the RWC and the enlarged RWC. More than this, there were refined "special contact" lists for the House Banking and Currency Committee, the House Rules Committee, and also of "key Senate phone contacts."[15]

There is much debate about the usefulness of masses of letters, wires, and phone calls to a legislator from his home district. Lobbyists themselves disagree widely on the usefulness of the tactic. Congressmen declare that it is not usually one of the most important influences on their decisions.[16] They are fully aware that any sudden barrage of communications has probably been contrived by an organization, even where pains have been taken to avoid standardization. ("Be specific," wrote Calvin Snyder of the RWC to the realty board secretaries. "Bring in local conditions. The personal element in your message is imperative. It avoids the appearance of mass production."[17])

Even so, few congressmen can be entirely impervious to a demonstration of the ability of a national organization to produce very large numbers of messages from their constituents. Typically, a congressman will use them for his purposes if they support his position. If they do not, he will frequently send out urgent pleas to people on his side to encourage mail from his sympathizers. To the legislator who is wavering on an issue, a sudden avalanche of mail may finally convince him (providing that it is

---

[15]House, *Hearings, Housing Lobby,* Exhibit 414, pp. 1008–1009; Exhibits 264–264-B, pp. 826–834; Exhibit 264-C, pp. 834–835; Exhibit 264-D, pp. 835–837.

[16]See, Lester W. Milbrath, *The Washington Lobbyist* (Chicago: Rand McNally, 1963). However, the prolonged difficulty of securing effective gun control legislation in the face of the National Rifle Association's massive letter-writing campaigns supports the evidence of the public housing study in questioning the validity of Milbrath's conclusions.

[17]House, *Hearings, Housing Lobby,* Exhibit 339, p. 942. See also *Headlines,* May 25, 1953.

not handled so clumsily that it produces a hostile reaction). In the public housing case, at least, the realtors believed that their technique was effective,[18] and they used it later on other issues. They were among the pioneers of a tactic which almost all national organizations have come to use in pursuit of their legislative objectives.

Moreover, the mass of congressional mail was but one aspect of the campaign conducted by the realtors and their allies. The barrage of letters and wires served merely to provide the backdrop for the more selective and sophisticated personal contacts from important people in the congressmen's districts. Sometimes these were personal friends. Often they were substantial contributors to the election campaign costs which, in the case of the representatives, had to be incurred every other year. These were people whose telephone call or visit could not be easily ignored by congressmen.

Taken together, the mass response to the requests for grass-roots messages, the selective contacts made by influential people in the home districts, and the traditional lobbying techniques in Washington added up to a formidable pressure campaign. This campaign built to a crescendo from 1945 through 1949, and though unsuccessful in that year, began again with renewed vigor and greater effect in 1951, with the results already described.

The Communities

As soon as the Taft-Ellender-Wagner Bill was passed, the Washington offices of several of the national housing associations sent appeals to their local units to mount campaigns against the implementation of public housing in the communities. The response in several cities was enthusiastic. Coalitions quickly

[18]Calvin Snyder of the Realtors' Washington Committee wrote to Herbert Nelson: "Too much cannot be said for the cooperation and support that we had from realtors at the grass-roots. This is not guesswork, because in the closing two weeks of the Congress Al Payne and I, as well as others making contact on Capitol Hill, came across the results of close and intimate letter writing between realtors and Members of Congress. Most of them sent us copies of their letters or telegrams and usually followed up with copies of replies received from their Congressmen. This gave us an opportunity to open the subject and, without exception, I found the effectiveness of the realtors to be far-reaching in the decisions made individually by Members of the House" (House, *Hearings, Housing Lobby,* Exhibit 315 p. 879).

formed, usually led by organizations affiliated with the national associations. The composition of the alliances varied from place to place (the lumber industry, for example, played a more prominent role in the Northwest than elsewhere), but in most cases the real estate board was very much involved; and often the local chamber of commerce played an active part.

The fact that these groups were related to national organizations was generally helpful to the opposition campaigns. NAHB, the RWC, and the USSLL supplied their members with packages of material providing arguments and techniques for attacking public housing.[19] The national offices also facilitated the flow of suggestions from city to city. The best of the locally prepared materials came from the Seattle Master Builders, who commissioned and made generally available a kit of materials giving a detailed description of their successful campaign, with copies of radio and TV spots, newspaper and billboard ads, and day-by-day news stories.

These processes brought a considerable measure of uniformity to the local campaigns. The same slogans appeared all over the country. Newspapers in various cities carried accounts of identical speeches made on the same day by local organization leaders.[20] Identical editorials on "socialized housing" appeared in Hearst newspapers in four of the cities where public housing was under attack.[21] In addition, staff members from the Washington offices showed up from time to time to lobby before city councils.

[19]NAHB prepared a packaged kit called "Home Builders' Information Material to Oppose Socialized Public Housing," which contained a basic manual, various pieces of mimeographed information about the program, accounts of successful opposition campaigns around the country, and reprints of articles and congressional speeches, some made available from the Realtors' Washington Committee, which was also sending out large numbers of reprints. In 1950 the USSLL too, produced a substantial kit containing sample slogans, advertisements, editorials, news stories, speeches, pamphlets, and articles, as well as a detailed manual on "How to Prevent the Spread of Government Housing."

[20]On April 1, 1951, the *Cincinnati Enquirer* and the *New Orleans Item* carried identical statements attacking public housing that were attributed to the president of the home builders association in each of those cities. Reprinted in "Home Builders' Information Material to Oppose Socialized Public Housing" kit.

[21]"Hearst Papers Use Canned Editorial," *Journal of Housing,* IX, no. 1, 1952), 17.

These various kinds of national intervention were pointed to by defenders of public housing as proof that the battles in the communities were merely part of a carefully planned and coordinated campaign that was controlled and directed from Washington, the local units of the associations acting without volition of their own. This assessment was not accurate. There were three important factors offsetting the influence of the national organizations.

First, the direct participation of staff members from Washington had to be handled circumspectly, for there was always the danger of arousing the traditional American hostility to carpetbaggers. "The people of Roanoke," said a city councilman in Virginia to a NAREB staff representative who asked to be heard, "can run their own city without getting foreigners to come down here."[22]

Second, there were communities in which the local organizations were unenthusiastic about the policies of the national leadership. In New York, despite the official stance of the City Real Estate Board against public housing, there has not been much opposition to public housing among realtors outside Queens. This has been true in several of the big Eastern cities; and there have been cases in which the realty board has worked closely with the housing authority in planning the program and selecting the sites.

Third, a number of community groups with no national affiliations were also involved in the battles against public housing. There were the owners, for example, of small rental properties (many of them dilapidated) which might be pulled down to make way for public housing or whose tenants might move into public housing. Thus, in Los Angeles "the dirty work in the fight was done by . . . the Small Property Owners League . . . which furnished the mass base which the other organizations lacked."[23] But there was an even broader mass base to be found in the associations of property owners who lived and worked in the vicinity of proposed housing projects. In Los Angeles, three such groups, two of them created for this purpose, engaged in a fierce

[22]*Journal of Housing,* VII, no. 6 (1950), 192.

[23]Richard Norman Baisden, "Labor Unions in Los Angeles Politics," unpublished Ph.D. dissertation, Department of Political Science, University of Chicago, 1958, p. 308.

attack on a projected public housing site close to their own neighborhoods.[24] In Chicago, about 200 neighborhood associations provided the bulk of the opposition, supported by the State Street Council, "a powerful group of merchants who were able to act in concert."[25] National leadership in the Chicago case was discounted by Meyerson and Banfield in their study of the controversy there: "Elaborate and ramified as it undoubtedly was, the national real estate lobby and its Chicago affiliates would have little direct influence in the struggle over sites in Chicago. . . . The organizations themselves would stay somewhat aloof from the struggle."[26]

Clearly, even had there been no national opposition to public housing, the program would have had its troubles in some communities. It was an element for change in residential areas; and whenever changes in the "character of the neighborhood" are proposed, the antipathies of local communities tend to be aroused.

Still, if it is necessary to refute the charge that the local campaigns were totally controlled from Washington, it does not follow that the story in the cities would have been much the same had there been no intervention from the national associations. Without that intervention, the local opposition might have been bitter, but it would have been spontaneous and sporadic. While it certainly would have prevented the selection of a number of specific sites, it might not have been sufficient to bring about the total rejection of the program in a number of major cities.

In fact, the combination of local initiative on the one hand and national guidance, encouragement, and coordination on the other, happened to be the most effective possible combination for the conduct of the local campaigns. Without the national involvement, local rejections of individual sites would have had only isolated significance. Without the locally based organizations the intensity and fury of the opposition could never have been pro-

See Monterey Woods Improvement Association, *Rose Hills Report* (Los Angeles: Monterey Woods Improvement Association, 1953).

Martin Meyerson and Edward C. Banfield, *Politics, Planning, and the Public Interest* (New York: The Free Press, 1955), p. 116.

Meyerson and Banfield, *Politics, Planning, and the Public Interest,* p. 117.

voked. Moreover, the financing of the campaigns was essentially local, for the national organizations did not command the resources to underwrite battles in so many communities.

In the course of these battles, all of the tactics typical of local pressure politics were employed by the opposition groups. Lobbyists argued, promised, and threatened in their dealings with members of city councils. Barrages of letters, telegrams, and phone calls were produced at both the local and the national level. And perhaps more important than all the efforts of paid lobbyists were the personal contacts of builders and realtors with their friends and acquaintances in city government. Thus in Los Angeles Fritz Burns, a leader of the opposition both nationally and locally, needed no intermediary to reach Mayor Norris Poulson on the public housing issue. Shared purposes and values made pressure superfluous.

When the phase of site selection was reached, the emphasis moved from informal discussions and behind the scenes maneuvering to noisy public confrontations. For this was the stage at which the private housing industry was clamorously joined by the small property owners and the neighborhood associations resisting the prospect of disruption of the tone and style of their communities. In Los Angeles in 1951 a succession of representatives of local residents testified against the selection of proposed sites. Council meetings were attended by 400 to 500 supporters of the Small Property Owners League, who created a tremendous uproar on several occasions. Despite the fact that it was the day after Christmas, hundreds had to be turned away from the packed council chamber when the city council first cast its vote against public housing. The same kind of atmosphere prevailed in hearings in Pittsburgh and Seattle. In Chicago, the Southwest Neighborhood Council sent out 12,000 notices to get people to attend city-council hearings on proposed sites, and the galleries were filled with anti-public housing forces, who cheered and booed constantly.[27]

The referendum campaigns, of course, demanded tactics very different from those of traditional lobbying. The referendum, after all, was originally designed as a way of preventing contro-

[27]Meyerson and Banfield, *Politics, Planning, and the Public Interest*, p.181-182.

by small numbers of professionals and activists and of placing the decisions in the hands of the many. By and large, the results have not provided an overwhelming demonstration of the validity of direct rather than representative democracy. Power has tended to shift to the few who have the money needed to hire the specialists in the arts of mass-media persuasion. The public housing referendum campaigns were painfully impressive illustrations of this new reality.

The Seattle referendum campaign was a small classic in this respect. The Seattle Home Ownership Council, a grouping of private housing organizations created just before the enactment of the Taft-Ellender-Wagner program, established a campaign structure under the chairmanship of an officer loaned by the Washington Land Title Association. The partners in a Seattle advertising firm worked with the chairman as his advertising and public relations counsel. Various services were made available to sympathetic groups: a speakers' bureau, pamphlets, background information and arguments, slogans. There was a stream of news releases, and letters to the editor were written and distributed to important men in the community, who in turn sent them to local papers. Political and civic clubs were contacted and their support enlisted. A site map was prepared containing the opposition's projections on which locations might be selected for housing projects if the program were pursued. This appeared in the metropolitan and neighborhood newspapers.

Then there was the advertising campaign. As explained by the firm conducting it, this was based on two main principles, the first of which was, "Keep it simple":

> We felt we had two problems to be solved to win the election. The first, and perhaps larger, was apathy, particularly among that group whose support was required. The second was lack of information. In order to penetrate that group, we chose to depend upon repetition—simple repetition. The public housing question is too complex to be presented in its entirety, or grasped by the semi-interested reader. We consequently resisted the frantic considerations of the moment and contented ourselves mostly with repetition of the key phrase, "Can You Afford to Pay Somebody Else's Rent?", borrowed from the New Jersey campaign, to

which was added, "Let's do the *most* good for the *most* people." This addition, in our opinion, gave an unselfish motivation to the "rent question" which, while unquestionably powerful, is entirely selfish.[28]

This was the approach, stated in forthright Pavlovian terms. The techniques flowed naturally from this basic principle. Billboards were used extensively during the two weeks before the election, sixty identical three-color billboards carrying the slogan "Can YOU Afford to Pay Somebody Else's Rent?" followed by "Vote NO on Referendum No. 3" and "The Seattle Committee for Home Protection." Radio time was bought not for speeches but for chainbreaks, with "live" spots featuring the basic slogan and dramatized transcribed spots carrying such messages as: "My name is Al Henderson. I am a mechanic. I have a place for every nickel I make. Now they want me to help pay for public housing, and I just can't *do* it! I am going to vote NO on Referendum 3." Newspaper space was broken into small repetitive ads until the evening before and the morning of the election. At that point large ads were used in the metropolitan newspapers. One carried the slogan, a cartoon, and seven points telling the "WHOLE TRUTH" about public housing. Another explained "what every homeowner should know about real estate lobbies" ("It's YOU, the homeowner, of course!").

In addition, the community newspapers and "class weeklies" were well covered; and scatter ads appeared in the classified section of the larger newspapers, especially the Sunday real estate section. For this last purpose a special appeal was made to realtors: "Regarding Classified: So as to leave no stone unturned, we are hoping to have a number of little 2-line 'Stingers' tied into the real estate ads between now and March 14. Both daily papers have agreed to help, and you will likely get a call asking that you allow one or more of these to be added to your classifieds which present and future homeowners are reading." Sample lines followed.

Only in the four-page *Home Protector* tabloid (distributed

---

[28]Keene and Keene Advertising, "Outline of Advertising," The Seattle Public Housing Fight (Kit of materials compiled for the Seattle Master Builders, 1950) (Mimeographed).

"to every home in Seattle" five days before the election) did the campaign organizers "seek even to approach a detailed story, and then anticipated that we had to depend on headline readership. . . . This is one place where we attempted to give the general public a complete story." Yet, it was admitted, this was not really a complete story but the presentation of "a variety of approaches so as to appeal to the greatest number of people." First among the "variety of approaches" was the map of alleged sites. Other features were a cartoon, reprints from the *Seattle Times* and *Post-Intelligencer,* an array of arguments against public housing, stories of other communities that had rejected public housing, and a quotation from Lincoln on the rights of property.

The second basic principle of the advertising part of the Seattle campaign followed naturally from the first. "Keep it short" was the firm injunction. Since a primary election would precede the referendum by two weeks, there was actually a period of little more than fourteen days in which to concentrate the campaign. Yet this limitation was regarded not with dismay but with satisfaction. The greatest impact, said the advertisers, could be obtained in a brief, saturation campaign. So, while billboards were used from two weeks before polling day, the most intensive efforts in newspapers and radio were left for the last few days.

Evidently the skillful application of these two principles worked. In the referendum, public housing was defeated by 57,-732 to 33,529. While there is no conclusive evidence that opinion in Seattle actually shifted drastically in this short period or that it might not have shifted with a different type of campaign, it was the view of leaders on both sides and of experienced observers of the local scene that there had, in fact, been a substantial change in attitudes and that the campaign had materially influenced this change.

The techniques used in Seattle found their counterparts in the campaigns in other cities. Advertising and public relations firms were heavily involved in Houston, Los Angeles, and in the 1950 statewide referendum in California on Proposition 10, which was aimed at compelling local referenda on all public housing programs not yet authorized. As in Seattle, heavy reliance was placed in these campaigns on the mass media. In Houston, extensive use was made of billboards, radio spots, and newspaper advertisements, and there were mass mailings of letters and postcards.[29] In California, the advertising campaign was concentrated in the metropolitan areas because of limitations of time and money. Billboards were rented wherever possible, but since good space was scarce, all kinds of display facilities were utilized, from twenty-four-sheet boards to window display cards. Radio and television spot announcements were concentrated into the last ten days of the campaign, with an increasing number in the last five days. A sixteen-page "Facts Booklet" went out to all newspapers, and the California Real Estate Association claimed that "many newspapers were ready at this time to take a stand against Proposition 10 simply because they did not understand the issue. This mailing caused many of them to wait until they could hear our side of the story."[30] Their side of the story was then presented in ads purchased in many of the major California dailies and weeklies.

In the placing of these ads, local housing groups were brought in. Mats of advertisements were prepared by the state-wide campaign committee and mailed to real estate boards throughout the state with the request that they obtain local sponsorship for them. Other ads were sponsored by real estate brokers in their community newspapers, while the papers were contacted with the suggestion that they try to sell ads to local sponsors. The local real estate boards and savings and loan leagues used their wide contacts and distribution systems to reach people in other ways, too:

> Perhaps our most potent literature distribution was that done by Realtors and members of the California Savings and Loan League. The Savings and Loan people took our basic campaign pamphlet and mailed it with passbooks to the great majority of their investors. In many cases they added their own personal letter, pointing out the property owner's

[29]National Association of Home Builders, "Home Builders' Information Material to Oppose Socialized Public Housing." Neighborhood workers were also pressed into service in Houston. A special mailing with postcards enclosed produced a 22 percent response of people willing to work at the precinct level, and they undertook the job of talking with their neighbors and passing out pamphlets.

[30]California Real Estate Association, "Summary of the Campaign for Proposition 10," n.d. (Mimeographed).

stake in Proposition 10. The Realtors took the great bulk of our literature and in some areas distributed door-to-door, and in other areas mailed it directly into the homes, and in hundreds of cases sent letters and folders to their clients—past, present and future. More than 1,500,000 campaign pamphlets were produced and distributed.[31]

THE PRO-PUBLIC HOUSING GROUPS

In public policy disputes in America, the organized group pressures are never on one side only. The public housing issue was no exception. The program would never have existed in the first place but for the initiative provided by a combination of labor unions, local housing officials, and various religious, racial, ethnic, and political groups who formed themselves into the National Public Housing Conference. In 1934 the conference issued "A Housing Program for the United States," acclaimed as "the first long-range and carefully considered program to be formulated in the United States."[32] It was this coalition that Senator Wagner relied on to do most of the work of drafting the public housing provisions of the 1937 housing act.

The component units of the coalition had grown considerably by the time they entered into the struggle over the Taft-Ellender-Wagner proposal. By 1949 there were well over 3000 members in the National Association of Housing Officials; by 1965 the organization, now the National Association of Housing and Redevelopment Officials (NAHRO), included 5000 individual members, working for 1000 local agencies. NAHRO's excellent monthly publication, the *Journal of Housing,* contains a great deal of information that has been invaluable over the years to the groups supporting public housing. Organizations of local government officials, such as the National League of Cities and the National Institute of Law Officers, expressed support for the program. Consistently fighting for public housing during its period of

[31]California Real Estate Association, *Summary of the Campaign for Proposition 10.*

[32]Timothy L. McDonnell, *The Wagner Housing Act* (Chicago: Loyola University Press, 1957), pp. 80–81.

greatest duress was the United States Conference of Mayors. Social workers, organizing as the American Association of Social Workers and the National Federation of Settlements, were vocal supporters, too.

Labor was a prime mover in the coalition. Until their merger in 1955, both the AFL and the CIO had housing committees, the AFL's directed by Boris Shishkin since 1935, the CIO's by Leo Goodman. In addition, an assortment of organizations usually numbered among the backers of welfare legislation were included in the pro-public housing coalition. There were church groups, Protestant, Catholic, and Jewish; women's organizations, such as the American Association of University Women and the League of Women Voters; Negro organizations, including the NAACP and the National Urban League; veterans' groups, including the American Legion and the American Veterans of World War II, both of which were at first hostile to the plan but changed their minds in time to support the 1949 act; and various others, including the National Association of Parents and Teachers, the American Council on Human Rights, and the National Association of Consumers.

Providing coordination between the pro-public housing groups was the National Public Housing Conference (later the National Housing Conference), which worked for both the Wagner-Steagall and the Taft-Ellender-Wagner Acts. During the struggles of the 1940s and 1950s, the conference had an able leader in its vice-president, Lee F. Johnson, an experienced Washington hand. While the housing conference included all the major organizations backing public housing, its membership and leadership were principally representative of officials of local housing authorities.[33] In addition, the Housing Legislative Information Service brought together informally about forty of the national organizations actively involved in the fight for public housing.

In the communities, too, large numbers of individuals and groups rallied to the defense of public housing, organizing themselves in coalitions under such titles as the Citizens League for Better Homes in Portland, the Citizens Housing Committee in

---

[33]Twenty-three of the fifty-two members of the conference's legislative committee in 1948 to 1949 were public officials. (See House, *Hearings, Housing Lobby,* Exhibit N-2, pp. 1338–1339.)

Seattle, the Citizens Housing Council in Los Angeles, and the Citizens Committee for Slum Clearance in Miami.

By and large, these local coalitions paralleled closely the combinations of groups supporting the program in Washington. Labor waged a strong fight in Los Angeles, Seattle, and other communities. Usually there was representation from veterans' groups, church, women's, civic, and minority group organizations, and sometimes Democratic clubs. Local housing officials were inevitably participants in the defense of their programs. In most places their involvement could not be overt, and the degree to which they provided behind the scenes leadership varied from place to place. In Los Angeles, however, the Citizens Housing Council was actually nothing more than a "list of prominent names which had no budget or workers," a paper organization through which the city housing authority worked.[34] Other official backing came from the commissioners of the housing authorities, lay people charged with the responsibility of establishing policy for the projects and of representing the programs to the public and the local governmental structure.

It was part of the standard argument of the pro-public housing forces that the techniques used by the opposition, nationally and locally, were essentially undemocratic and manipulative. Yet, none of the tactics utilized by the opposition was neglected in the defense of the program. Lee Johnson and Leo Goodman sent repeated appeals to their constituent units in the NPHC and the CIO for masses of communications from the grass roots. They cultivated their personal contacts with congressmen, and maintained a careful surveillance of legislative developments.

In the cities the public housing forces did all they could to match the opposition's tactics in influencing city-council decisions. Employees of the housing authorities sometimes turned out in force at the hearings.[35] Labor unions encouraged their members to attend, reminding them that public housing meant jobs for unemployed plumbers and other craftsmen. Nor were distortions and oversimplifications limited to the opposition side in the referendum campaigns. In Los Angeles, the brochures and other materials used by public housing's supporters were redolent with half-

---

[34]Baisden, "Labor Unions in Los Angeles Politics," p. 369.

[35]Monterey Woods Improvement Association, *Rose Hills Report*, p. 9.

truths and high-pitched language. In California, officials of the housing authorities who spearheaded the attack on Proposition 10, quickly decided that the truth could not be left to speak for itself, and they hired a leading advertising agency. In Seattle, the Citizens Committee, which conducted the defense of the program, did so without recourse to the skills of the professional publicist but with subsequent regret: "We should have developed a counter slogan," said the secretary of the committee, "or, in the alternative, we should have concentrated much earlier on the 'real estate lobby.' "[36]

PLURALISM?

Any examination of the forces engaged on both sides of a public policy issue must lead to a test of the two rival theories concerning the group process in American politics. On the one hand, it is postulated that, by and large, there is a reasonable balance of interest groups and that no one, or combination, of them dominates the rest.[37] Against this, it has been argued that American politics reflects the fact that ours is essentially a business society, and that organizations representing business interests tend to prevail in the struggle over public policy.[38]

Both sides in this controversy can find evidence for their positions in the public housing case, as will be demonstrated here. In the view of the present writer, however, the group balance theory ultimately provides a less satisfactory interpretation of this case than the opposite thesis.

The Group-Balance Thesis

It is clear that the public housing program was by no means a helpless, motionless prey, waiting to be devoured by marauding

[36]Kenneth A. MacDonald, "Report on the Seattle Referendum Campaign," Seattle 1950, p. 11 (Mimeographed).

[37]See John Fischer, "Unwritten Rules of American Politics," *Harper's Magazine* (November 1948), pp. 27–36; and Earl Latham, "The Group Basis of Politics: Notes for a Theory," *The American Political Science Review,* XLVI, no. 2 (1952), 376–397. See also David B. Truman, *The Governmental Process* (New York: Alfred A. Knopf, 1951).

[38]Elmer Eric Schattschneider, *The Semi-Sovereign People* (New York: Holt, Rinehart and Winston, Inc., 1960).

private housing interests. Impressive coalitions, representing vast memberships, worked vigorously on behalf of the program, fighting back with all of the methods employed by the opposition. Moreover, the forces aligned on the public housing side did not consist only of private organizations. The federal bureaucracy helped them substantially. During the congressional campaigns on behalf of the Taft-Ellender-Wagner Bill, counsel for the federal housing agencies were made available as advisors to the Senate and House Banking and Currency Committees, and "their knowledge of the legal problems involved and their judgments as to desirable courses of action doubtless exercised strong influence on the course of the legislation."[39] And, of course, the White House worked vigorously for the cause from the New Deal period through 1952, and again from 1961. In the local communities, the housing officials were fighting for their own programs, sometimes for their very jobs. Additional help was quietly given in a number of places by the field offices of the federal housing agencies.

Nor was there monolithic unity among private business interests on the public housing question. Nationally, it was true that the major business organizations testified against the program. But this antipathy was not always matched in the communities, especially in the older cities of the East and Midwest, where the major business concerns have often displayed a sense of civic responsibility and a willingness to support programs designed to help low-income people and minority groups.

To a considerable extent, the business hostility to public housing was a regional phenomenon, mostly evidenced in cities of the West and Southwest which were growing at a phenomenal pace.[40] Consequently, they were communities in which the real estate, home building, and home finance interests were flourishing and politically aggressive.

This was especially true of Los Angeles, and it is not surprising that Los Angeles should be the city that reverberated to the most bitter charges that behind the opposition to public housing was a conspiracy of power and money. Mayor Bowron set forth

---

Martin Meyerson, Barbara Terrett, and William L. C. Wheaton, *Housing, People, and Cities* (New York: McGraw-Hill, Inc., 1962), p. 277.

The trend in the 1950s was for cities to lose population to the surrounding suburban communities. But the big public housing defeats in Los Angeles, Houston, and Seattle (and later, in Dallas and San Antonio) occurred in cities whose populations increased substantially between 1950 and 1960.

the indictment. At the center of the conspiracy, he declared, wa the *Los Angeles Times* and its publisher, Norman Chandler. Th Chandler family was the proprietor of a vast financial empir encompassing large holdings of land and interests in a grea diversity of businesses. It was their purpose, he said, in conce with a small number of other wealthy people, to take over the cit government and use it for their financial benefit. As the campaig developed, Bowron and others made a more specific accusation a plot by the "real estate syndicate."[41] They pointed out that ver little had been heard from the opposition groups until the cit council had taken the steps necessary to condemn the sites und eminent domain. Once this had been done, areas that had bee occupied only by shacks and other dilapidated housing becam extremely valuable parcels of land, close to the downtown are and suitable for business and expensive residential developmen It was then that the opposition had made their move again: public housing, hoping, said Bowron, to turn the sites over private developers. And it was to thwart this plan, Bowron ex plained, that he made his lame duck appointments to the cit housing authority after his defeat: "I felt it was my duty . . . protect and preserve the public property for public uses . . [against] a scheme afoot to sell three or more of the parcels property acquired for public housing projects to real estate specu lators or subdividers."[42]

The charges took on a degree of plausibility from the fac that the 1949 housing act made provision for private redevelop ment programs following government slum-clearance action. An the *Los Angeles Times* in July 1953 suggested that:

> The city may buy the sites on which no public housing wi be built, paying the cost of the land to the Housing Authori ty. Or, if the city does not want to buy, the sites may be sol to private persons at public sale. There is time for us to com to a sensible decision on this matter.[43]

However, the issue was shrouded in a fog of legal doubt. If th very large amount of money spent to defeat public housing in Lc Angeles is to be viewed solely as a financial investment, it woul

[41]Text of KNBH telecast, May 12, 1953.

[42]*Los Angeles Times* (June 24, 1953), Pt. I, p. 1.

[43]*Los Angeles Times* (July 30, 1953), Pt. II, p. 4.

have been a very risky kind of speculation. Before the final settlement was reached, Mayor Poulson had to reassure city councilmen who contended that the housing authority had no legal right to sell land it had acquired by condemnation for a specific public purpose. The mayor announced that he would oppose the sale of the properties to private parties.

In subsequent transactions, this understanding was not strictly adhered to. The largest of the cleared sites, Chavez Ravine, was used later for the construction of a privately owned baseball stadium, and the terms under which this was arranged were to be the occasion of another angry controversy. Still, Walter O'Malley and the Dodgers could hardly have been manipulating the public housing issue from Brooklyn during the early 1950s.

While the possibilities of private exploitation of the sites may have been in the minds of some of public housing's opponents from the outset, the *Los Angeles Times*' concern with the issue was more likely political than financial. Certainly it displayed an extraordinary preoccupation with the matter, thundering its denunciations in no less than twenty editorials from August to December 1951. It also applied strong pressure on recalcitrant councilmen; and the conversion to the opposition side of the two swing votes on the council was probably due less to the sudden revelation that public housing was socialism than to hopes for the *Times*' endorsement in future elections. Still, a conspiracy theory is not needed to explain the newspaper's role. Public housing, apart from being the kind of government-sponsored program that the then very conservative *Los Angeles Times* would dislike instinctively, provided a very convenient issue with which to defeat Bowron and install a more acceptable candidate.

In no other city was there such a massive assault on public housing by business interests as in Los Angeles. Nowhere else was the press such a formidable foe. In many places, in fact, newspapers were by no means hostile to the program. In Miami, both the *Herald* and the *Daily News*—and in Toledo, the *Blade* and the *Times*—supported the program editorially and were powerful factors in keeping the opposition on the defensive. In Madison, the opposition of the *Wisconsin State Journal* was balanced by the support of the *Capitol Times*. Although all Hearst newspapers were opposed to the program (vigorously so in Los Angeles),[44]

---

[44] The *Daily News* was the only Los Angeles newspaper to support public housing.

the Hearst *Post-Intelligencer* in Seattle showed only mild displeasure and generally was much fairer in its coverage than the persistently hostile *Seattle Times*. Eastern papers like the *New York Times* and the Washington *Post* were generally friendly to public housing over the years.

Further support for the group-balance thesis can be found in the final outcome of the public housing controversy. The program still exists and continues to grow. While it was totally rejected in several communities, it was approved in many others. In the biggest local conflicts of all—those in Chicago and Los Angeles—the result was a compromise. The Chicago settlement provided for the construction of 12,500 units. In Los Angeles, almost half of the original program was salvaged. In large measure this happened because, while the opposition gained control of some of the decision points, it was unable to establish its hold on all of them. No sooner had the anti-public housing forces gained control of the mayor's office than their power in the city council slipped away. Of the three vacancies on the council which were in serious contention in the 1953 election, the *Los Angeles Times* endorsement bore fruit in only one, while the other two victors were backed by labor and could be relied on to support the housing authority. The public housing struggle provides yet one more illustration of the lack of a single, concentrated power structure in Los Angeles.

At the national level, both sides continued in their intractability for several years. But slowly a more conciliatory spirit began to emerge. While the private housing groups still told congressional committees that they disliked public housing, after 1954 other aspects of housing legislation commanded more of their attention. Urban renewal, for example, entailed higher stakes and bigger issues for the housing industry. Furthermore, once public housing had been reduced to minor proportions and provided shelter for people displaced by other programs favored by private housing groups, it hardly could continue to be regarded as a major threat to private housing interests. So, the home builders and the savings and loan leagues and most of the other organizations that had been so militant in the early years grew increasingly mellow in their attitudes toward public housing. Only NAREB maintained the appearance, at least, of unyielding and total hostility; but even they were devoting much less time to the issue by the end of the 1950s.

By the time of the hearings on the 1965 housing legislation, group opposition to public housing had dwindled still further. The United States Savings and Loan League was now opposed only "to any public housing program beyond the rate of 35,000 units per year."[45] While the National Association of Home Builders continued to argue that private builders could do a better job than the PHA, a NAHB spokesman declared in 1965 that public housing needed "a thorough overhaul of its financing and construction requirements. New and existing projects should be revamped to provide much more effective housing relief for the poor and destitute families in our land."[46] This was hardly the unyielding language of the Taft-Ellender-Wagner days. This was a call for reform, not abolition. The United States Chamber of Commerce continued to invoke its research findings against public housing.[47] Yet, in clarifying comments on his House testimony, a chamber director was anxious to emphasize that his "wasn't a sweeping condemnation . . . at all"; that the program simply "left work undone" which might be better done by other government programs; and that a public housing program comprising, as it did, about 1 percent of the total housing inventory of the nation was no cause for alarm.[48] The National Lumber and Building Material Dealers Association argued against further authorizations, but went on to concede: "We also realize that Congress saw it to approve this years ago and that the program will undoubtedly continue."[49] NAREB still inveighed against public housing, but

[45]U.S. Congress, Senate, Banking and Currency Subcommittee, *Housing Legislation of 1964, Hearings on S. 2468,* 88th Cong., 2d sess., 1964, p. 1165; hereinafter referred to as: Senate, *Hearings, Housing Legislation of 1964.*

[46]U.S. Congress, House of Representatives, Banking and Currency Subcommittee, *Housing and Urban Development Act of 1965, Hearings on H.R. 5840 and Related Bills,* 89th Cong., 1st sess., 1965, Pt. I, p. 548; hereinafter referred to as: House, *Hearings, Housing and Urban Development Act of 1965.*

[47]See *The Impact of Federal Urban Renewal and Public Housing Subsidies* (Washington, D.C.: Construction and Community Development Department, Chamber of Commerce of the United States, 1964).

[48]House, *Hearings, Housing and Urban Development Act of 1965,* Pt. 2, pp. 1006–1007.

[49]U.S. Congress, Senate, Banking and Currency Subcommittee, *Housing Legislation of 1965, Hearings on S. 1354,* 89th Cong., 1st sess., 1965, p. 518; hereinafter referred to as: Senate, *Hearings, Housing Legislation of 1965.*

its 1965 testimony on the subject was cursory and lacked the old self-confident ring.[50]

Moreover, as the provisions of the 1965 act went into effect, and as they were supplemented by new administrative rulings from the PHA, some of public housing's traditional foes saw new business opportunities for themselves in the program. Home builders, realtors, and apartment owners in several cities began to work closely with the local housing authorities in developing these opportunities. Thus, the opposition's drift, first apparent in the mid-1950s, toward acceptance of a limited public housing program was strongly in evidence by the mid-1960s.

This movement toward a more conciliatory posture was matched on the other side among the proponents of public housing. To some extent, their declining zeal was the product of sheer exhaustion. The battle to establish the program had been debilitating. The effort to keep it alive in the face of years of hostility in Washington and of a series of rejections in the communities was bound to sap the vitality of the movement sooner or later. But along with depleted energies went an emerging disappointment with the program.

Among the most disappointed was Catherine Bauer, whose credentials as a supporter of the program were unimpeachable. She had been one of the key people in the establishment of the original public housing program during the New Deal. She served as the U.S. Housing Authority's director of research and information. She had been deeply involved in the program as a leading member of housing organizations, as a government consultant, and as a writer and teacher. But in 1957 she wrote an article entitled "The Dreary Deadlock of Public Housing." She suggested that the reason the program "drags along in a kind of limbo, continuously controversial, not dead but never more than half alive" was partly the obstructionism of the real estate lobby and "the neuroses that come from chronic fright and insecurity" inflicted on housing officials by the incessant attacks on their program.[51] But there were also, she contended, certain "inner weaknesses" in the program itself that rendered it incapable of ever accomplishing its purposes.

---

[50]Senate, *Hearings, Housing Legislation of 1965,* p. 608.

[51]*Architectural Forum,* CVI, no. 5 (1957), 140.

Catherine Bauer's criticisms were echoed by a number of other people who hitherto had been among the most vigorous spokesmen for public housing, including Charles Abrams, one of the great figures of the movement. Like Miss Bauer, Abrams recognized that much of the problem was attributable to the opposition:

> By the time you get through all of this [lobbying for laws, fighting court cases, and pushing to get funds] it is too hard to start things all over again with a program that makes common sense.[52]

Yet, the essential point in Abrams' argument was that, in the light of experience, public housing in its existing form no longer seemed to make common sense.

Many housing officials resented this public airing of dissatisfaction; but privately there was a growing readiness in the housing agencies to recognize the weaknesses identified by the liberal critics.[53] These weaknesses were serious, and they grew worse as time passed. Most important, however, they compelled the emergence of a new empirical spirit among the public housing forces. Ideas that previously had been regarded as anathema (many of them notions first introduced by the opposition groups as substitutes for public housing) were now seriously considered as ways of modifying or supplementing the public housing program. It was this new resiliency that led to the changes in legislation and administration under President Kennedy and to the fresh approaches built into the 1965 act.

This willingness to accept modifications on the public housing side, combined with the granting of recognition to the program by the private housing industry, transformed the climate of relationships between the public and private housing forces. In the past there was little contact between them in Washington. Today, there are matters of mutual concern to discuss, and staff members from the various organizations are known to meet on occasion in a spirit of amicability.

[52]*The Housing Yearbook, 1952* (Washington, D.C.: The National Housing Conference, 1952), pp. 10–11.

[53]The nature of these weaknesses will be developed in the chapters which follow.

So, in this perspective, the public housing case is an exemplification of pluralism triumphant. At the outset there had been rival alliances which, in the view of one group of scholars, were "evenly balanced."[54] They confronted each other intransigently, with no common ground and with no desire to establish any. But with the passage of time, continued pressures from both sides, changes in Congress and administrations, at last it was made clear that neither side could achieve total victory. Once this was recognized, the way was clear for that process of conciliation, compromise, and—ultimately—consensus which is the special genius of American politics. The result of this process was the 1965 housing act. The provisions of the act were not, of course, completely satisfactory to either of the contending parties. Nonetheless, the legislation gave all of the organized interests some part of their original demands, and the final product was at least tolerable to each of them. Indeed, the 1965 act ought to be seen not merely as a safe midpoint between competing claims. The public housing program under the new legislation was recognized on all sides to be a better, more imaginative and flexible instrument than it had been before. If it was a smaller program than had been provided for in 1949, it had gained in quality what it had lost in quantity. It was a compromise settlement but compromise at its most constructive and most creative.

The Group-Imbalance Thesis

The evidence just presented convincingly refutes allegations that the public housing conflict was completely one-sided and that the enemies of public housing had everything their own way. Yet, it does not necessarily contradict the view that there is a general bias in the American political system in favor of business groups. In fact, it would appear to this author that the public housing case provides more support for the group-imbalance thesis than it does for the group-balance, or pluralist, theory. Though there were strong coalitions on both sides, this does not mean they were evenly matched. If the private housing interests had to accept a compromise, it can still be argued that they got very much the best of the bargain.

[54]Meyerson, Terrett, and Wheaton, *Housing, People, and Cities,* p. 278.

First, then, the pro-public housing groups suffered from some
important disadvantages. Unquestionably, both nationally and locally they had less money and staff at their disposal than the
opposition, although few precise figures are available. Lobbying
reports reveal only part of the story. Financial statements of the
organizations are not very revealing, for most of the groups
engaged in the struggle are not single-purpose organizations, and
their statements do not make clear which of the items reported
might have some relation to the public housing campaigns. Nonetheless, as the available information is pieced together, it reveals
greater expenditures against the program than for it.[55] The difference is not of the proportions claimed by the public housing
forces, who used traditional liberal rhetoric in insisting that they
were heroic but puny defenders of the public welfare against the
ravages of massively staffed and monied special interests. In fact,
the funds committed to the attack in Congress on public housing
were not unlimited, and the opposition staffs seem to have been
remarkably effective in creating the impression of far greater
numbers of men than were actually deployed. Just the same, the
opposition groups obviously had substantial sums committed to
the struggle and did not suffer from the chronic shortage of funds
that afflicted the National Housing Conference, which lived in a
perpetual state of financial crisis and periodically sent out emergency appeals for money simply to enable it to survive. In the
communities, too, the sheer scale of some of the opposition cam-

[55]From 1947 through 1950, $40,000 a year was allocated from the general
budget of NAREB to the Realtors' Washington Committee, and an additional $90,000 a year came in from special contributions of $5 a member
solicited through the local boards. The lobbying reports reveal that approximately $260,000 was spent in 1949 to influence legislation by NAREB,
NAHB, USSLL, the Associated General Contractors of America, the Building Products Institute, the Producers' Council, the National Apartment
Owners' Association, and the U.S. Chamber of Commerce. On the other
side, the CIO and AFL housing committees and the National Housing Conference registered lobbying expenses of over $112,000. These figures do not
accurately reveal the scale of activity on both sides. On the one hand, all
the organizations mentioned had concerns that went beyond public housing.
On the other hand, a great deal of effort and money expended by both sides
did not go into the records, including activities defined as "education" or
"public relations" and the kind of grass-roots involvement, paid for by individuals, which was an especially strong feature of the realtors' campaigns.

paigns, especially in the very expensive context of the referendum, was everywhere greater than the efforts to defend the program.[56]

Another factor favoring the opposition was the greater internal cohesion of the various opposition groups. None of them, of course, was single-minded. There is invariably a gap between leaders and many of the followers. It has already been noted that some of the local units of the private housing associations did not follow the lead of their national officers; and within the local organizations there were individuals who either acted against the positions taken by the organizations or did not care very much one way or the other. Still, the private housing groups were relatively homogeneous, and their primary interest was housing. On the public housing side, this could be said only of the housing officials. For social workers and mayors and veterans, housing was but one of many issues they must be concerned with. Furthermore, in the mass-membership organizations declaring their support for the program, the claims of the leadership to speak for their members were often dubious in the extreme. Church social action groups tend to be far more liberal than the general congregation; and in the local battles, clergy and prominent church laymen were often openly hostile to the official stands of their ministerial associations on behalf of public housing. Voting patterns in the local referenda made it obvious that not all members of labor unions agreed with their national leaders on this issue.[57] So, while the list of organizations declaring for public housing was always much longer than the opposition list, both nationally and locally, this was an illusory asset.

[56]In Los Angeles, the AFL alone spent $73,000 in the 1952 referendum campaign, mostly from the building trades workers. (See Baisden, "Labor Unions in Los Angeles Politics," p. 369.) But the scale of their opponents' campaign required resources very much larger than this. In Portland it was estimated that the proponents raised $8500, the opposition $15,000. (See Chester Rapkin, "Rent-Income Ratio–Should Formula for Public Housing Be Changed?" *Journal of Housing,* XIV, no. 1 [1957], 8.) The Seattle Citizens' Housing Committee could only raise about $6000. (See MacDonald, "Report on the Seattle Referendum Campaign," p. 3.)

[57]Nor did all local unions follow the lead of their national organizations with enthusiasm. Even in Seattle, where labor was a mainstay of the defending alliance, the unions did not contribute much money, and some locals were uninvolved.

To some extent, the support of public housing by the federal and local bureaucracy redressed the balance of forces. Yet even this was not quite as solid a factor as the public housing side would have wished. During the critical years of the 1950s, the housing officials responsible for the program in Washington were so harassed that they could hardly be an effective force for their program. Moreover, after 1953, their top leadership pursued policies which, if not hostile to public housing, were cautious and austere.

In the communities, the officials responsible for the operation of the projects suffered from other liabilities. In the smaller cities, many of the housing officials had come into their jobs without prior public service experience. Some, indeed, came from the private housing industry and lacked a full commitment to the purposes of those who had created the public housing program. In the larger communities, on the other hand, the housing authority tended to be staffed by people with backgrounds in public administration, social work, community planning, law, and engineering. This helped to give them an understanding of the goals of public housing, but it did not always provide them with the political experience that was so necessary when the program was under attack. The problem was especially complicated because the local housing authorities were not part of the regular governmental framework. Partly because of the fear of municipal corruption, partly because most cities were close to or had reached the limits of their borrowing powers, the housing authorities had been established as semiautonomous agencies, financed through their own bond issues. They were not subject to the direct control of the local mayors and councils, although the housing commissioners were appointed by the mayors. This could be useful on occasion; but it meant that the program was denied a natural power base in the community. In some places—Los Angeles, for example—the housing authority staffs refused to be inhibited by the peculiarity of their situation. But in Chicago, as Meyerson and Banfield show, the housing authority's political rootlessness and the emphasis by the staff on professional and technical considerations to the neglect of political factors were damaging to the program's prospects.[58]

[58]Meyerson and Banfield, *Politics, Planning, and the Public Interest,* pp. 260–267.

Of course, the housing commissioners were supposed to provide the link between the staffs of the housing authorities and the political community. Yet, preponderantly they represented the established local interests. Almost half of the national total of housing commissioners in 1948 came from business, banking, and industry, with a substantial number from the private housing field. Only 15 percent were wage earners or labor officials. A mere 6 percent were public officials and civic leaders.[59] This is not to say that in general the commissioners did not support public housing. Indeed, some worked with dedication in its behalf.[60] Yet, when the heat was on, when an ostensibly nonpolitical program became the focus of intense political controversy, the kind of people appointed to the housing commissions could not always be expected to supply the staunch defense so urgently needed. To enter the lists vigorously on behalf of public housing might not only alienate them from lifelong friends, but might also have continuing adverse political, personal, and professional effects. Thus, confronted with the ferocity of the attacks, many of the housing commissioners were, in fact, intimidated and failed to undertake the necessary counterattack.

Nor does a favorable interpretation necessarily emerge from the fact that the public housing forces managed to prevent the dismantling of the program, and that the struggle actually produced some improvements in the program between 1949 and 1965.

For one thing, the quantitative price that had to be paid was very high. The 1949 program, which was to have been completed in six years, has not been fully carried out in twenty. Second, while the process of group conflict has produced improvements in the program, the fact that this could only be accomplished by such an abrasive and prolonged confrontation does not reflect well on representative government. Conflict is an inevitable concomitant of democratic politics. But it can be questioned whether

---

[59]*Journal of Housing,* VI, no. 1 (1949), 9.

[60]Thus, in New Jersey a pamphlet defending public housing against some proposed hostile legislation carried the note: "This brochure is published by the commissioners of local housing authorities in New Jersey, acting as citizens with a responsibility for answering misrepresentations and distortions" (New Jersey Association of Housing Authorities, *What's Wrong with the Hillery Bill?* [New Jersey Association of Housing Authorities, n.d.]).

the conflict need be as harsh and unremitting as it was in this case and so replete with irrationality and oversimplification, especially in the referendum campaigns.

Finally, and most important, the terms of the conflict were biased from the outset against the interests of those who were most affected by the problem—that is to say, the poor themselves, who were the only ones who could qualify as tenants in the projects. The reasons for this bias, and its consequences, are the subject of Part II of this book.

PART II
THE CLIMATE
OF IDEAS
AND ATTITUDES

Chapter 3
Poverty

Public housing is not the only program both to have experienced difficulties in the legislative arena and to have attracted heavy interest-group opposition. Obstruction is the norm rather than the exception in the American system. Yet, the trials of public housing were arduous far beyond the norm. The basic reason for this is that the program was designed exclusively for the poor, for those of very low income. In the 1937 and 1949 housing acts, 'the term 'families of low income' means families who are in the lowest income group and who cannot afford to pay enough to cause private enterprise in their locality . . . to build an adequate supply of decent, safe and sanitary dwellings for their use."[1]

On the face of it, this is reasonable enough. Many of the poor were badly housed. Public housing would give them better housing. If it were offered only to the very poor—to those who

Section 2 (2).

needed it most—why should this be a source of weakness for the program?

The answer, of course, is that in the American context a program that serves only the very poor is built on a fragile political foundation. The health of any undertaking established by the government depends in large measure on the strength of the constituency that it serves. But, until very recently at least, the poor have constituted a politically weak constituency.

Generally speaking, the poor have not been political activists. This inevitably lessens the thrust of such programs as public housing. Congressmen need votes, campaign workers, and money; but the poor have a low incidence of voting, are apathetic about campaigns, and obviously are not a source of funds. Again, in the group struggle that surrounds all questions of public policy, the poor are underrepresented. They are the least likely to join organizations or to be chosen as organizational leaders. While there were many groups fighting on behalf of public housing, very few of those eligible for public housing were either members or active participants in those groups. Housing officials, university women, and clergymen are not among the very poor; social workers deal with the lowest-income group, but are not of them; even labor unions do not have many members who could qualify for public housing, except in times of economic depression.[2] These various groups worked diligently on behalf of the poor. But since the clientele of the program were not directly represented in the shaping of its policies, it is not surprising that their interests were inadequately reflected.

Even more damaging than the political quiescence of the poor is their isolation. Although the poor are still very much with us, their numbers have been reduced to a minority of the popula-

[2] A CIO spokesman in the late 1940s said: "Labor unions are interested in housing because cost of shelter is the largest single item that workers pay each month. . . . Sociologists studying the question have found that when a family is paying more than 20 percent of its income for shelter they are taking those funds from other necessities of life. The continuing housing shortage which we have had in this country has made it necessary for those workers to pay more than 20 percent of their income for housing," U.S. Congress, House of Representatives, Select Committee on Lobbying Activities, *Housing Lobby, Hearings Pursuant to H. Res. 298,* 81st Cong., 2d sess., 1950, Exhibit 349, p. 151; hereinafter referred to as: House, *Hearings Housing Lobby.* But by the early 1950s, employed union members could not qualify for public housing, and few of them would want to.

tion. (The size of this minority is subject to dispute: The federal government estimates it as close to 20 percent; some conservatives insist that it is around 10 percent; whereas Leon Keyserling and others have argued that, if we include those living in "deprivation" as well as unalloyed economic misery, over 35 percent of our population suffer from obvious material insufficiency.)[3] Nonetheless, it remains true that, by almost any definition, the United States has attained the almost unparalleled achievement of lifting the majority of its people out of poverty. This majority regard themselves as either middle class or, at least, respectable working class[4] and clearly different from those at the bottom of the economic scale. And the majority, with a self-image of having made themselves secure from poverty by their own efforts, tend to be somewhat disdainful of the minority who have been less successful. The poor are widely thought to have only themselves to blame for their poverty.[5] They are viewed as a burden, a major cause of the high level of federal, state, and local taxes.

[President Lyndon B. Johnson, "The Problem of Poverty in America," in *Economic Report of the President, January 1964* (Washington, D.C.: Government Printing Office, 1964), pp. 55–84. See also Rose D. Friedman, *Poverty: Definition and Perspective* (Washington, D.C.: American Enterprise Institute for Public Policy Research, 1965), pp. 29–36, 38–42; Herman P. Miller, "Who Are the Poor?" *The Nation* (June 7, 1965), p. 609; and Leon H. Keyserling, *Progress or Poverty* (Washington, D.C.: Conference on Economic Progress, 1964), chap. IV.

Polls which had indicated that the overwhelming majority of Americans identify themselves with the middle class have been contradicted by a study of the 1964 presidential election made by University of Michigan Survey Research Center. According to this study, 56 percent of the American electorate claimed working-class status, while only 39 percent said they were middle class. Evidently there is not a homogenized middle-class society in the United States, and statements made throughout this book about majority attitudes must be viewed as very broad generalizations. These qualifications, however, do not alter the fact that the poor constitute a low-status minority in America.

Two Gallup polls in 1964 indicated that the electorate was divided into three, roughly equal, portions on the question, "In your opinion, which is more often to blame if a person is poor—lack of effort on his own part or circumstances beyond his control?" A third blamed the poor for lack of effort; a third, circumstances; while another third believed that both factors were important. Among those with incomes over $7000, however, there were far more who blamed the poor themselves than their circumstances. A Harris poll in 1964 revealed that 64 percent of the electorate believed that welfare and relief payments tend to make people lazy.

This is not to say that the majority refuse to accept any obligations toward the poor. Organized charity exists on a vast scale. And when the Depression made it clear that private charity was not enough, the majority were willing to take several strides down the path toward the welfare state. Today America is far advanced on that journey. The federal government's welfare activities consume many billions of dollars a year and engage the energies of vast armies of bureaucrats in innumerable departments and agencies. Succor to the poor is also available on a large and rapidly increasing scale from state and local units of government.[6]

Just the same, the relative success of the majority has meant that the development of social services in America is much less comprehensive than in other industrialized countries. Thus, Medicare, the great legislative achievement of 1965, provided for Americans over sixty-five fewer benefits than were given to the entire working and retired population of Britain by the National Insurance Act of 1911.[7]

Moreover, Medicare was enacted not only because the poor needed it, but also because many in the middle-income groups lived in constant fear that they would be ruined by their parents' medical bills. The prospects for social legislation have, in fact, always been enhanced when its sources of support were not limited to the very poor, but when other significant constituencies would also benefit.

In contrast to Medicare, no other broad constituencies shared the benefits of public housing. The majority are reasonably well housed. Government, through the Federal Housing Administration, the Federal National Mortgage Association, the Veterans Administration, and so on, has played an active part in making this possible. But that, for the majority, is another matter. Public housing is for those who cannot afford to take advantage of other

[6]The Harris survey cited in footnote 5, which showed that almost two-thirds of the electorate believed that welfare and relief payments tend to make people lazy, also indicated that 68 percent thought that "government must see that no one is without food, clothing, or shelter."

[7]Great Britain, The Law Reports, *National Insurance Act of Britain* (December 16, 1911), XLIX *The Public General Statutes* (London: Eyre & Spottiswoode [Publishers], Ltd., 1911), 337–452.

government aids. It has always been only for the poor. As such it has lacked the potential for broad-based support. More than that, it has been a natural target for the widespread attitude of distaste for the poor. The antipublic housing groups skillfully exploited this attitude in the local conflicts. In the Seattle campaign, for example, it was claimed that the private housing forces

> constantly berated the initiative, intelligence and character of occupants of public housing units. Such people were pictured as spineless ingrates who had found a nest within "government compounds"—people who, in truth, did not have the American abilities to go out and buy their own homes. These people were pictured as people of low and vicious habits.[8]

Nothing could have captured the distrust and disdain for the poor better than the slogan, "Do You Want to Pay Somebody Else's Rent?" which was used with minor variations in cities all around the country. It does not convey the loftier aspirations of American civilization. It is directly opposed to the Judeo-Christian ethic. Yet it expresses with clarity and force a number of the strands that went into community hostility to public housing: Would not the program undermine the recipient's independence and initiative? Was it fair to impose an additional burden on the already hard-pressed homeowner? Why should his own thrift and hard work be penalized to support people who were shiftless and irresponsible—slum dwellers who would make slums out of public housing, too?

Thus the slogan, and the opposition campaigns generally, had a good deal of resonance in the communities. The campaigns, no doubt, were skillful exercises in the process of persuasion. But people did not need very much persuasion. Where they voted against public housing, it was not primarily because of Pavlovian conditioning, but because they had a perfectly clear perception of the issues. They did not want to pay somebody else's rent. The private housing groups were the catalysts of deep-seated community feelings toward the poor.

Kenneth A. MacDonald, "Report on the Seattle Referendum Campaign," Seattle 1950, p. 9 (Mimeographed).

EXCEPTIONAL CIRCUMSTANCES

If this were so, if public housing was the target and symbol of such hostile attitudes, how was enough backing secured to establish the program in the first place, and then to bring about even the modest growth that was accomplished? The explanation is to be found in some special circumstances that developed at crucial times in the program's history.

Attention has already been drawn to the two requirements of the legislative system that must be satisfied before much can be done about public housing. These are, first, a President who strongly supports the program and, second, a large Democratic majority in the House of Representatives. But these alone are not completely sufficient. A substantial degree of support in the country at large is also necessary.

This measure of national support for public housing was available for short periods on a few key occasions. It was there in the 1930s. Not many people in those years scorned the poor. Poverty was no distant threat, known only to the lazy or incompetent, but a socially produced calamity threatening vast numbers of the previously secure middle class. The result was a general empathy for the poor, evoking ready support for government welfare programs, such as public housing, which aimed at the amelioration of social injustice. Moreover, the preamble to the 1937 housing act included among its purposes "the reduction of unemployment and the stimulation of business activity." This was the key factor in securing approval for public housing, for the program would generate jobs. And since unemployment was still of major concern in 1938, further public housing authorization was easily obtained.

The condition of support quickly evaporated, however. When the Administrator of the United States Housing Authority asked for still more money in 1939, the House of Representatives refused. The economic situation had eased somewhat, and although there was still heavy unemployment, the slightest improvement was sufficient to bring the program's momentum to a halt. Realtors and savings and loan associations pressed their opposition to public housing on Congress, and in 1939 they found a receptive atmosphere in the House.

After World War II, hopes for an expansion of the program

could not be based on general economic conditions. The fears which existed in 1945 that the conversion to peace would bring another depression were quickly replaced by buoyant optimism as the long-denied yearning for consumer goods provided an assured foundation for continued prosperity. However, in place of economic crisis there was a widespread housing crisis. The poor were not the only ones who worried about housing. The war had slowed residential construction drastically. For a period following the war, some construction materials were in short supply, so the building industry was slow in getting back into full operation. Yet, housing demand had increased enormously. People who had roomed with relatives in wartime were no longer willing to do so. Veterans were returning from the service, getting married, and wanting homes of their own. Hundreds of thousands of them were denied the opportunity. Many were compelled to live in "attics, basements, chicken coops and boxcars."[9] Chicago reported over 100,000 homeless veterans. In Los Angeles in December 1945, the city council appropriated $100,000 to construct temporary shelters, and one councilman complained that this was insufficient: "By Christmas you will see veterans by the hundreds bivuacked in Pershing Square."[10] While this dire prediction did not materialize, the situation in Los Angeles as well as in other cities remained critical. A general condition of scarcity persisted, affecting many from the middle class. At the beginning of 1947 an opinion poll revealed that housing was one of the top issues in the public mind.[11] All over the country the problem was front-page news.

Consequently, large numbers of people were ready to turn to government for help in increasing the supply of homes. So intense was the public concern that it provided President Truman with a powerful issue which he used with increasing fervor against the

Richard O. Davies, *Housing Reform During the Truman Administration* Columbia, Mo.: University of Missouri Press, 1966), p. 41.

Los Angeles Times (December 11, 1945), Pt. I, p. 12. It was Councilman Davenport who made this statement. He went on to say, "I think the situation is critical. Let's do something realistic, not make a gesture." It was his same councilman who later discovered that public housing was socialistic and provided one of the decisive votes against the program.

Journal of Housing, IV, no. 5 (1947), 129.

Republicans. The 80th Congress' failure to act on the Taft-Ellender-Wagner Bill was cited by him as a perfect illustration of its "do-nothing" character. He berated the Republicans as tools of the "real estate lobby" and repeatedly criticized Dewey during the 1948 campaign for his failure to say anything on housing beyond bland generalities.

Truman's handling of the issue before the public was especially effective in the way it tied the need for more public housing to the general housing crisis. For the majority it would no longer take a great leap of the imagination to see that if the middle class had a housing problem, there might be a problem at the lower end of the income scale. While it would be too much to claim that the President and his supporters made public housing into a great popular cause, a national poll in January 1949 indicated general approval of government action to provide more low-rent housing.[12]

Despite this, there was the narrowest possible margin for public housing in the House of Representatives. And this margin almost certainly included some who accepted public housing only grudgingly, as part of a package which included the continuation of FHA and other programs for the private housing market. Title I of the Taft-Ellender-Wagner Act, dealing with a new program of urban redevelopment, also had its own group of enthusiasts in the House. And by no means all of these favored public housing, for redevelopment opened up a number of new and interesting possibilities for private business.

It was obvious, then, that the tenuous congressional support for public housing would dissolve if there were no general concern in the country over the housing problem. As it transpired, this concern faded rapidly after the passing of the 1949 act. By the time the act was on the books, the housing crisis was already passing its peak. Despite the shortage of materials following World War II, housing production gradually increased. Almost

---

[12]*Public Opinion Quarterly,* XIII, no. 1 (1949), 159. The question was: "It has been suggested that the new Congress should provide government money for slum clearance and low-rent housing. Do you think Congress should provide this money?" Of those polled, 69 percent said yes, 21 percent said no, and 10 percent had no opinion. The same question posed in March 1949 revealed support among union members (79 to 13 percent) and farmers (56 to 29 percent). *Public Opinion Quarterly,* XIII, no. 2 (1949), 351

3½ million units were constructed between 1946 and 1949, and previous records were broken in 1950 with the production of 1,400,000 units. There was a dip during the Korean conflict, but the annual residential construction rate by 1954 was well over one million. Critics argued in the 1950s that this was far below what was needed and that much of the new building was incredibly shoddy. Even so, for the majority the pressure was gone. By 1952, housing was no longer listed as one of the dominant issues in the public mind.[13] The normal state of affairs had returned, and once again the poor were isolated in their plight. The new construction had done little to improve their living conditions, but in the absence of either an economic calamity or a general housing crisis, their claims to better housing were received apathetically.

Indeed, once the issue was taken into the communities and the neighborhoods, it became apparent that apathy sometimes gave way to active hostility. And when this hostility had been given a chance to express itself in the referendum, the remaining support for public housing in Congress was still further eroded. From 1953 until 1958, in fact, the House was reluctant to go along even with the modest Eisenhower proposals. Had it not been for a further set of unusual circumstances in 1956, it is unlikely that there would have been congressional approval of a two-year, 35,000 units a year, authorization. For in June, after favorable action in the House Banking and Currency Committee, Jesse Wolcott, the ranking Republican on Banking and Currency, once again talked to Judge Smith, and the Rules Committee voted to table the bill.

At first, this was greeted by the private housing groups with satisfaction. The National Association of Home Builders told their members that, if the housing bill stalled, "few repercussions would be felt in the home building and lending industry."[14] Then in July FHA Commissioner Norman Mason warned that serious harm

---

[13]Elmo Roper, *You and Your Leaders* (New York: William Morrow & Company, Inc., 1957), p. 249; *Congressional Quarterly Almanac*, IX (1952), 484. *The Reader's Guide to Periodical Literature* lists 238 articles on housing in the United States from May 1945 to April 1947. This had fallen to 101 articles in the period April 1953 to February 1955.

[14]National Association of Home Builders, *Newsletter* (June 19, 1956).

would come to the FHA programs if there were no housing legislation in 1956. Within two weeks of Mason's warning, the bill began to move again. The Rules Committee reported it favorably, including the Administration's public housing request. On the floor, Wolcott and other archfoes of public housing meekly voted for a bill that included 70,000 (35,000 a year) units of public housing.[15]

Of course, in voting for 35,000 units a year Wolcott and his supporters were not conceding anything close to the 1949 program. And the 35,000 units a year pace was not exceeded even under the sympathetic Kennedy and Johnson administrations until the late 1960s, when the impact of the riots in the cities had generated a new urgency in the federal government's approach to the plight of the poor. Even today, with the program more securely established than in the past, it is also clear that no politician can look to public housing, as Harry Truman did, for a profitable campaign issue.[16]

It was fortunate for public housing that it could be a viable issue in 1948 and that on a few other occasions there were unusual conjunctions of conditions sufficient to bring the program into being and keep it alive. But if these special circumstances were enough to give it life, they could not endow it with real vitality. The reasons for this were endemic in the prevailing attitudes toward the poor.

THE BUILT-IN DEFECTS OF PUBLIC HOUSING

"I have never seen anything the matter with the public housing program of the federal government." This kind of ringing assertion could still evoke enthusiastic applause at a National Housing Con-

---

[15]Among other long-time enemies of public housing to vote for 70,000 units in 1956 were Congressmen McDonough, Hiestand, Allen, Ellsworth, and Latham.

[16]Unless it be as a target for hostility. In a speech in Chicago in October 1967, Governor Ronald Reagan pronounced public housing a failure with a high crime rate. (See *Los Angeles Times* [October 28, 1967], Pt. I, p. 7.)

erence meeting in 1954.[17] But not long after that it came to be generally acknowledged that there was a great deal wrong with public housing. A body of criticism evolved that commanded support across a broad spectrum of informed opinion. And the most anguished cries of disappointment came from some of public housing's earliest and warmest supporters.

No doubt any program on the scale of public housing would have its problems, and those who became so acutely disillusioned had perhaps never faced up to the fact that their program could not be exempt from the shortcomings of all forms of human organization. Still, the deficiencies of public housing went far beyond any normal degree of malfunctioning. It was bound to be so from the beginning. Public housing was never able to break away from the sources of trouble that were built into it initially. It was born with profound defects, and the hostile environment in which it grew aggravated its congenital ailments.

At the heart of its problems, as has been indicated, was the general view of poverty as reflecting personal failure and as deserving alleviation by society only under carefully controlled and limited conditions. This attitude permeated the legislation as it was written by Congress. It manifested itself in the rules established for the program by its administrators. It expressed itself in the shrill and angry voices of the people as they voted against the program in referenda or demonstrated against the selection of particular sites. In every arena, the common attitude toward public housing was grudging and restrictive. Harsh limits were imposed on the program, and these limits gave rise to a mounting chorus of criticism as the 1950s progressed.

Income Restrictions

When the authors of the 1937 housing act said that public housing was for families of "the lowest income group," they did not explain exactly what they meant by that term. They specified that the net income of a family at the time of admission was not to exceed five times the rent to be paid (including utilities), unless there were three or more minor dependents, in which case

[17]"How Should Low-Income Families Be Housed?," *The Housing Yearbook, 1954* (Washington, D.C.: The National Housing Conference, 1954), p. 26.

the ratio would be 6 to 1.[18] Exact limits, however, were left to the administrator of the program.

In making his decision, the administrator could be guided partly by legislative intent. After 1949, the intent of Senator Taft was a powerful consideration. Taft believed that the program should serve only those who could not afford to provide their own housing. However, he had in mind primarily the "deserving poor"—those who were in more or less regular employment but whose income was not high enough to pay for decent private housing. Though he would not exclude families on relief, he resisted efforts to make the projects into homes for indigents.

This view coincided with the preferences of most of those responsible for administering public housing. They did not see the housing projects as almshouses, Poor Law institutions. They wanted success stories, families who would find new hope through the opportunity to live in a clean, soundly built dwelling and be inspired to better themselves and eventually move up to good private housing. Moreover, the federal subsidy assumed that a large proportion of the cost of public housing would be met by the tenants' rents; thus, if the occupants fell behind on their payments, the projects would be faced with financial difficulties.

Consequently, eligibility requirements were imposed that denied admission to some of the chronically poor—and also to those who might cause trouble in the projects because of prison records or social behavior which, by middle-class standards, was unacceptable. This became a source of criticism of the program by the opposition groups. Public housing, they said, was not really for the poor; and they cited examples of tenants who, because of exemptions granted by virtue of having several children, actually

---

[18]For discussion of the rent-income ratio, see Robert Moore Fisher, *20 Years of Public Housing—Economic Aspects of the Federal Program* (New York: Harper & Row, Publishers, 1959), pp. 223–227. The requirements of the 1937 and 1949 acts were modified by the 1959 amendments, which substituted for the rent-income ratio requirements the following statement: "Income limits for occupancy and rents shall be fixed by the public housing agency [LHA] and approved by the Authority [PHA] after taking into consideration (A) the family size, composition, age, physical handicaps, and other factors which might affect the rent-paying ability of the family, and (B) the economic factors which affect the financial stability and solvency of the project" (U.S. Congress, House of Representatives, *Conference Report on the Housing Act of 1959,* H.R. Rept. 566, 86th Cong., 1st sess., 1959, p. 29).

1ad higher incomes than many of the people who lived outside he projects.[19]

Just the same, the projects have housed the very poor, if not always the poorest. After the 1937 act was passed, the administrator of the program fixed a maximum of $1400 a year for larger cities, less for smaller communities. During the prewar years, the median annual family income of the tenants was around $800. In 1950 it was approximately $1700. Even by the standards of those periods, these figures were below the poverty evel. The 1949 act essentially maintained the stringency of the income limits, and in 1966 the median was close to $2700.[20]

The key to holding the figure at these levels was that, as the tenant's income rose beyond the permissible limits, he was subject to eviction. Again, the opposition gave much publicity to cases in which families were not promptly ejected after surpassing the maximum allowed earnings. Yet, the general rule was that people whose income rose beyond a certain point had to leave the projects. This had undesirable results both for the tenants who had to move out and for the projects they left behind. For the families faced with the prospect of eviction there was an obvious disincentive effect. "An increase of income . . . has become a tragedy, for it invites eviction, loss of neighborhood associations, shifts in the schooling of the children and other inconveniences."[21]

[19]In 1963 the Comptroller General of the United States submitted to Congress critical comments along the same lines. (See Comptroller General of the United States, *Review of Eligibility Requirements, Rents, and Occupancy of Selected Low-Rent Housing Projects,* Report to the Congress of the United States [Washington, D. C.: General Accounting Office, April 1963].)

[20]See "Few Ineligible Tenants," *The Housing Yearbook, 1954,* p. 60; Housing and Home Finance Agency, *16th Annual Report* (Washington, D.C.: Government Printing Office, 1962), p. 211; U.S. Congress, Senate, Banking and Currency Subcommittee, *Housing Legislation of 1967, Hearings on Proposed Housing Legislation for 1967,* 90th Cong., 1st sess., Pt. I, 1967, p. 116; hereinafter referred to as: Senate, *Hearings, Housing Legislation of 1967.* The median for 1966 was $2709 for all families. However, the median for elderly tenants was only $1500, for the nonelderly $3293.

[21]Charles Abrams, "Public Housing Myths," *The New Leader* (July 25, 1955), p. 6. See also Lawrence M. Friedman, *Government and Slum Housing* (Chicago: Rand McNally & Company, 1968), pp. 132–138; Lawrence M. Friedman, "Public Housing and the Poor: An Overview," *California Law Review,* LIV (May 1966), 642.

It could also mean a decline in their standard of living, for outside the projects rents for comparable housing would be considerably higher. "Eviction of over-income families," said one report, "throws many of them into a housing no-man's land."[22] This being so, the desire to improve themselves by getting a better job—one of the ostensible purposes of the public housing program—would be reduced.

Nonetheless, there were many who did increase their income and who went out into the private housing market. Their departure represented a serious loss to the quality of life in the projects, for they tended to be the more energetic, ambitious, and "responsible" tenants. They included a high proportion of the "leadership families," who set the pattern of attitudes in the projects and were active in providing structure and organization in the public housing communities. Those left behind were, to a large extent, families who would never be successful by the usual tests of achievement in America. Their condition was marked not only by a lack of income, but also by the entire syndrome known as the "culture of poverty."

The development of this culture (or subculture) reflects, according to Oscar Lewis, the combined effect of a variety of factors, including not only low income, but also segregation and discrimination, fear, suspicion, and apathy. It is typified by low expectations about the future and mistrust of the institutions and practices of the larger society—including marriage. Thus, a high proportion of the children born into the culture of poverty grow up without a father.

The poverty culture is by no means without positive aspects. It develops its own modes of providing protection against a hostile environment. There is a gregariousness which provides warmth and human contact; and "living in the present may develop a capacity for spontaneity and adventure, for the enjoyment of the sensual, the indulgence of impulse, which is often blunted in the middle-class, future-oriented man." Nonetheless, in Lewis' view it is "a comparatively thin culture," containing "a great deal of pathos, suffering and emptiness. . . . Its encouragement of mistrust magnifies individual helplessness and isolation." Thus the

[22]California, Department of Industrial Relations, Division of Housing, *Report of the Governor's Conference on Housing* (June 1960), p. 37.

individual who grows up in this culture has a strong feeling of fatalism, dependence, and inferiority.[23]

These are the traits that have contributed to the political impotence of the poor. But the consequences for public housing are social as well as political. People who have come out of generations of slum living do not necessarily rid themselves of their sense of dependency and inferiority and their patterns of social disorganization simply because they have been given better housing. As Kenneth Clark has pointed out, "merely to move the residents of a ghetto into low-income housing projects without altering the pattern of their lives—menial jobs, low income, inadequate education for their children . . ."[24] does not break the cycle of poverty.

So, inevitably, some of the attributes of the slum were brought into public housing. Michael Harrington conceded "the tendency toward violence, and juvenile crime in particular."[25] Harrison Salisbury complained that in some of the housing projects in New York, "we have merely institutionalized our slums." They are, he said, "forcing centers of juvenile delinquency. They spawn teen-age gangs. They incubate crime. They are fiendishly contrived institutions for the debasing of family and community life to the lowest common mean. They are worse than anything George Orwell ever conceived."[26] The Pruitt-Igoe project in St. Louis, considered to be one of the best public housing facilities in the country when it was built in 1954, was described by a perceptive reporter in 1967 as the worst slum in "the entire north half of St. Louis." His story tells of the surrounding land being "strewn with broken bottles, empty cans and piles of miscellaneous debris," of hallway floors filled with litter and "overrun by rats and mice and bugs," of broken windows and inadequate

[23]Oscar Lewis, *La Vida* (New York: Random House, Inc., 1966), pp. xlv–xlviii, li–lii.

[24]Kenneth Clark, *Dark Ghetto: Dilemmas of Social Power* (New York: Harper & Row, Publishers, 1965), p. 253.

[25]Michael Harrington, *The Other America* (Baltimore: Penguin Books, Inc., 1963), p. 159.

[26]Harrison Salisbury, *The Shook-Up Generation* (New York: Harper & Row, Publishers, 1958), pp. 74–75.

heating, of vandalism by bands of roving youths, of 60 percent of the families without a male head.[27] And one of the most frequently heard criticisms among the tenants of Pruitt-Igoe was that, because of evictions resulting from increased income, "we have lost the most needed, most stable element in our community —families that are beginning to make it."

Now, the entire burden of the problem of social disintegration cannot be placed on the fact that overincome families were evicted. It would have been a travesty of the purposes of the housing programs if public housing had not included a high proportion of the most hostile and alienated members of the poverty culture. This could not help but mean that life in many of the big-city projects would be ridden with tension and difficulties. But with the systematic removal of the more successful families, the element making for cohesion and stability was gone.

This problem has grown steadily more acute as the nature of poverty has changed in America. In the 1930s, when poverty was still widespread, many of those in public housing were the "deserving poor," who would be able to advance themselves when the job situation improved. Then World War II and the postwar boom sharply reduced the numbers of the poor. By the early 1950s, as the young married veterans who had come into the projects in the postwar years moved out, the remaining clientele for public housing consisted primarily of those who, despite the general affluence, were still unable to break out of poverty. Many of them were on welfare, and in some projects a majority of the rents were paid by the local welfare agencies.

So the desire of housing officials to maintain a more balanced, representative community in the projects was thwarted. They had less and less choice in the matter as the character of the eligible group changed. Moreover, after 1954, housing legislation placed increasing emphasis on the function of public housing as a repository for slum dwellers who were uprooted from their homes by urban renewal, redevelopment, and other public programs. People in this category were given high priority by the law, and the opportunities were reduced for screening out the most disruptive "problem families." After the late 1950s, too, legislation opened the way for single, elderly people to live in

[27]D. J. R. Bruckner in the *Los Angeles Times* (February 2, 1967), Pt. I, p. 22.

public housing. These, at least, were no threat to the peace and order of the housing projects, but neither were they a source of leadership to replace the younger families who had moved out because of higher earnings.

So the grim pattern of social disorganization, though by no means universal, has become an undeniable malignancy in some of the housing projects in New York, St. Louis, and other major cities. The danger was always there, for the seeds of disaster are constantly present in the culture of poverty. But since the law insisted that only the very poor be permitted to enter and to stay, and since the number of the very poor came closer and closer to the hard core of those trapped in the culture of poverty, disaster became unavoidable. The worst might not have occurred if, as their incomes rose, people had been permitted to pay higher rents and stay in the projects. But this would have been contrary to the intent of the laws establishing the program. It would have conflicted with the view that anything government does for the poor must be within the most carefully circumscribed conditions—for more than this would be an undue burden for the majority and a dangerous undermining of the initiative of the poor.

Whatever possibilities might have emerged for a mellowing of this attitude were, in any case, frustrated by the drastic cutting back of the program's appropriations following 1951. Where there was so little public housing, only those in the most urgent need could be provided for. Tenants with incomes beyond the allowable limits were obviously not those with the greatest need. Only a much larger program might have provided room for the socioeconomic balance which is found in public housing in other countries but which is so determinedly absent from the American program.

Site Restrictions

If the first complaint of the liberal critics was that public housing was segregated by income, their second was that it was segregated by location. In most of the big cities, the housing authorities wanted to locate some of the sites outside the poverty areas. Even with the power of eminent domain, slum clearance is expensive. With the advent of urban renewal, public housing could sometimes take advantage of slum clearance undertaken with other federal funds (although many urban renewal projects have ignored the need for low-cost housing).[28] But in the years immediately following the passage of the Taft-Ellender-Wagner Act, the public housing program itself had to carry most of the expense of preparing sites. Then, too, leveling a dilapidated area takes time, as does building new housing. If the new were to be built on the sites of the old, where were the people who lived in the slum dwellings to go until the new housing projects were ready for them? Finally, public housing proponents did not want to accept the prevailing residential patterns that kept the poor and the minority groups penned within ghettos. Public housing, they earnestly believed, was a means by which integration could be promoted.

As previously seen, their hopes ran into fierce local resistance. The introduction of *anything* new into an existing residential community would have been sufficient to stir some antipathy. Almost every proposal that brings an element for change into a neighborhood—be it a highway, school or park, or even a private housing development—must make its way over the suspicions and fears of local property owners. City-council chambers filled with angry homeowners protesting zone changes are a frequent spectacle in America.

But public housing in a suburban area would be a particular threat. The incursion of the poor could undermine the typical neighborhood preoccupation with "maintaining property values." There was a predisposition to accept the view offered by the National Association of Home Builders that "Nobody wants property near public housing projects. When nobody wants it, property loses value."[29] Actually, the impact of a public housing project on neighborhood property values is not necessarily harmful.[30] But the neighborhood associations were not prepared to examine

[28]Martin Anderson, *The Federal Bulldozer: A Critical Analysis of Urban Renewal* (Cambridge, Mass.: The M.I.T. Press, 1965), pp. 91–105.

[29]National Association of Home Builders, "Home Builders Information Material to Oppose Socialized Public Housing" (Mimeographed kit of materials).

[30]See "'Canned' Campaign Killed in Miami," *Journal of Housing*, VII, no. 7 (1950), 226, which quotes a Chicago study in which thirty-four realtors were interviewed, thirty-two of whom said that land values in the vicinity of public housing projects were either not affected or actually increased by the presence of the projects.

dispassionately all economic evidence on both sides of the question. They were only too ready to accept the impression of financial danger, for their concern was more than financial. Behind the phrase, "maintaining property values," was the even more potent concept, "maintaining the character of the neighborhood." The character of the suburban neighborhood had been established by people who wanted to keep the poor at a safe distance. The poor, in their view, were a group with a higher-than-average incidence of criminality, delinquency, illegitimacy, and school dropout. They tended to be dirty, disorderly in public places, and given to the use of profane language. They had different customs, manners, ways of dress and speech. If allowed into the suburban neighborhood their children would attend the local public schools and lower the social and educational level. In short, the poor would bring the entire culture of poverty with them into the housing projects, and soon the projects would themselves become slums.

Now, as we have just seen, this stereotype is not entirely divorced from reality. The culture of poverty is not ennobling. Its virtues are not readily compatible with middle-class standards. Its vices are inevitably regarded as a threat by the dominant community in America. Public housing projects did, in some cases, take on some of the worst attributes of the slum. Yet, most of the harrowing examples of conditions in the projects did not materialize until later. The experience of public housing up to the time the site battles were occurring in the early 1950s was by no means bad. The fears aroused in the communities were based at least as much on myth and status anxieties as upon reality. Yet, whatever their causes, the fears were themselves a reality, and the opposition groups were especially skillful in playing upon these fears in the referendum campaigns.

In Seattle in 1950, for example, the opposition took advantage of the fact that no announcement had yet been made of public housing locations to construct a site map of their own. The campaign organizers called more than fifty real estate agents in residential districts and asked them if there were any vacant land in their area that might conceivably be available for the projects. Fifteen possible locations were discovered, and an artist was hired to draw a map of the city indicating the fifteen sites. Six days before the election, the *Seattle Times* carried a three-column cut of this map with the caption *Map Indicating Possible Sites for*

Proposed 1221 Housing Units." The accompanying story quoted the chairman of the Seattle Real Estate Board: "It seems unlikely," he was quoted as saying, "that the entire project will be located in one spot. . . . As so much of the land shown in the survey has proved unsuitable for housing of any kind because of slide and marshy conditions, it appears that the projects may be forced close to high-grade residential sections, damaging property values."[31] The same map and an accompanying story was carried by neighborhood newspapers in the vicinity of the possible sites.

The mayor and the housing authority indignantly insisted that the sites had not yet been selected and that most of those suggested in the map were extremely unlikely ones.[32] Yet, the opposition's tactic had a powerful impact. There was a great outcry in some of the districts indicated on the map. While there would have been opposition had the sites actually been announced, the failure to select them before the election left the way open for the opposition to provoke hostility in communities that would have had nothing against the idea of public housing were it not for the possibility that it might be brought into their neighborhood.

The ploy of speculating on where the sites might be had been borrowed from the campaign in St. Petersburg. There, in November 1949, a newspaper carried a map indicating a number of possible locations, and asked:

> Where in St. Petersburg will the proposed new housing project be located? The location of the Housing Project on which you voters of St. Petersburg will be called upon Friday, November 18, to vote either "yes" or "no" has not been designated. WHY? Will the location of the project be Shell Island—will it be in North Shore—will it be in the Mirror Lake section—will it be in the West Central section—or Maximo Point—or near Bahama Beach? Will it be adjacent to YOUR property? You should be told before you vote.[33]

[31]*Seattle Times* (March 8, 1950). Reprinted in Seattle Master Builders Kit, 1950.

[32]*Seattle Times* (March 10, 1950). Reprinted in Seattle Master Builders Kit, 1950.

[33]*St. Petersburg Independent* (November 14, 1949). Reprinted in Seattle Master Builders Kit, 1950.

Then the idea moved on from Seattle to Portland, Oregon. In their special tabloid, the *Portland Shopping News,* the private housing groups asked, *"Why Don't They Tell You* BEFORE *Election?"* followed by:

> 30 sites within the Portland city limits have been tentatively approved by the Public Housers. IS ONE OF THEM IN YOUR NEIGHBORHOOD? . . . Naturally, you suppose that all this Public Housing will be built in some other section of the city and that your own neighborhood will remain just as it is. Why don't they tell you before election just where they intend to build 2000 units of public housing?[34]

The site issue was a powerful element almost everywhere in the controversies over public housing. In Los Angeles the first city councilman to defect from the unanimous approval for the program represented a district in which a project was to be located.[35] In Chicago, Philadelphia, Detroit, and Grand Rapids, the attempt to locate public housing projects on vacant land outside of the slum areas was the prime source of much of the trouble the program faced.

The consequence was that housing authorities in most of the big urban centers had to draw back from their efforts to build projects outside the poverty areas and to restrict them to older, more dilapidated neighborhoods. This was a factor in reducing the opposition of the private housing groups to public housing. But it increased the disenchantment with the program of many of its earliest proponents.

Cost and Design Restrictions

The decision to build a housing project within the existing slum boundaries reinforced some of the other inhearent defects of public housing. Slum sites were costly to prepare, and the money available from Washington was severely limited. When a site was finally available, it was natural to want to use it to the full by

---

[34]*Portland Shopping News* (May 16, 1950). Reprinted in Seattle Master Builders Kit, 1950.

[35]This was Councilman John Holland, in whose district was located about one-third of the proposed Rose Hills project.

building high-rise apartments.[36] But this was precisely the wrong kind of housing for the children and youths of the slums. Mothers found it difficult to watch children playing many stories below. Large numbers of teen-agers were brought together in a small area, resulting in an intense concentration of gang problems.[37] It was suggested that public housing actually increased crime and delinquency, a charge repeatedly voiced by the opponents of public housing in Los Angeles and elsewhere. Actually, there is evidence to suggest that the rates are higher in neighborhoods adjacent to projects *where income levels are similar.*[38] Even if this is so, the concentration of the poor in high-rise projects made more visible the social disorganization which previously had been dispersed throughout a number of slum neighborhoods and made the target for the opposition more obvious.

The problem was exacerbated by restrictions on design. While high-rise apartments are not the best environment for families with young children, intelligent design can minimize this difficulty and, at the same time, provide pleasing, attractive surroundings. But two factors inhibited a concern about design. First, a grudging attitude accompanied aid to the poor. Sound construction, adequate air and light must meet the standards for publicly sponsored buildings. Yet, many felt, it would not be fitting to give too much attention to esthetic factors when dealing with the poor. The basic legislation makes it clear that every "project shall be undertaken in such a manner that it will not be of elaborate or extravagant design or construction." While no one would argue for an "elaborate or extravagant" approach, in practice this has generally been taken to mean that public housing style should be Spartan and unadorned. The 1949 act also provides that "economy will be promoted both in construction and administration." Some economists have suggested that, in this respect at least, Congress was unduly permissive and did not impose sufficiently

[36]The argument for high densities was reinforced by the fact that slums are generally overcrowded; and if public housing is to provide more space per person, pulling down the slums would result in a net loss of housing for the poor unless the projects were high-rise.

[37]Drayton S. Bryant, "The Next Twenty Years in Public Housing," *Social Work,* IV, no. 2 (April 1959), 46–54.

[38]See Albert Mayer, "Public Housing as Community," *Architectural Record,* (April 1964), pp. 169–178.

clear cost limits, leaving too much leeway to the USHA Administrator.[39] In practice, under Raymond Foley and Albert Cole there was little danger of a relaxed approach to expenditures. Even if they had been more expansive themselves, the tiny appropriations granted the program from 1951 would have given them few opportunities for extravagance.

The worst consequences of these restrictions were all too visible in some of the big cities of the East and Midwest. *Progressive Architecture* complained that "low-cost public housing in New York . . . most often has been a collection of monolithic, institutional apartment structures about as inviting to live in as Wormwood Scrubs."[40] James Baldwin described public housing in Harlem as "colorless, bleak, high and revolting."[41] The contrast between the early hopes of the public housing groups and the later realities was graphically stated by Albert Mayer, an architect and a public housing consultant since 1933:

> Planners had, in the incubating New Deal days, seen in public housing the chance of creating developments that would be large enough and freely enough designed to form brave new communities—uncluttered, throbbing with new life and vigor, beacons of urbane living. But . . . instead of a neighborhood cynosure, imaginatively planned and inviting, we had large, monotonous, pared-down institutions of single economic level.[42]

Here, then, the esthetic and the social dimensions of the problem came together. The projects *looked* forbidding. Their size was beyond "human scale," the environment too big for individuals to adjust to, especially those already alienated, hostile, dependent.

In addition, the appearance and sheer physical bulk of the projects increased the impression of separateness. The buildings

Fisher, *20 Years of Public Housing,* pp. 138–140.

"Making Public Housing Human," *Progressive Architecture* (January 1965), p. 177.

James Baldwin, *Nobody Knows My Name* (New York: The Dial Press, Inc., 1961), p. 63.

Albert Mayer, "Public Housing Architecture," *Journal of Housing,* XIX, no. 8 (1962), 450.

towered above their neighborhoods—indeed, "turning their backs' on them, declared Catherine Bauer.

All of this heightened the antipathy to public housing in middle-class neighborhoods. It was bad enough that the project tenants were poor. But public housing might bring a heavy concentration of poor people, inundating the community with their numbers. Furthermore, the proximity of high-rise apartments in themselves is an anathema to neighborhoods of single-family houses. In the Los Angeles struggle, the very notion that some of the proposed projects would rise to thirteen stories caused a great roar of outrage in the newspapers and among homeowners' associations. This would breach the city's traditional insistence on low-density construction. Since that time, of course, the Los Angeles skyline has been strikingly changed by buildings reaching forty stories or more. But these were privately constructed, and they were not for the poor. It was totally unacceptable that a program designed for the poor should be the innovative factor in the life style of the city.

Administrative Restrictions

In many projects, the harsh, institutional appearance was matched by harsh, institutional administration. Even before the Eisenhower period, the prevailing view was that the projects should be conducted according to the requirements of sound real estate management, and the local housing authorities tended to "emphasize the efficiency of its real estate operation rather than the extension of its achievements in social welfare."[43] With the advent of Eisenhower to the White House and Cole and Slusser to the housing agency, there was even more emphasis on efficiency and the elimination of "frills." The frills included social welfare services of various kinds. Without these there could be little hope of countering the social disorganization in the projects other than through harsh regulation and eviction in case of unmanageable misconduct.

Yet, the blame cannot be placed entirely on the rigidities of some of the administrators. Since there were income limits and since tenants who transcended those limits had to be evicted, some mechanism had to be used to enforce this. Procedures

[43]John P. Dean, "The Myths of Housing Reform," *American Sociological Review*, XIV, no. 2 (April 1949), 281–288.

varied from city to city, but typically they included credit checks, scrutinies of income tax statements, and written declarations of income that had to be completed to comply with the demands of the housing authorities.

Moreover, the conditions described by Harrison Salisbury and others were bound to lead to an emphasis by project managers on preserving the peace and protecting property. The very existence of the social order was threatened by some of the juvenile gangs. Many tenants, coming from the Appalachians and the rural South, lacked experience not only with decent housing but with urban living in general. So, a variety of rules and regulations was established. In Los Angeles, says Paul Jacobs,

> The "rules and regulations" which the Housing Authority attempts to use to control the tenants encompass nearly every detail of daily life. Tenants who do not put trash cans out alongside the house are charged for having it done by the maintenance crews; tenants who don't clean up their own yards are charged for having that done. If a maintenance man decides a lawn needs watering and turns on the hose, the tenant is charged for that; if a stove is broken and it is the property of the Authority, the tenant is charged for the repairs. The tenants may put only those screen doors on the apartments which are supplied and installed by the Authority, and they must pay for both the door and installation at the usual commercial rates. "We must have uniformity in the project so that the apartments all look more or less alike," says the director.[44]

Housing authorities in many other cities imposed restrictions on painting and alterations and forbade pets. "Some tenants," said one observer, "find this to be precisely a confirmation of their greatest anxiety, that they were being offered decent housing in exchange for their independence."[45]

The atmosphere inside some of the projects, then, reinforced the charity stigma that their physical appearance generated. As

[44]See Paul Jacobs, *Prelude to Riot: A View of Urban America from the Bottom* (New York: Random House, Inc., 1966), pp. 158–164.

[45]U.S. Department of Health, Education, and Welfare, Social Security Administration, Division of Research Statistics, *Slums and Social Insecurity,* by Alvin L. Schorr, Research Report no. 1 (Washington, D.C.: Government Printing Office, 1963), p. 112.

this stigma intensified, a smaller and smaller proportion of those eligible for public housing were willing to apply. In Boston's West End, for example, only one-sixth of the low-income people displaced by urban renewal (and therefore eligible for public housing) applied for admission. The "respectable" poor of West End "those characterized by normal family structure, residential stability, steady employment, and a commitment to the place where they live and the people they live with" had no use for public housing.[46] Though they were mostly apartment dwellers themselves, living in crowded slums, they objected to the congestion in the projects. They did not like the kind of people living there "riff-raff," they said, given to "common law marriages." Though they themselves lived in substandard housing, at least they were free from the institutional quality of life in the projects, with its multitude of rules and regulations. So, despite the paucity of decent housing for the poor, there were some cities with an unduly high vacancy rate in their public housing projects.[47]

These criticisms of public housing added up to a dismaying indictment; and the liberals who had championed the program from its origins were, by the late 1950s, among its principal accusers. To some extent their disenchantment caused them to overstate the deficiencies. While there is abundant documentation for each of the charges mentioned, they are by no means the whole story. The appalling conditions reported by Salisbury in New York and by others in St. Louis are not unique, but they are among the worst; and there are many that are very much better. Salisbury himself praises the conditions in other New York projects. Lee Rainwater, who has directed a major research study of Pruitt-Igoe, agrees that "no other public housing project in the country approaches it in terms of vacancies, tenant concerns and anxieties of physical deterioration."[48] The high-rise monstrosities

[46]Chester Hartman, "The Limitations of Public Housing," *Journal of the American Institute of Planners*, XXIX, no. 4 (November 1963), 283–296.

[47]See Robert K. Brown, *Public Housing in Action: The Record of Pittsburgh* (Ann Arbor, Mich.: University of Pittsburgh Press, 1959), p. 83.

[48]Lee Rainwater, "Poverty and Deprivation in the Crisis of the American City," Occasional Paper no. 9. A statement presented to the U.S. Senate Committee on Government Operations, Subcommittee on Executive Reorganization, Washington, D.C., December 6, 1966, p. 3.

are by no means characteristic of public housing in the West or in small- or medium-sized towns generally. Many housing officials have displayed imagination and sensitivity in their administration of the projects. As for the appearance of the big Eastern projects, this was not very different from many middle-income apartment houses. Some of the disillusionment of the original housing advocates stemmed from their hope that the projects would not accept the prevailing shoddy standards of architecture but would provide models of delight and grace for their communities. It is an understandable desire. But, generally speaking, public buildings in America have not been tastemakers for the country at large; and it was too much to expect that a program designed for the poor would prove the exception.

Furthermore, in spite of all its deficiencies, public housing has represented a vast improvement in the way of life of a great many people. Alvin Schorr reports:

> When they are asked, the majority of families who live in public housing say that they like it. They appreciate its facilities; their general morale is higher than it was in substandard housing. One must, of course, take into account that those who would object most to public housing never enter it, or they leave. Nevertheless, for those who take up tenancy, public housing represents a considerable improvement in physical surroundings. Moreover, the aspects of the environment which are offensive to some families may be secondary or even functional for others.[49]

And, if there are many who refuse the chance to live in public housing, there are plenty of others who want to get in but cannot. There may be high vacancy rates in some cities, but in Washington, D.C., the number of families awaiting admission has at times exceeded the total number of housing units. New York and many other communities have long waiting lists which cannot be much reduced with the present construction rates. In the nation as a whole, according to Secretary Weaver in 1968, "Ap-

---

[49] U.S. Department of Health, Education, and Welfare, *Slums and Social Insecurity*, p. 115.

plications for additional units are being submitted at an annual rate of about 140,000 units."[50]

Nonetheless, by the end of the 1950s, the defects of public housing were widely admitted even by its allies. As for its long-term foes, they could claim that they had predicted from the beginning that the hopes invested in the program would be disappointed. But, after all, this was something of a self-fulfilling prophecy. It was the restrictions built into the program from the outset and the environment of hostility which enveloped it as it struggled to grow that had contributed so largely to its failures.

RECENT EFFORTS TO IMPROVE THE PROGRAM

The housing acts of 1961, 1965, and 1968, and the new leadership in the Public Housing Administration have done a great deal to remedy the deficiencies that showed up so painfully in the experience of the 1950s. Greater flexibility has been introduced at several points. The 1961 act, for example, gave local housing authorities the right to allow low-income families whose income rose beyond the eligibility levels to stay on at increased rents. This was only if they were "unable to find decent, safe and sanitary housing within their financial reach after making every reasonable effort to do so,"[51] and most overincome families were

[50]U.S. Congress, Senate, Banking and Currency Subcommittee, *Housing and Urban Development Legislation of 1968, Hearings, on Proposed Housing Legislation for 1968,* 90th Cong., 2d sess., 1968, Pt. I, p. 76; hereinafter referred to as: Senate, *Hearings, Housing and Urban Development Legislation of 1968.* The National Commission on Urban Problems, under the chairmanship of Paul H. Douglas, looked into three aspects of the public housing program—the average vacancy rate, the average turnover rate, and the number of applicants. In each of these areas the Commission's findings were favorable. The figures for applicants were especially impressive. In 1967 there was an average of 28 applicants for every vacancy. In New York City there were 762 applicants per vacancy, in Chicago 126.

[51]Housing and Home Finance Agency, *15th Annual Report* (1961), p. 213. According to HHFA's *16th Annual Report:* "At the end of December 1962, 3143 families, or approximately six-tenths of 1 percent of the families in occupancy, had incomes exceeding the limits applicable. Of these, 962 families were unable to find private housing; the remainder were asked to move" (Housing and Home Finance Agency, *16th Annual Report* [1962], p. 211).

still asked to move. Still, the provision has enabled some people to remain in public housing who otherwise would have been evicted.

In addition to legislative adaptation, various devices have been used to break away from the old pattern of large, high-rise projects, which set their inhabitants apart in isolation from the surrounding community. The emphasis has been increasingly on "vest-pocket projects," built on small, scattered sites. In one of these, "maximum advantage was taken of existing neighborhood facilities by the device of building along established streets or individual scattered lots which were either vacant or occupied by unusable structures."[52] Some new public housing structures have been designed to blend into established neighborhoods. And the 1968 act specifically prohibited the HUD Secretary from approving high-rise elevator projects unless there was no practical alternative. Other new programs departed completely from the construction of special public housing projects: Apartments in private housing were leased, sometimes after rehabilitation, for eligible tenants and the difference between the market rent and the amount that the tenant could afford to pay was made up by the local housing authority. Even Los Angeles showed interest in the money provided in the 1965 housing act for this purpose, and in 1966 its housing authority applied for funds to lease 1000 units.

Initiatives were also taken to improve the quality of life in the existing large-scale projects. The 1961 act permitted the inclusion in housing projects of neighborhood facilities such as stores and other private commercial undertakings. This could help to change the projects from mere aggregations of dwelling units to communities in the full sense.[53] At the same time, project administrators were encouraged to make fuller use of the resources of the surrounding communities for the well-being of the tenants. This applied especially to social services, which were no longer viewed as unnecessary frills. Cooperative arrangements were

[52]Housing and Home Finance Agency, *15th Annual Report* (1961), pp. 208–209.

[53]However, implementation of this provision has been slow. Local housing authorities often have been hesitant about taking on yet another set of conflicts that might result from promoting competition with existing neighborhood enterprises. And, in some cases, black residents have felt that making the projects more self-sufficient sets them even further apart from the rest of the community.

entered into at the federal level with the Department of Health, Education, and Welfare to facilitate the fuller availability of welfare services to public housing tenants in the communities.[54] And to combat the habits of noninvolvement and alienation which characterized so many of the poor, the word went out from Washington that tenant associations ought to be encouraged in the projects.

Great stress also came to be placed by the new Public Housing Commissioner, Mrs. McGuire, on better design. Her first annual report conceded the validity of the criticism that public housing construction had generally lacked imagination in design and was institutional in appearance.[55] She moved vigorously to hire imaginative architects, to make them available at the local level, and to have her staff confer with committees of the American Institute of Architects and other professional groups. Important changes have taken place under these policies. Projects in New York and in Marin County, California, have won architectural awards. Bleak, deserted areas in some New York City projects became, with Rockefeller Foundation support, graceful plazas and recreational centers.

This is all to the good. The public housing program today is, at least potentially, an instrument of sufficient flexibility and variety to make a major contribution to the re-housing of the poor. Yet there is little prospect in the near future that this potential will be fully realized. It cannot free itself from its past reputation. It is still in thrall to the weaknesses of the 1950s.

The massive institutions of the Eastern cities are still there. Whatever their defects of design they were built to last. Their financing is for at least forty years. Ayn Rand's architect hero in *The Fountainhead* destroyed his low-rent housing project when his design was subverted, but this recourse is not open to commissioners of public housing. Welfare services can be greatly improved. But all the panoply of our existing welfare structure has

[54]U.S. Department of Health, Education, and Welfare, and U.S. Housing and Home Finance Agency, *Services for Families Living in Public Housing* (Washington, D.C.: Government Printing Office, 1963). The 1968 act included authorization for $15 million in 1969 and $30 million in 1970 to upgrade management and tenant services. However, the funds for 1969 did not survive the 1968 appropriations stage.

[55]Housing and Home Finance Agency, *15th Annual Report* (1961), p. 203.

failed to make deep inroads into the culture of poverty, and the disintegration of the family, which is such a marked feature of the big project, will not easily be cured or compensated for. The dismaying conditions in Pruitt-Igoe in St. Louis prevailed in 1967, after years of struggle with the problem.[56]

While the trend of the housing program today is strongly against the construction of large projects, the factors that produced them have not been eliminated. Even in the 1960s the Chicago Housing Authority prepared plans for several new high-rise projects, and Jane Jacobs told the National Housing Conference:

> I should think you would all get so bored with yourselves, with what you hear over and over again, you could not stand it. . . . Let us take, as an example, all the to-do about vest-pocket housing. We have been hearing about this for years, yet Chicago right now has under construction the largest low-income public housing project it has ever built. It is 97 acres. It will house around 20,000 people. . . . Why is this? . . . I think it is owing to two reasons. One is the poor ideas that have carried over and have not been examined. . . . The other thing at fault is too much wishful thinking. In another culture our public housers would be rain dancers.[57]

Yet, if the housing officials' rain dance was an irrational ritual, the drought that made them go through the ritual was very real. The dearth of sites has not been relieved. There is still resistance, probably even more powerful than in the 1950s, to allowing the poor and minority groups to move into the suburbs. In August 1967, 2000 residents of suburban areas in New York City thronged to city hall to protest the building of eleven projects in their communities. *"Public Housing Is Immoral"* declared one of their placards. "We worked and saved to get the money to buy our homes here and get out of the slums," said one of the protestors. "Now the mayor wants to bring the slums back to us."[58]

[56] See *The Housing Yearbook, 1963,* pp. 33–35.

[57] *The Housing Yearbook, 1962,* pp. 10–11.

[58] "The Mayors' Dilemma," *Newsweek* (August 14, 1967), p. 22.

The notion of vest-pocket projects clearly reduces the threat that great concentrations of the poor will move into other neighborhoods and change their character. But even in small numbers, the poor are not always welcome. The leasing proposal has evoked some of the same fears. The National Lumber and Building Material Dealers Association complained in 1965 that "the new proposal . . . to acquire or lease existing homes for public housing in scattered communities could give to the public housing agency the authority to interject public housing in practically every area of a city. We have some misgivings about the effect of this program on the value of surrounding homes in the area."[59] The trend away from large projects, in other words, means a larger number of sites to which there can be opposition.[60]

Similarly, most of the other improvements that the 1960s have brought to the program have served to attract new hostilities to the program. Even the improved designs that won plaudits and architectural awards aroused the envy of those who could see no reason why the poor should be more graciously housed than many of the more respectable people in the community. The Comptroller General of the United States expressed himself indignantly on this issue when he wrote a strongly critical report on the beautifully designed project in Marin County, California.[61]

The only change that did not evoke new resentments was the extension of opportunities for low-income elderly people to get into public housing, for geriatrics is excellent politics. Otherwise

[59]U.S. Congress, Senate, Banking and Currency Subcommittee, *Hearings, Housing Legislation of 1965*, on S. 1354, 89th Cong., 1st sess., 1965, p. 518; hereinafter referred to as: Senate, *Hearings, Housing Legislation of 1965*.

[60]However, the United States Commission on Civil Rights reported in 1961 "Today some 10,000 units in scattered site projects are either completed or under construction in more than 15 communities. . . . Sacramento, Calif. has recently moved 46 Negro and 4 white families into scattered, single family rental homes with a high degree of success." One advantage of scattered housing was cited by a public housing official: "We get them built before people who oppose public housing find out about them" (U.S. Commission on Civil Rights Report, *Housing* [Washington, D.C.: Government Printing Office, 1961], Book 4, p. 115).

[61]Comptroller General of the United States, *Review of Selected Activities of the Low-Rent Housing Program in the Nine-State Area Administered by the San Francisco Regional Office, Public Housing Administration*, Report to the Congress of the United States (Washington, D.C.: General Accounting Office, March 1962), pp. 14–28.

no matter how public housing has changed and no matter what it does to take into account the suggestions of its critics, it cannot expunge its fundamental liability, namely, that when the poor are helped by public policy, the help is proffered grudgingly and restrictively.

In 1965, the Johnson administration tried to solve the problem by breaking out of the public housing framework completely and offering rent supplements as the instrument for a major new assault on the housing problem of the poor. But before the rent-supplement program could be securely established, it too had provided one more depressing example of the political weakness of the poor.

Rent Supplements

The purpose of rent supplements, as the Johnson administration explained it, was to make housing "available for lower income families who are elderly or handicapped, who are displaced from their homes by public action or who are occupants of substandard housing."[62] As with the case of public housing, the federal government would make supplemental rental payments to bridge the gap between the normal rent and what the poor could afford to pay.[63] Unlike public housing, however, the program would not be built or operated by the government. Ownership was to be vested in nonprofit, limited-dividend or cooperative organizations, which would be able to utilize FHA-insured market-interest-rate mortgages. FHA was to be the responsible agency, so the onus attached to the public housing agency would not damage the new program. There was freedom, too, from an irksome restriction that had handicapped public housing so severely: As the income of an occupant in a rent-supplement project rose, he would pay a higher rent rather than be forced to move.

The proposal was stalled almost immediately, for the Administration wanted to limit the program to the income group just above those eligible for public housing. It was to be for the poor, but not the very poor. Both the National Association of Real Estate Boards and the National Association of Housing and Re-

[62] Senate, *Hearings, Housing Legislation of 1965,* statement of Robert C. Weaver, p. 57.

[63] Tenants would pay one-fourth of their income for rent.

development Officials objected to this,[64] and the Administration, faced with impending defeat, changed its mind, and amended the proposal to apply only to the lowest-income group.

With this change made, the prospects for rent supplements looked very favorable. The year was 1965, so the conditions needed to overcome legislative obstruction were overwhelmingly present. The change in income requirements won over the realtors and the housing officials; and all the other groups that had opposed public housing favored rent supplements from the beginning. Thus, there was no organized national pressure against the proposal. The difficulties facing public housing that were set forth in Part I of this book appeared to be completely absent from the rent-supplement case.

Yet, the new program was approved on the House floor in 1965 by 208 to 202—a margin reminiscent of the 1949 voting on public housing. No money at all was appropriated that year. In 1966, the President asked for $30 million for the program. The House Appropriations Committee approved $12 million. This was retained on the House floor by 198 to 190. But now there was trouble in the Senate, which had almost invariably been a bulwark of strength for public housing. The Senate Appropriations Committee deleted the $12 million by a vote of 15 to 12, and the Administration had to lobby furiously to get this reversed on the Senate floor—on a vote of 46 to 45.[65]

These actions were quickly followed by a further Administration request for fiscal 1967. This time $20 million was approved, but the margin in the House was four votes; in the Senate, thirteen. And to gain its margin in the House, the Administration had to agree to a provision that gave veto power to locally elected bodies over any rent-supplement project not located in

[64]NAREB felt that the groups to be subsidized by government would now be reaching upward dangerously close to the normal clientele of the private housing market. NAHRO argued that since government housing funds were so limited, none should be diverted from the income group whose need was greatest. Nor were the housing officials happy about the vesting of responsibility in the Federal Housing Administration, which had had no experience in housing the poor and whose contacts had been primarily with representatives of the private housing field.

[65]Senator Bartlett of Alaska voted against the funds in the Appropriations Committee, then changed his mind when the bill reached the floor after gaining Administration promises of support for Eskimo housing.

an urban renewal area. Thus, the requirement of local approval was built into the rent-supplement program as it had been in the case of public housing.

Housing officials were perturbed about this amendment. Their perturbation was even greater the next year, for the 1966 elections took away an essential condition for low-cost housing legislation—a very large Democratic majority in the House. It was still sizable—248 to 187—but this would not be enough to offset the reemergence of the traditional conservative coalition. Nobody was surprised when, in 1967, the House voted for no new appropriation for rent supplements. The Senate, encouraged by Senator Dirksen's change of heart on the issue, responded with a large majority for the Administration's full request of $40 million, but the final compromise was for only $10 million.

There were two basic reasons for the unenthusiastic response to the rent-supplement idea even in the generally docile 89th Congress. First, the cost of Vietnam had become formidable by 1966 and posed the same problem for rent supplements that Korea had represented for public housing. Housing for the poor rates a low priority when a war is on. The *Los Angeles Times* had editorialized against one public housing proposal in 1950: "This money earmarked for the transformation of Chavez Ravine will do the country far more good if it goes to pay soldiers' wages and to buy armor-piercing shells [for Korea]."[66] Similar arguments reverberated in 1966.

Second, there was the fear that this program, too, could be used to break down existing residential patterns which kept the poor and the middle class apart. In its original form in 1965, the proposal to aim at a clientele one step up the income ladder from the public housing tenants led Senator Tower to complain that the program would "get low-income, middle-income and high-income groups all living together."[67] This dread prospect was alleviated by the lowering of the income-level requirements, although a tenant could still earn more and not be evicted. But the change did not address itself to the question of sites, and as long as the possibility remained that sites for the program would be sought in

---

[66]*Los Angeles Times* (August 9, 1950), Pt. II, p. 4.

[67]Congressional Quarterly, *Housing a Nation* (Washington, D.C.: Congressional Quarterly Service, 1966), p. 82.

the suburbs, fears would persist among congressional conservatives that rent supplements were designed to produce socioeconomic integration.[68]

From the conservatives' viewpoint, the new program might be even more dangerous in this respect than public housing, for it was freed from some of the liabilities that had kept public housing in check. Suddenly the conservatives were finding profound virtues in public housing, and the congressional debates were lavish in their testimonials to that tried-and-true, historically tested program from which rent supplements represented such a "radical change." It was this ironic contrast, in fact, that at least partly accounted for the general congressional acceptance of public housing in 1965. It was the devil they knew—but by now a relatively safe, controlled devil. The rent supplement was a new, and as yet unmeasured monster. It must be watched closely and, if possible, starved of funds.

President Johnson had introduced the rent-supplement idea with the promise that it was to be "the most crucial new instrument in our effort to improve the American city." The initial construction target was 375,000 units by 1969, but the achievement fell as far short of the aspiration as did public housing under the Taft-Ellender-Wagner program. Secretary Weaver told Congress in 1968:

> The rent supplement program is rapidly acquiring momentum. By the end of fiscal year 1969, 384 rent supplement projects with nearly 27,000 supplemented units located throughout the country are expected to be ready for occupancy. The remaining 18,000 units provided under approved contract authority through fiscal year 1968 will be ready for occupancy in fiscal year 1970.[69]

Perhaps, as Weaver suggests, the momentum is finally there. In 1968, $30 million was appropriated for rent supplements, three times the 1967 figure. Congress may be overcoming its initial suspicions of the program and soon may be ready to see it

[68]See comments of Representative Fino, quoted in Richard Wilson, "What Would Taft Have Done?" *Los Angeles Times* (May 3, 1966), Pt. II, p. 5.

[69]Senate, *Hearings, Housing and Urban Development Legislation of 1968,* Pt. I, p. 75.

as a necessary auxiliary of other federally aided enterprises, such as the Model Cities program[70] and of the kind of initiative from the private sector to be discussed in Chapter 5.

Yet the 1968 appropriation for $30 million represented a sharp reduction from the Administration's request for $65 million. There was also the painful fact that a program which was to have built 375,000 units by 1969 would not reach 45,000 until 1970—and this despite the absence of the national opposition that for so long had harried public housing. The inventors of rent supplements had done what they could to remove from their program the weaknesses built into public housing. But there was one source of political weakness that they were not able to expunge: Like public housing, the rent-supplement program is available only to the poor.

The stigma of charity surrounds the program. The congressional debates reflect the attitudes of the larger culture toward the poor, and the votes in Congress are repeated testimony to the fundamental weakness of the low-income groups in the American political system.

[70] The Model Cities program is a good example of the new integrative approaches to problem solving. The program goes beyond the view of public housing, urban renewal, and OEO projects as separate packages and treats them as aspects of a total effort to remake blighted areas of cities.

Chapter 4
Race

Chapter 3 indicated that public housing was treated exceptionally harshly by legislators and lobbyists because it served only the poor. Now one more source of political weakness must be introduced: The poor include a disproportionate number of certain minority groups—Puerto Ricans, Mexican-Americans, and, most of all, blacks.[1] This fact further intensified the travails of the housing program. The public housing case is a study in race as

[1] The problem under discussion in this chapter is clearly not limited to blacks. Many of the same factors apply to Puerto Ricans in New York and Miami, and to Mexican-Americans in Los Angeles and in parts of Texas. However, the concentration of Puerto Ricans and Mexican-Americans is primarily in a few regions, whereas blacks are present in significant numbers in most of the cities referred to in this study. Thus, while mention is made where appropriate to other minority groups, the race problem will be discussed here primarily in terms of the black American.

ell as poverty. The conflict contained all of the major features aught up in the overriding domestic issues of our time—the onfrontation between the races in our urban centers.

There was no way of keeping the race question out of the ublic housing controversy. The program was a response to bad ousing; and in general blacks in America live in worse housing an whites. In 1950, 72 percent of the nonwhite population ccupied substandard dwelling units. The 1960 census figures dicated that in ten years considerable improvement had been corded, for by the end of the decade the proportion of non-hites living in substandard units had declined to 44 percent.[2] till further advances have been achieved subsequently, and by 966 the proportion had fallen from 44 percent to 29 percent.[3] ven so, a wide qualitative disparity remains between the housing f whites and nonwhites. In 1950, the proportion of whites in ıbstandard housing was 32 percent; it was down to 13 percent y 1960, and to 8 percent in 1966. Today housing is no longer ıted as a major problem for most of the white population. But is is clearly not the case for blacks. Polls indicate persistent

J.S. Housing and Home Finance Agency, *Our Nonwhite Population and s Housing* (Washington, D.C.: Government Printing Office, 1963), p. 10.
he Statistical Research Division and the Housing Division of the Bureau f the Census in 1966 questioned the accuracy of the Census data, sug-esting that the 1950 figures represented an overcount and the 1960 figures substantial undercount. This would lead to a reassessment of the picture progress revealed by the earlier figures, and the 1966 study suggested at no substantial change had been brought about. However, these figures lated to the category of "dilapidated" housing, which is a much narrower ıtegory than "substandard" housing. (See U.S. Department of Commerce, uality of Housing, Second Draft [Washington, D.C.: U.S. Department of ommerce, Bureau of the Census, April 1966].) Also, the 1967 report on ıe social and economic conditions of blacks (see footnote 3 following) ıll used the figure of 44 percent for nonwhites in substandard units in 966.

J.S. Department of Labor and U.S. Department of Commerce, Bureau of abor Statistics and Bureau of the Census, *Social and Economic Condi-ıns of Negroes in the United States,* BLS Report no. 332, Current Popu-tion Reports, Series P-23, no. 24 (Washington, D.C.: Government Print-ıg Office, October 1967), p. 53; hereinafter referred to as: U.S. Depart-ıents of Labor and Commerce, *Social and Economic Conditions of Negroes the United States.*

dissatisfaction among blacks with their housing conditions.[4] An
a Harris survey in the aftermath of the 1967 Newark and Detro
riots indicated that 68 percent of the black community believe
that "lack of decent housing" was one of the major causes of th
riots.[5]

WHY BLACKS ARE BADLY HOUSED

It is not difficult to find the reasons for the miserable housing
so many Negroes. First, blacks are much more likely than whites t
be poor. Their average income is considerably lower. Thoug
impressive gains have been made in the last generation, it wa
still the case in 1966 that 32 percent of black families had a
annual income of less than $3000, as compared with 13 percer
of white families.[6] Consequently, a very high proportion of the
cannot afford decent housing in the private market.

Second, nonwhites, especially Negroes, are discriminate
against. The United States Civil Rights Commission declared i
its 1959 report that "housing . . . seems to be the one commodit
in the American market that is not freely available on equi
terms to everyone who can afford to pay."[7] Nonwhites a

[4] According to a Harris poll in 1963, 43 percent of the black communit
believed that their housing conditions had improved during the previo
five years. Yet another Harris poll in 1966 indicated that not only did th
same figure prevail, but that housing was the one area out of six studied
which "the Negro's sense of well-being [failed] to show a gain" ("A Maj
Survey of U.S. Racial Attitudes Today," *Newsweek* [August 22, 1966
p. 23).

[5] "After the Riots: A Survey," *Newsweek* (August 21, 1967), p. 19. In th
report, 67 percent of the blacks interviewed mentioned lack of jobs as
major cause; 72 percent, lack of equality; and 61 percent, inadequate edu
cation. Only 39 percent of the whites interviewed thought that bad housin
was a major cause, although this was still among the most frequently me
tioned.

[6] The proportion of nonwhite families earning less than $3000 (in 196
dollars) has fallen from 65 percent in 1947 to 44 percent in 1960 to 3
percent in 1966. An additional 24 percent earned between $3000 and $500
in 1966 (U.S. Departments of Labor and Commerce, *Social and Econom
Conditions of Negroes in the United States,* p. 18).

[7] U.S. Commission on Civil Rights, *Report* (Washington, D.C.: Gover
ment Printing Office, 1959), p. 534.

charged more than whites for equivalent housing. "The dollar in a dark hand," said the Commission, does not "have the same purchasing power as a dollar in a white hand." And much of the housing market is closed to blacks at any price. Partly this is the result of the kinds of attitudes in white communities as discussed earlier—attitudes prevalent not only in middle-class areas, but also in the working-class neighborhoods which might be within the financial reach of many Negroes. The private housing groups have reinforced and institutionalized these attitudes. Until 1950 it was actually part of the NAREB "Code of Ethics" to discourage integration. Article 34 of the code stated that: "A Realtor should never be instrumental in introducing into a neighborhood a character of property or occupancy, members of any race or nationality, or any individuals whose presence will clearly be detrimental to property values in the neighborhood." Even after the deletion of this article, realtors were expelled from local real estate boards for selling homes in "exclusive" areas to members of minority groups. The right not to sell to minority groups was still regarded as inalienable in NAREB's "Property Owners' Bill of Rights" in 1963.[8] A further dimension of the problem was the reluctance of home-finance agencies (with such notable exceptions as the Bowery Savings Bank in New York) to extend credit for the purchase of housing for minorities outside the segregated areas.

So strongly entrenched were these policies and so great was the support from organized groups and from the white community in general that government housing agencies were for many years unwilling to contradict them. Until 1947, the official FHA "Underwriter's Manual" specifically warned federal officials not to insure property unless it was protected from "adverse influences," such as "inharmonious racial groups"; and the manual declared

[8]Blacks and other minority groups were not specifically mentioned in the NAREB document, but they were obviously the prime target of "the right to determine the acceptability and desirability of any prospective buyer or tenant of his property [;] . . . the right of every American to choose who, in his opinion, are congenial tenants in any property he owns—to maintain the stability and security of his income [; and] . . . the right to enjoy the freedom to accept, reject, negotiate or not negotiate with others." The California Real Estate Association reprinted this document in 1964 for use in the campaign for Proposition 14, repealing the state's fair housing law. The electorate in voting 2 to 1 for repeal had no doubt about the point the realtors were making.

that, to preserve the stability of a neighborhood, it was necessary that "properties shall continue to be occupied by the same social and racial classes." The manual even contained a model restrictive covenant, whose inclusion in real estate sales contracts became a prerequisite of FHA mortgage insurance. Officially FHA policies have changed, restrictive covenants have been found legally unenforceable, and the FHA in 1949 declared that the racial composition of a neighborhood was not to be a consideration in establishing eligibility. After that, the agency moved toward expressly encouraging open occupancy. Nonetheless, FHA's policies have been considered a major factor in increasing segregation, for they have concentrated on increasing the supply of new housing in the suburbs, from which minority groups have generally been excluded.[9]

A breakthrough in federal government policy came with President Kennedy's executive order on housing in 1962, which forbade discrimination in all FHA or VA-insured housing, in federally owned or operated housing, and in housing constructed with federal loans. Yet this covered only about 18 percent of new housing construction.[10] Nor was the pattern changed significantly by the 1964 Civil Rights Act, despite Title VI of the act, which bars discrimination under any program or activity receiving federal assistance against any person because of his race, color, or national origin. Only in the context of continued outbreaks of fury in the cities and the assassination of Martin Luther King was the Administration at last able, in 1968, to overcome intense congressional resistance to open-housing legislation.

Notwithstanding the bad housing conditions to which low income and discrimination condemned urban blacks, a great migration of Southern blacks to Northern cities has been taking place throughout this century and has been accelerating since World War II. They have flocked into the center of the cities, for those were the only places available to them. As they came in, the whites left in such numbers that, despite the inexorable trend toward urbanization of the American people, the population of

---

[9]U.S. Commission on Civil Rights, *Housing Report* (Washington, D.C.: Government Printing Office, 1961), pp. 62–65.

[10]Largely because it did not extend to the housing built through savings and loan and commercial bank loans. Furthermore, FHA loans are being used for a declining proportion of new housing.

most big cities has declined since 1950. Yet, because of the influx of blacks from the South, and because the birthrate of blacks has been higher than that of whites, the black population of the Northern cities has been rapidly increasing. In 1950, Negroes constituted 12 percent of the total population of central cities in metropolitan areas. By 1960 the proportion was 17 percent; by 1966, 20 percent. Within another decade, a number of cities will probably have black majorities. These will be black communities surrounded by white suburbs.[11]

Most of the bad housing will continue to be found within the city core. The demand for decent housing will grow, but the supply will not keep pace. The ghetto will expand, but not fast enough to ease the pressure. So, the combination of low income, discrimination, and urban immigration has produced the contemporary metropolitan crisis. And a festering ingredient of that crisis is the housing problem of the black American.

THE HOPES OF THE REFORMERS

It was the hope of the pioneers of public housing that their program would play an important part in reversing the segregation trend. These pioneers were liberals whose desire to undertake an attack on bad housing conditions was an expression of their total system of values. Those values were intrinsically hostile to racial prejudice and discrimination. Through public housing they sought to build integrated communities that could serve as models for the larger society.

They had some successes. The PHA has worked assiduously in the field of race relations:

> In striking contrast to the FHA, which for years seemed to think of minorities only as a threat to real estate invest-

---

[11]U.S. Departments of Labor and Commerce, *Social and Economic Conditions of Negroes in the United States,* pp. 10–11. Among the thirty largest cities, only Washington, D.C., had more blacks than whites by 1965. In most of the others, blacks comprised considerably less than one-third of the population. However, in almost all large cities, the percentage of blacks has been increasing, and in some there is already a majority of black children in the public schools.

ments, the administration of public housing has always operated on the principle that the minority groups were entitled
to share in the program. . . . The Administration supported
its racial relations officers in working for a maximum degree
of equity for minority groups, community by community.[12]

PHA insisted that the number of housing units available to Negroes
be proportionate to their need—not merely to the black population in the area—and that physical facilities, proximity to schools
and parks, and other requirements must be provided to blacks
equally with whites.

Wherever it could, PHA went beyond the policies of insuring
racial equity to promoting integration. By 1960 it was able to
report that thirty-two states operated their public housing projects
on an open-occupancy basis. New York, Los Angeles, Cleveland,
Pittsburgh, Seattle, Boston, and Newark were among the cities
that introduced official anti-segregation policies following World
War II.

Many of these cities told of heartening success with their
integration efforts. Annual reports showing black and white children playing happily together did not lie. There were far fewer
racial incidents in the integrated projects than had been predicted, and harmonious relationships were the rule in many places.[13]
In some of its projects, reported the Chicago Housing Authority,
adjustment is made "within a surprisingly short time, despite the
fact that many of the tenants are living in Chicago for the first
time, and that many came from small communities where interracial living was unheard of."[14]

Yet these successes were limited. On the whole, public housing
has not been able to withstand the factors producing segregation,
in either the North or the South. The susceptibilities of the South
had to be respectfully observed from the beginning. In 1949,

[12]Weldon Davis McEntire, *Residence and Race* (Berkeley, Calif.: University
of California Press, 1960), pp. 317–318.

[13]See Morton Deutsch and Mary Evans Collins, *Interracial Housing* (Minneapolis: University of Minnesota Press, 1951).

[14]National Community Relations Advisory Council, *Equality of Opportunity
in Housing* (New York: National Community Relations Advisory Council,
June 1952), p. 22.

liberals were compelled to resist efforts by the enemies of public housing to write an antidiscrimination clause into the bill, for this would have cost the support of Southerners whose votes were crucial. Although many of the Southerners were irreconcilable in any case (congressmen from Mississippi, South Carolina, Virginia, and Texas were overwhelmingly opposed to the program throughout the congressional struggle), there were votes to be gleaned among Democrats in the House from Alabama, Georgia, and Tennessee. Without those votes, public housing would have no chance; and they could be obtained only as long as the projects in the south could be segregated. The consequence of any breach in this understanding was revealed in 1954 when Senator Maybank, a leader in the fight for public housing, defected from the cause when the Supreme Court refused to overrule a California court decision that blacks must be admitted to a San Francisco housing project.[15] "Now that the Supreme Court has seen fit to reverse an acceptable and working pattern," said Senator Maybank, " . . . I must oppose my own amendment . . . and thereby abandon a fight to which my energies and devotion have been dedicated for a quarter of a century."[16] However, the case was interpreted as upholding California rather than federal law, and the Southern states continued their segregation policies in public housing.

The Kennedy executive order in 1962 applied to public housing specifically, and the Mississippi legislature promptly passed a law forbidding any further authorizations by municipalities for public housing with federal funds. But even after that and after the 1964 Civil Rights Act, there were still plenty of devices by which segregation could be preserved de facto in public housing in the South.

Nor were all-white and all-black housing projects found only in the South. In the Northern cities, too, the forces producing the ghettos fixed public housing in a vise of racial separation; and no matter what devices they tried, housing officials could not shake their program free from that vise.

[15]*Housing Authority of the City and County of San Francisco et al.* v. *Banks et al.* (U.S.) (May 24, 1954).

[16]*Congressional Record,* C, Pt. 6, 83rd Cong., 2d sess., June 3, 1954. 7618.

THE RACIAL MIX IN THE PROJECTS

The hope of preserving a reasonably diverse racial composition in public housing could not long survive the sheer number of black applicants. "Arithmetic is against us," said Joseph S. Clark, Jr., then mayor of Philadelphia.[17] The low incomes of most blacks gave them the dubious privilege of eligibility for public housing. Many who might have been able to afford better private housing were shut out by discrimination. Then, as urban renewal, highway and other government-aided programs expanded in the 1950s, Negroes were displaced in large numbers. "Urban renewal is Negro removal" was the common cry.

Public housing might have its faults, but blacks could not afford to be as fastidious in the matter as whites. There was nowhere else to go for remotely comparable housing at public housing prices. More and more Negroes applied for admission to the projects. In 1952, nonwhites occupied 38 percent of all public housing units. By 1961, the percentage was up to 46 percent.[18] It had reached 51 percent by 1965.

At first the increase did not necessarily exclude the possibility of racial balance. But as the numbers of blacks grew, the same phenomenon occurred in public housing that has taken place in private housing. Once the "tipping point" was passed, the whites began to leave.[19] And, in most cases, they were replaced by blacks, for there were few whites willing to move in once the blacks had attained a majority in a project. Most of the whites who were displaced by urban renewal and were poor enough to be eligible for public housing refused to apply. They did not like the institutional atmosphere; the loss of privacy; or the appearance of the projects. They disapproved of the kind of people who lived

[17]Quoted in Herbert Hill, "Demographic Change and Racial Ghettos: The Crisis of American Cities," *Journal of Urban Law 231,* XLIV (Winter 1966), 262.

[18]See U.S. Commission on Civil Rights, *Housing Report,* 1961, p. 110.

[19]"The Low Rent Housing Program and the Great Society," address by Abner D. Silverman, Assistant Commissioner for Management, Public Housing Administration, to the annual meeting of the Pennsylvania Association of Housing and Redevelopment Authorities, January 27, 1965 (Mimeographed), p. 6. In a number of projects the "tipping point" was reached when black occupancy passed 40 percent.

there—especially when these were Negroes. And they had heard of violence and disorder in the public housing communities.

There is insufficient data to determine whether the social disorganization of the projects in New York, St. Louis, and elsewhere was an outgrowth simply of the culture of poverty or whether the terrible damage inflicted on the Negro by discrimination and by the fragmentation of his family structure has introduced an additional and distinctive element. Moynihan and others contend that the undermining of the fabric of the family has been especially harmful to the culture of the Negro; public housing projects with their extraordinarily high proportion of fatherless black families would give abundant support to their view. On the other hand, Oscar Lewis emphasizes that most of the disruptive characteristics of Negro life are to be found in a great many cultures of poor people. And Harrison Salisbury suggests that, in the gang conflicts found in one of the New York projects, "color seems to play only a secondary role":

> Before Red Hook Houses were built about twenty years ago this was an Irish-Italian neighborhood with a long record of combat among street gangs of the same ethnic composition. The first tenants of Red Hook Houses were mostly Jewish. Conflict broke out between the native Irish and Italians and the incoming Jewish residents. Hostility was common among adults. There was gang fighting between the adolescents.
>
> The population of Red Hook Houses today is two-thirds Negro and Puerto Rican. The hostility between project and neighborhood has not lessened. Ethnic lines have changed. Lines of combat have not.[20]

It is not necessary here to decide whether blacks are behaving like other ethnic groups before them or whether there are some special characteristics of the black's culture which make him unusually vulnerable to social disorganization. The fact is that, increasingly, other ethnic groups have been leaving public housing, and blacks have taken their place. From the perspective of people outside the projects—and ultimately of the politicians—it could not be gainsaid that in some public housing projects whose

[20]Harrison Salisbury, *The Shook-Up Generation* (New York: Harper & Row, Publishers, 1958), pp. 84–85.

tenants were primarily or entirely black there was a high incidence of social disorder.[21]

The problem existed. And any tendency toward social disorganization which might already be present in the culture of the people in the projects would certainly not be checked by the bleak, towering monoliths which engulfed them and which brought together, in one concentrated area, the various and mutually reinforcing hostilities of poverty families. Whites who could find any other place to live, however unsatisfactory, would tend to do so, for their preexisting prejudices would find ample confirmation in what they heard about life in the projects. So they moved out or refused to move in; and the consequence was that a majority of the project tenants today are blacks and the larger number of tenants today are living in projects which are all-white or all-black.

In their desperate efforts to preserve some degree of integration, housing authorities have resorted to a variety of tortuous and sometimes self-defeating techniques. New York City, for example, introduced occupancy controls based on a racial formula in 1959. The housing authority's open-occupancy policy (state laws forbade discrimination in public housing) had produced a tenant body that was 39 percent Negro and 17 percent Puerto Rican.[22] To combat this trend, the housing authority tried to control the number of whites and nonwhites admitted to those projects that were not already irrevocably and completely comprised of one race only. Race replaced need as the prime consideration in these cases. In some projects, whites were given priority over blacks and Puerto Ricans. In others, no more blacks or Puerto Ricans were accepted at all, and apartments were even held vacant until suitable white applicants appeared. In others again—where there was a low proportion of nonwhites—the latter were given priority for one-third of the vacant apartments. A further variable was introduced in some projects where Puerto Ricans were given precedence over Negroes.[23]

[21]The St. Louis newspapers carried many reports of the trouble in the Pruitt-Igoe development where, in 1967, all but one of the families in the entire community of 2000 families were black.

[22]The city's population at the time included 12 percent blacks and 8 percent Puerto Ricans.

[23]Bernard Roshco, "The Integration Problem and Public Housing," *The New Leader* (July 4–11, 1960), pp. 10–13.

The motives behind this were understandable and even laudable. Integration is an avowed ideal of American society. Public housing was becoming identified with blacks and Puerto Ricans only. Similar efforts to prevent a community's becoming totally segregated have been made by liberal groups in a number of racially mixed areas of private housing, and usually these attempts are highly praised.

Yet efforts of this kind are always extraordinarily difficult to sustain, and in the public housing context the problem is especially acute. Quotas or any other formulas based on race cannot readily be defended in publicly owned facilities, whatever the justification. A housing authority will be hard put to it to explain why a large black family should be passed over in favor of an elderly white couple. When thousands of nonwhites are clamoring for admission, it will seem palpably absurd to leave an apartment vacant for months in the hope that a suitable white applicant will turn up. Not surprisingly, New York quietly abandoned these efforts in 1964 after protests by black rent strikers.[24]

The Newark Housing Authority had somewhat more success with its efforts along these lines, but could not avoid the inevitable cross fire of opposition. There the housing authority was also the urban renewal agency; and housing authority director Louis Danzig was anxious to prevent Columbus Homes, a new project in a predominately Italian area, from becoming mainly black in its composition, for this would discourage private development in the neighborhood. So, the housing authority launched a vigorous campaign to seek out white tenants for Columbus Homes, agreed to give preference to eligible families from the original slum site that had been cleared to make way for the project, and opened the project by moving in 300 white families. At this, black leaders descended on Danzig's office and bitterly attacked the policy. Danzig responded that Columbus Homes was not intended as an "Italian project," that the best way to assure racial balance was to move whites in first, and that the next group of tenants would be largely black. The following year black families were moved in. This was the signal for an outcry from Italian political and civic leaders in the area, who charged that their original understanding had been betrayed. The local Italian newspaper denounced the housing authority for removing people from the

[24]Hill, "Demographic Change and Racial Ghettos," p. 261.

site area under false pretenses and for giving priority to "recent immigrants" over "long-time city residents."[25]

The housing authority's policy in Columbus Homes held up, but it was against the trend of the racial mix in Newark as elsewhere. Between 1951 and 1954 the percentage of black public housing tenants in Newark tripled. By 1955 there were more blacks than whites in public housing, and the flight of white tenants and their replacement by blacks continued. The hostility that the Columbus Homes effort evoked from both sides made it clear that it could not be generally emulated.

RACE AND SITE SELECTION

"In reality," says Herbert Hill of the NAACP, "the policy of reserving apartments in all-Negro projects for a small number of whites is a feeble attempt to avoid grappling with the real problem of housing integration. . . . The meaningful solution is not the reserving of apartments for a few white tenants, but rather in site selection, that is, to decide where to construct the new projects while they are still in the planning stage."[26] The United States Civil Rights Commission has taken the same position, recommending to the PHA that it "take affirmative action to encourage the selection of sites on open land in good areas outside the present centers of racial concentrations. PHA should put the local housing authorities on notice that their proposals will be evaluated in this light."[27] PHA, while having no mandatory site-selection requirements, has discouraged site selection in racially stratified areas. As Commissioner McGuire has explained: "PHA has long been aware that the selection of sites in areas of predominant occupancy by one race or another makes for de facto racial segregation. . . . It actively encourages the use of vacant land, [and] sites outside of areas of racial concentration."[28]

[25]Harold Kaplan, *Urban Renewal Politics: Slum Clearance in Newark* (New York: Columbia University Press, 1963), pp. 152–153.

[26]Hill, "Demographic Change and Racial Ghettos," pp. 261–262.

[27]U.S. Commission on Civil Rights, *Housing Report*, 1961, p. 113.

[28]U.S. Commission on Civil Rights, *Housing Report,* 1961 p. 113.

This is a consummation devoutly to be desired but not easily achieved. Efforts to locate projects outside the poverty and racial ghettos have been repeatedly frustrated precisely because of the factors that produced the ghettos in the first place—including the hostility to minority groups in the white suburbs.[29]

This was an element in all of the site conflicts reviewed in Chapter 3. In Seattle, the issue involved primarily Japanese-Americans. There was no overt mention of this in the public campaign. But a large part of any political campaign is made up of unrecorded, informal conversations; and in this case there was a great deal of talk about the feared impact of a large influx of Japanese-Americans on neighborhood property values.[30] In Los Angeles, the final compromise excluded the two biggest sites—both outside the existing Negro ghetto areas. Those which were retained were mostly within the districts with heavy concentrations of blacks and Mexican-Americans.

Chicago is the most instructive case of all in this respect. The dominating question here, once the issue had reached the point of site selection, was "where would the CHA program move Negroes?"[31] The aldermen of Chicago, while agreeing that public housing was a fine thing for their city, did not want a heavy incursion of blacks into their wards, and this would be the almost inevitable concomitant of a housing project. So great was the onus that on some occasions aldermen sought to punish their enemies on the council by voting to locate housing projects in their wards. A Jewish alderman who had been among the most ardent advocates of bringing more public housing to Chicago faced strong

---

[29]The issue of racial integration was also an unstated aspect of congressional debate about rent supplements. In the case of that program, too, some conservatives worried about integration resulting from the selection of sites in white suburbs.

[30]In a personal interview with the author, the Seattle Housing Authority Director, Charles Ross, expressed his belief that this issue had not affected many votes, since Seattle had a good race-relations record, having absorbed large numbers of Japanese and then 4000 to 5000 blacks with a minimum of tension. However, other observers (including some realtors) disagreed. The acceptance of the influx of minority groups into certain areas of the city did not mean that they could readily be absorbed into the kinds of neighborhoods featured in the site map.

[31]Martin Meyerson and Edward C. Banfield, *Politics, Planning, and the Public Interest* (New York: The Free Press, 1955), p. 121.

resistance to the location of a large project in his ward, for his Jewish constituents regarded their being singled out for this attention as a sign of discrimination against them. Even a Negro alderman opposed a site in his ward, for the middle-class Negroes in his constituency were themselves afraid of being engulfed in the culture of poverty from which they had escaped.[32]

The final settlement of the site battles, which endorsed only one-third of the units originally proposed, allowed one-sixth of the units to be built on vacant land instead of the requested two-fifths. Confronted with this reinforcement of ghetto patterns, the Chicago Housing Authority nonetheless reaffirmed its open-occupancy policy and pledged that applicants could select any project in which there were vacancies. In 1953 it reiterated that blacks could apply for projects previously limited to whites.

In August of that year the attempt to move the first black family into Trumbull Park Homes, a project in the steel-mill belt of Chicago's south side, touched off a pattern of violence and riots that caused a police guard to be maintained in the area for many months.[33] The opposition ranged from "political opportunists and race haters to businessmen, surrounding residents, and those who say, 'It's not the time; we must educate first.'"[34] The Chicago Housing Authority stood its ground. The family which had been the occasion of the uproar moved out, but more black families moved in. Blacks were also admitted to other previously all-white projects. Yet the resistance from the surrounding communities was too great to allow for much more than token integration. By 1960 there were still only a few blacks in several of the projects. Indeed, the new housing authority director who took over in 1958 explained that: "We are not going to use public housing as a wedge to integrate all white neighborhoods. Our role must be one of a friend to the community."[35]

[32]Meyerson and Banfield, *Politics, Planning, and the Public Interest,* pp. 175, 199, 217–218.

[33]See Alfred P. Klausler, "When Racial Tensions Flare," *Christian Century* (January 6, 1954), pp. 11–14; Robert Greenberg, "Chicago Fiddles While Trumbull Park Burns," *The Nation* (May 22, 1954), pp. 441–443; Charles Abrams, "Slums, Ghettos, and the G.O.P.'s 'Remedy,'" *The Reporter* (May 11, 1954), p. 27.

[34]Klausler, "When Racial Tensions Flare," p. 12.

[35]Hill, "Demographic Change and Racial Ghettos," p. 266.

During the 1950s, 31,000 new public housing units were built in all-black wards in Chicago. Three and a half miles of them extended in a solid row "along the expressway, a favorite site for public housing in all our cities."[36] Among these was the Robert Taylor project, housing 28,000 blacks in high-rise buildings and referred to by some of its residents as "the Congo Hilton."[37] Then in the 1960s, the Chicago Housing Authority proposed the construction of four additional high-rise public housing buildings adjoining the Robert Taylor Homes, and the PHA gave its approval.

Civil rights organizations protested bitterly. The American Civil Liberties Union filed complaints asking the federal courts to enjoin this proposal, citing the Fifth and Fourteenth Amendments to the Constitution and the 1964 Civil Rights Act. "The authority has deliberately chosen sites for such projects," said the ACLU, "which would avoid placement of Negro families in white neighborhoods for 15 years."[38] The issue was caught up in the demonstrations against housing discrimination led by Martin Luther King in the summer of 1966. The conflict was concluded by a "summit agreement" among religious, civic, business, labor, and civil rights leaders. The agreement approved the principle of open housing in Chicago, and this had important implications for public housing:

> The Chicago Housing Authority will take every action within its power to promote the objectives of fair housing. It recognizes that heavy concentrations of public housing should not again be built in the City of Chicago. Accordingly, the Chicago Housing Authority has begun activities to improve the character of public housing, including the scattering of housing for the elderly across the city, and initiation of a leasing program which places families in the best available housing without regard to the racial character of the neighborhood in which the leased facilities are provided. In the future, it will seek scattered sites for public housing and will

[36]Wolf von Eckardt, "Black Neck in the White Noose," *The New Republic* (October 19, 1963), p. 15.

[37]Hill, "Demographic Change and Racial Ghettos," p. 270.

[38]Hill, "Demographic Change and Racial Ghettos," p. 270.

limit the height of new public housing structures in high density areas to eight stories, with housing for families with children limited to the first two stories. Wherever possible, smaller units will be built.[39]

At last this would mean the end of the high-rise obsession of the Chicago Housing Authority. Yet it did not dispose of the reasons leading to that obsession. It remained to be seen whether enough of those scattered sites could be found to provide for the number of public housing units that the city wanted.

There was a similar problem in New York. Negro organizations have protested the trend toward building more and more projects within the ghetto. Yet, as has been already noted, Mayor Lindsay's efforts to spread the projects to outlying suburbs have encountered bitter resistance. The underlying cause, said an Urban League official, was "plain bigotry." A protester from Queens denied this: "What we don't want is the lower-class Negroes. We wouldn't be bothered by middle-class Negroes."[40] But middle-class Negroes are not public housing tenants. Bigotry or not, opposition to suburban sites remains high.[41]

So the patterns of segregation persist in public housing. In Detroit the housing commission reported: "We do not anticipate any significant number of white families moving into predominately or all-Negro projects in the forseeable future." In Balti-

---

[40]"The Mayors' Dilemma," *Newsweek* (August 14, 1967), p. 22.

[41]In Portland, Oregon, minority groups and liberal organizations were able to veto plans in 1961 and 1963 for the construction of a housing project in Albina, a district with a high proportion of black families. Then the problem arose of how to insure that black tenants would be accepted for Northwest Tower, a senior citizens' public housing project in a part of the city containing almost no black families. President Kennedy was to have visited Portland in September 1963 to dedicate Northwest Tower. But when the NAACP and other groups failed to get satisfactory assurances on the integration question, the ensuing uproar was so great that the President cancelled his visit. (See Richard T. Frost and Janet McLennan, "The Northwest Tower Dispute," in Rocco J. Tressolini and Richard T. Frost [eds.], *Cases in American National Government and Politics* [Englewood Cliffs, N.J.: Prentice-Hall, Inc., 1966], pp. 216–226.)

[39]Subcommittee to the Conference on Fair Housing Convened by the Chicago Conference on Religion and Race, *The "Summit" Agreement* (Chicago: Leadership Council for Metropolitan Open Communities, August 26, 1966), Commitment to Action, Step 3.

more: "the percentage of nonwhites in all four of the integrated public housing projects has increased in the past year. Local housing authority officials doubt that integration can be maintained without occupancy controls"; and, "local housing authority officials in Baltimore have been unsuccessful in attempts to encourage nonwhites to apply for the city's three all-white projects. All three are located in far-out areas where no other facilities are available to nonwhites."[42]

The Civil Rights Act of 1964 has not reversed the trend. The Public Housing Administration did send out to all local housing authorities and managers instructions on procedures to be followed in pursuance of the no-discrimination clause of Title VI of the act.[43] It asked for the "establishment of a plan for selection of applicants and assignment of dwelling units to insure non-discrimination on grounds of race, color or national origin."[44] It also indicated that site selection should be undertaken in accordance with the policy established in Title VI. Nonetheless, the National Committee Against Discrimination in Housing charged in 1967 that the public housing agency (by then the Housing Assistance Administration) had been unwilling to enforce Title VI, that local authorities were allowed to flout the law, and that there were no signs that there would be any significant shift away from the dominant pattern of racial segregation.[45]

[42]U.S. Commission on Civil Rights, *Housing Report,* 1961, pp. 112–113.

[43]U.S. Housing and Home Finance Agency, Public Housing Administration, *Circular,* December 30, 1964, and August 27, 1965.

[44]Housing and Home Finance Agency, *Circular,* August 27, 1965.

[45]Richard Margolis and Diane Margolis, "The Ghetto and the Master Builder," in "How the Federal Government Builds Ghettos," *Trends in Housing,* XI, no. 2 (1967), 1–3. However, a further tightening of the regulations came by an amendment to the Low-Rent Housing Manual (paragraph 4g, Section 205.1) in February 1967: "Any proposal to locate housing only in areas of racial concentration will be *prima facie* unacceptable and will be returned to the Local Authority for further consideration and submission of either (1) alternative or additional sites in other areas so as to provide more balanced distribution of the proposed housing or (2) a clear showing, factually substantiated, that no acceptable sites are available outside the areas of racial concentration." In May 1968, another notice declared that the policy could not easily be circumvented "because of denial by city officials of necessary rezoning or other site approval." Department of Housing and Urban Development, Office of the Assistant Secretary for Renewal and Housing Assistance, *Circular,* May 3, 1968.

It may be that the federal agencies have been unduly timid in their approach to the problem. Yet the weight of community forces is so great, the site alternatives so few, and the enforcement powers so questionable that it will take more than the issuance of instructions from Washington to make the tide of segregation recede. So public housing, far from breaking down the barriers of segregation, today stands accused of actually reinforcing them. No more cruel charge could be leveled at those pioneers of public housing who, in the grim but optimistic days when the country was struggling out of the Depression, believed that this program could lead the way to a new era of harmony and understanding between the races.

SEPARATE BUT EQUAL AGAIN?

The debate over public policy in the field of race and housing is entering a new phase. Until the 1950s the doctrine of "separate but equal" was in effect. Then came the period beginning with the change in FHA regulations, progressing through the 1962 Executive Order and culminating in the 1964 Civil Rights Act, when it was thought that government action could shatter the walls of segregation. Those were the years of the rise of the civil rights movement, and the movement could point to major accomplishments. It achieved the beginning of the end of segregation in public accommodations, parks, and other facilities. It was a prime agent of change leading to the War on Poverty and an impressive array of new social welfare programs. Yet, in the crucial realm of housing, which determines so many other elements in the pattern of segregation, the civil rights movement has accomplished little. There are more black ghettos today than ever before. A high proportion of the bad housing of the country is within those ghettos. The drive for integration in housing has produced neither integration nor good housing. Indeed, it is often suggested that the stress on integration has been counterproductive, resulting in less, rather than more, new housing for the poor.

Accordingly, a profound disillusionment with desegregation attempts has set in, and many voices are suggesting that the goal of integration be subordinated to the improvement of housing conditions. The new doctrine was well stated by the late Senator Robert F. Kennedy:

> It is important that Negroes who have achieved financial and social security should have complete freedom to choose where to live. But it is far more important that the vast majority of Negroes be enabled to achieve basic financial and social security where they live now. It will be the work of years, and of all Americans, white and black, to decide whether most people will live in substantially homogeneous neighborhoods. But there should be no question that black neighborhoods, as well as white, must be places of security and dignity and achievement and comfort.[46]

The same view was cogently expressed in a December 1966 article in *The New Republic* by Frances Fox Piven and Richard A. Cloward of the Columbia University School of Social Work.[47] In their view, "the desperate need for better housing and facilities in the ghetto has been and continues to be sacrificed to the goal of residential integration." Piven and Cloward point to the failure to complete the public housing provisions of the Taft-Ellender-Wagner Act as a horrible example of the problem: "The ghetto poor have paid in this way for the struggle over whether Negro and white shall mingle, neighborhood by neighborhood." They have paid because of the efforts to integrate the projects—which have merely led to the departure of whites—and because of the search for sites in the white suburbs. The hostility that this provoked has been the principal cause of the setbacks in the program. "It seems clear, then, that reformers must apply what political pressure they have to secure relief in the ghetto itself. . . . If reformers can be persuaded to forfeit for a time the ideal of desegregation, there might be a chance of mustering political support and money for low-income housing."

[46]U.S. Congress, Senate, Government Operations Subcommittee, *Federal Role in Urban Affairs, Hearings,* 89th Cong., 2d sess., 1966, Pt. 1, p. 34; hereinafter referred to as: Senate, *Hearings, Federal Role in Urban Affairs,* 1966.

[47]Frances Fox Piven and Richard A. Cloward, "Desegregated Housing: Who Pays for the Reformers' Ideal?" *The New Republic* (December 17, 1966), pp. 17–22.

The "reformers" were bound to be disturbed by this argument, especially since it was expounded in the pages of the liberal *New Republic*, and letters in a subsequent issue expressed the sense of shock that some of them felt.[48] Still, liberals could hardly ignore the possibility that the pursuit of their integrationist ideal might be inflicting a severe loss on the people of the ghetto. Moreover, they could not even be sure that the ideal was as sound as it had once seemed. In earlier years the liberals had been the carriers of advanced, progressive thought. Now they were being made to appear obsolete by a new concept—the doctrine of Black Power. There are many versions of the Black Power creed, but at the heart of them all is the belief that, for the time being at least, the concentration of effort must be within the ghetto. Only within their own community, say the Black Power spokesmen, can black people discover their identity and build their political base. This potential power would be destroyed if blacks were integrated into predominately white communities.

So a strange conjunction of attitudes has emerged, with the conservative resistance to integration being matched by the militant blacks' insistence on blacks keeping to themselves. Confronted by these positions, it is not surprising that many liberals would retreat from long-held beliefs. It was clear to them that even the 1968 open-housing legislation and the subsequent Supreme Court decision pressing further still in the direction of housing integration would do little for the majority of the ghetto dwellers in the next generation. Piven and Cloward cite statistics which reveal the prodigious numbers of families who would have to move *in both directions* to reverse current trends toward separation of black cities and white suburbs.[49] Obviously this reversal is not going to happen on such a scale in the foreseeable future. Arithmetic is most certainly against us.

For some time to come, then, government programs addressed to low-income blacks will undoubtedly emphasize jobs, education, and housing over integration. Recent proposals in the low-cost housing field such as those by the late Senator Robert Kennedy and Senator Charles Percy,[50] have sought to improve

---

[48]"Correspondence," *The New Republic* (January 14, 1967), pp. 44–45.

[49]Piven and Cloward, "Desegregated Housing," p. 18.

[50]See this book, Chapter 5.

conditions where the problem is felt most acutely now—in the ghettos. And with respect to public housing, if the choice has to be made between segregated housing or none at all, it will be difficult to reject the case for the former.

However, the case for the new realism cannot be accepted entirely without qualification. The position developed by Piven and Cloward as well as others contains some flaws. First, their history is not unimpeachable. The race question has indeed been inextricably embroiled in the tribulations of public housing, and it was the most abrasive element in the local struggles over the program. But it is an oversimplification to see race as the sole or even the dominant reason for the failure to implement the public housing program on schedule. The most severe blow suffered by the program was not in Chicago in 1952–1953, but in Washington, D.C., in 1951, when the Appropriations Committee opened the way for Congress to cut back the requested funds. Racial animus was present on the floor of Congress at that time. But the basic difficulties, as we have seen, were the unremitting attacks by the private housing groups and, even more important, the low priority given to funds for the poor. The problem since then has not been merely to get a commitment to integrated housing, but to get any commitment at all to low-cost housing. Thus, it does not follow that removing the pressure for integration will smooth the way automatically for a rapid expansion of government programs to rehouse the poor.

Next, even if a commitment is made to massive efforts to improve ghetto housing, this will not necessarily obviate racial tensions. One of the shortcomings of ghetto life is congestion. The space criteria of federal housing agencies may be unduly generous;[51] still, there is unquestionably overcrowding in the housing of blacks, and this becomes worse as yet more blacks flock to the central cities of the North. One of the corollaries of upgrading housing conditions in an area is almost invariably a reduction of the number of units available—unless there is recourse to the now

---

[51]Nathan Glazer points out that the threshold we now consider "crowded" is one person per room, and he argues that it is very doubtful that densities of more than one person per room in themselves create social problems and family disorganization. (See Nathan Glazer, "Housing Problems and Housing Policies," *The Public Interest,* no. 7 [Spring 1967], 24–25.)

unacceptable high-rise construction.[52] The only solution remaining is that the ghetto will have to expand outward. But this cannot happen without causing the resistance and tension that the realists are so eager to avoid.

Then, it has yet to be shown that the black ghettos can, as a result of intensive investment, become what Senator Robert Kennedy called "places of security and dignity and achievement and comfort." The jobs are increasingly in suburbia. Senator Kennedy recognized this and proposed ways of creating jobs in the central cities;[53] but it is not known whether this can work on the scale needed. There is the problem, too, that segregated housing creates de facto segregated schooling; and the data from the Coleman report appears to lead to the conclusion that children educated in low-income, all-black schools are doomed to fall further and further behind the children of the suburbs.[54] This conclusion has been strongly challenged,[55] and it could be that a shift to local community control of ghetto schools, combined with massive infusions of federal funds will bring about a dramatic improvement in the education of black children. Yet the possibility remains that, no matter what is done within the central cities, the

[52]There are other possibilities, including row housing, but it is doubtful that major improvements can be achieved without some reduction in the number of units available unless high-rise construction is adopted. One other significant proposal has been suggested by Senator Joseph B. Tydings: the release of federal government land holdings in the cities for public housing. (See U.S. Congress, Senate, Banking and Currency Subcommittee, *Housing and Urban Development Legislation of 1968, Hearings, on Proposed Housing Legislation for 1968,* 90th Cong., 2d sess., 1968, Pt. I, p. 651.)

[53]He introduced legislation designed to bring industrial plants into poverty areas.

[54]U.S. Department of Health, Education, and Welfare, Office of Education, National Center for Educational Statistics, *Equality of Educational Opportunity,* by James S. Coleman *et al.* (Washington, D.C.: Government Printing Office, 1966). See a review of the Coleman report by Christopher Jencks, "Education: The Racial Gap," *The New Republic* (October 1, 1966), p. 21.

[55]See for example, Joseph Alsop, "No More Nonsense About Ghetto Education!" *The New Republic* (July 22, 1967), pp. 18–23. In this article Alsop approvingly quotes Piven and Cloward. His position was challenged in a subsequent article: Robert Schwartz, Thomas Pettigrew, and Marshall Smith, "Fake Panaceas for Ghetto Education: A Reply to Joseph Alsop," *The New Republic* (September 23, 1967), pp. 16–19.

perpetuation of the ghetto means the reinforcement of the culture of poverty.

Finally, we cannot escape indefinitely the moral issue which the integrationists, albeit unsuccessfully, have tried to confront. Nathan Glazer has questioned "the overall importance of the residential integration aim" and has suggested that the gains it brings are dubious "in light of the persistent tendencies of ethnic and racial groups in the past to prefer some degree of concentration, though nowhere the degree that is imposed by discrimination on Negroes."[56] But the last qualification is crucial. The Negro is concentrated to an extent far beyond the experience of any ethnic group in the past. He encounters encirclement and containment as though he were an alien force. This may well help the black to develop the identity, self-confidence and power base which he so sorely needs. But it does not follow from this that the full weight of government should be thrown behind policies of segregation.

Of course, Piven and Cloward are not segregationists, nor was Robert Kennedy. They were asking for only a temporary shift, leaving intact the ultimate ideal of integration. The problem is that, so powerful are the forces now working toward segregation that even a temporary endorsement by government of those forces (and the time period in question can hardly be less than ten to twenty years) would tend to produce permanent rigidities in the system. Blacks today constitute about one member in nine of our total population. Within a few years, the figure will be one in eight. The official acceptance of the separation of such a very large minority from the rest of the population is clearly incompatible with the values and institutions that have characterized the United States thus far.

Obviously it is not yet politically feasible for the federal government to compel integration everywhere, and the objections raised here to the Piven-Cloward position qualify, but by no means destroy, their central thesis. Integration will clearly not have the highest priority among the objectives of national housing policy. But this is not to say that it should be eliminated from the list of priorities. Public policy, while accepting the necessity of major investment within the ghetto, can still seek to open doors to desegregation. Too much of the current debate has been within a

---

[56]Nathan Glazer, "Housing Problems and Housing Policies," pp. 43–44.

context of all or nothing. A variety of options can still be provided.

Urban renewal, for example, can be used to promote a bringing together of races and classes by placing public housing or rent-supplement projects next to, or even as part of, middle-income developments. This has been done in all too few cases thus far, but HUD has indicated that it will apply greater pressure in the future to bring this about. Scattered public housing sites, the leasing of existing housing, rent supplements—all can be used in a number of communities to facilitate integration, as the Kerner report suggests.[57] In many places the resistance will be too great to overcome for the time being. But enough successes have already been achieved with these techniques to suggest that, with careful community study before the attempt is made, the risks can be considerably reduced. More ambitious long-range hopes have been tied to the creation of complete new towns that would be racially integrated from the outset.

Finally, the principle of open housing can be clearly established by vigorous enforcement of the legislation and Court decisions of 1968. It is true that the immediate significance of this principle is for middle-income rather than poor blacks. But this is no inconsiderable matter, for, outside the South, 38 percent of black families had incomes of $7000 or more in 1966.[58] The task of enabling these families to integrate is not encumbered by most of the difficulties we have been considering in this chapter in relation to public housing. Most black families with incomes of over $7000 are not crippled by the culture of poverty. Their movement into a white, middle-class community does not threaten to bring about a large increase in delinquency and vandalism or to undermine seriously the quality of education or to nurture those other forms of community deterioration that were popularly (and to some extent plausibly) associated with public housing. Denial to middle-income blacks of equal access to the private housing market is thus attributable only to status anxieties, prej-

[57]U.S. Commission on Civil Disorders, *Report of the National Advisory Commission on Civil Disorders,* Otto Kerner, chairman (New York: Bantam Books, Inc., 1968), p. 482.

[58]For the nation as a whole the percentage was 28—a fivefold increase from 1947 to 1966 (U.S. Departments of Labor and Commerce, *Social and Economic Conditions of Negroes in the United States,* p. 17).

dice, and erroneous assumptions about the threat to property
values. Clearly, if the principle of integration cannot be sustained
for those higher up the income scale, all hope that the poor black
might some day be able to move out of the ghetto will have to be
abandoned.[59]

[59]Herbert Gans argues in favor of opening up the suburbs to blacks, not
only the middle class, but also (through rent supplements) poor blacks.
Gans's starting point is not the standard criticism that the homogeneity of
the suburbs is deplorable; on the contrary, he believes that the very homogeneity is what gives satisfaction to suburbanites. Yet, he insists that politics
does not have to respond to only this kind of satisfaction and that public
policy can change attitudes by providing leadership: "When it becomes
politically feasible for the federal government to require 'open housing,'
. . . not only will the legal imperative persuade many suburbanites to accept
the inevitable, but if all communities must integrate, no one can expect
to live in all-white communities" (Herbert J. Gans, *The Levittowners* [New
York: Pantheon Books, 1967], pp. 427–428).

Chapter 5
Public Ownership

There is still one more characteristic of the public housing program that has helped to place it eternally on the defensive, forever trying to justify its place in the American scheme of things. Public housing is publicly owned; yet, government ownership and operation is very much the exception in the United States. There is a certain amount of municipal ownership, though less than in most other countries; but there is remarkably little federal management of economic enterprises outside the post office and TVA. There is substantial intervention in the economy. There are many kinds of regulation of industry and commerce. The awarding of huge government contracts has led to the evolution of an almost symbiotic relationship between the federal government and many kinds of business. Federal aid in the form of subsidies and price supports has been accepted—even demanded—by agriculture, railroads, airlines, shipping, and other industries. But the United States has not moved with the trend in most other industrialized countries, where railroads, coal mines, utilities, airlines, radio, and television[1] are partially or wholly nationalized.

To some extent, this is because private enterprise has been much more successful here than in other countries. However, the pragmatic result has not been the only test. The idea of free enterprise has taken a powerful hold on the American imagination. This idea, shaped by nineteenth-century experience, has been expressed not only in terms of the economic tools of capitalism—the market mechanism, competition, profit, supply and demand, and so on—but also as a set of value concepts or fundamental principles of morality. Free enterprise, in other words, has come close to being an ideology, a total system of beliefs and doctrine, within which are to be found the modes of thought and conduct indispensable to the achievement of freedom, as well as abundance.

At the heart of the ideology is a hostility to the power of government. All concentrations of power are feared in America, including concentrations of business and labor. However, governmental power is viewed as the overriding danger. This is especially so where the essential condition of free enterprise—competition—clearly prevails. This has generally been the case in the field of housing. It is not surprising, then, that direct public involvement came much later here than in Britain, for example, whose cities with financial support from the national government have been building houses for the working class since the 1890s. In the United States, the federal government did construct some low-rent housing during World War I as a result of an acute housing shortage, but even then only after a great deal of hesitation and muddle. When the war ended, however, almost all of this housing was sold to private owners. "Normalcy" had returned, and in the normal condition of things, government had to get out of business. In the 1920s there was action at the state level in New York,[2] but there was no support from the federal government.

[1]However, federal support of the Public Broadcasting Corporation is a limited step in this direction.

[2]"New York Housing Law," *Monthly Labor Review*, XXIII (July 1926), 77; Edwin L. Scanlan, "Public Housing Trends in New York City," unpublished Master's thesis, Graduate School of Banking, Rutgers University, 1952, p. 3.

It was only when the Depression dealt a savage blow to the economic system and to the ideology that conditions were created that made public housing possible. Still, apart from TVA (which mixed public and private enterprise), public housing was the only form of actual government ownership that emerged from the New Deal. It is thus antithetical to the dominant economic practices in the United States. Even as the role of government in the economy has steadily expanded, the charge that public housing is socialistic and therefore alien to the American creed has continued to reverberate. The consequence is that the proponents of public housing have always been at least half-apologetic about it, constantly explaining that it exists only out of dire necessity, that the construction contracts are placed with private firms, and that its accommodations are merely way stations for tenants who will move up in time to private housing. If their case has not carried conviction, sometimes it is because, in the context of an unfavorable ideological climate, they have seemed to protest too much.

For the opposition groups, on the other hand, the factor of public ownership provided another weapon with which to belabor the public housing program. It was not in itself as potent as the prevalent animus toward the poor and the black. But in public discussion at least one could not decently argue one's case on the basis of status fears and hostilities. To attack socialism was more respectable than to sneer at the unfortunate or to stir up racial prejudice.[3] Moreover, the ideological appeal provided the motivation which the leaders of the opposition groups needed to energize their rank and file members.

So the charge of socialism was persistently made against public housing by the opposition. Now, the doctrine of socialism has taken many forms and has been expressed in a very wide range of institutional forms and values. Almost all of them have included some degree of public ownership,[4] so there is no ques-

---

[3] Of course, a central element in socialist theory is the elimination of class barriers; the opposition's attack on public housing (and, later, on rent supplements) as encouraging "socioeconomic integration" could be placed in this context.

[4] Much of the guild socialist theory in Britain in the 1920s was based on pluralist alternatives to centralized government. And in the 1950s and 1960s some British Labour party theorists talked more in terms of a mixed economy, with the government's exercising a decisive role in economic

tion but that public housing is a small socialist element in the American system. Yet, as it was formulated by the opposition, the cry of socialism became a strident warning against a multitude of dangers.

THE ROAD TO SERFDOM

It was a constant theme of the opposition groups that public housing undermined private property, free enterprise, and the American way of life. It would speed the trend, they said, toward the eventual taking over of the entire economy by the government. Had not Britain and other countries of Western Europe followed the road to socialism by way of public housing? The Taft-Ellender-Wagner proposal, said a Republican congressman in 1949, should be entitled "a bill to further enslave the people of the United States."[5]

These forebodings were expressed in the inevitable anti-public housing resolutions passed at every annual conference of each of the opposition organizations in the 1940s and early 1950s. They were echoed by the predominately conservative speakers selected to address those conferences. Newsletters and trade journals brooded over the danger. Boards of directors and executive committees were militant on the subject.

So were the professional staffs. Herbert Nelson of NAREB had the misfortune to write a much-publicized letter to the president of his association in 1949 in which he said:[6]

> I do not believe in democracy. I think it stinks. I believe in a republic operated by elected representatives who are per-

---

policy but not owning and operating more industries than were already nationalized. Other European socialist parties have similarly drawn back from their earlier insistence on nationalization of all industry.

[5] Congressman Frederick C. Smith (Ohio), "Delay in Rules Committee Slows Down Action on H.R. 4009," quoted in *Journal of Housing,* VI (June 1949), 178.

[6] U.S. Congress, House of Representatives, House Select Committee on Lobbying Activities, *Housing Lobby, Hearings pursuant to H. Res. 298,* 81st Cong., 2d sess., 1950, Pt. 1, p. 25; hereinafter referred to as: House, *Hearings, Housing Lobby.*

mitted to do the job, as the board of directors should. I don't think anybody except direct taxpayers should be allowed to vote. I don't think women should be allowed to vote at all.

Morton Bodfish of the USSLL had also expressed in writing his distaste for popular government and democracy.

These strictures against democracy in no way inhibited Nelson and Bodfish from urging their local units to make use of the referendum—that ultimate device of direct democracy—in the attack on public housing. Still, this was an unfortunate necessity of politics, and public housing was viewed by Nelson and Bodfish as a product of mob rule which must do grave damage to the American system. So, together with the Home Builders' Frank Cortwright, they sought to build broadly based coalitions of conservative groups, which would attack public housing along with other kinds of government ownership and control. There was liaison with the National Association of Manufacturers, which resulted in some joint action, as well as abortive discussion with the American Medical Association. NAREB established the National Committee to Limit Federal Taxing Powers and the National Home and Property Owners Foundation. Help for the anti-public housing cause was solicited and received from the Committee for Constitutional Government (which helped to pay the costs of a widely distributed reprint of an attack on public housing by Representative Ralph Gwinn) and from the very conservative radio commentator, Fulton Lewis.[7]

Such allies may well have damaged the private housing cause more than they helped it, and the espousing by NAREB of a variety of quixotic causes alienated many moderately conservative people. Still, the claim that public housing represented a grave menace to the entire economic and political order served an important function in the battle against the program. It provided the messianic fervor that held the memberships of the housing groups together for sustained combat. No doubt it also helped the leadership, for leaders typically need a cause to gain reputations and enlarge their staffs and budgets. Some realtors in many

---

[7]For data on these various kinds of collaborations see House, *Hearings, Housing Lobby*, Exhibit 21A, p. 47; pp. 223–226; Exhibit H246, p. 281; and Exhibit H205-A, p. 287. (The suggestion for soliciting Fulton Lewis' help came from Los Angeles builder Fritz Burns.)

communities were, in fact, not in tune with the leadership. In one Midwestern city, for example, "several individual realtors admitted to those backing the proposal that they favored the housing ordinance, but could not come out publicly for it because of fear of retaliation from fellow realtors."[8] Nonetheless, the gap in ideological consciousness that usually exists between leaders and members was much less in evidence in the case of NAREB than with most organizations. Realtors tend to be numbered among the more conservative elements in any community. Campaigns against higher public expenditures or racial integration almost invariably include representation from the real estate profession. Like most home builders, they are characteristically small businessmen; and associations of small businessmen tend to be strong bastions of militant hostility to government action. It is true that, left to their own devices, most realtors, home builders, and savings and loan officers might not have spent much of their time fighting public housing. Still, in many communities they were ready enough to be aroused by the drumfire of statements, newsletters and speeches directed at them by their national leaders and to form local organizations with such titles as the Council for the Preservation of Free Enterprise or the Committee Against Socialized Housing.[9]

It was the contention of the public housing supporters that these antigovernmental crusades were hypocritical. No industry, they pointed out, has received more help from government than the business of housing. NAREB had advocated a federally chartered mortgage discount bank in the 1920s and early 1930s and was strongly supportive of the Federal Housing Administration and other agencies which employed the resources of the federal government to underwrite the credit structure of the housing industry. To the Home Builders, FHA was indispensable. They were also firm believers in the Federal National Mortgage Administration and the VA mortgage program. While the savings and loan leagues had no use for most of these programs, they had promoted and supported the Home Loan Bank in the 1930s, and

[8] Donald H. Bouma, "The Social Power Position of a Real Estate Board," supplemented paper delivered at the Sociology Section, Annual Meeting, Michigan Academy of Science, Arts and Letters, Wayne State University, March 24, 1961, p. 5.

[9] St. Petersburg, Florida, and Los Angeles, respectively.

it became one of their main props.[10] The housing industry maintained close and intimate association with all of the government agencies whose support to the private sector was so vital, and several members of the agency staffs and consultants came from some branch of the private housing field.[11] It was no wonder that Charles Abrams concluded that the housing industry believed in "socialism for the rich and private enterprise for the poor."[12]

The industry had an answer. There was a fundamental difference of principle, they contended, between the two kinds of government support. Public housing was paid for by government, owned by government, operated by government. The various aids to private industry did not entail government ownership or even direct subsidy. They did nothing more than apply the public credit to underwrite and insure the housing market. The programs were self-supporting and cost the taxpayer nothing.

This is a debatable proposition. The limitation of the programs to the underwriting of credit does not remove all traces of socialist taint. FHA, FNMA, and the rest represent government intervention in the economy, an interference with the free operation of the market. To some banks and insurance companies, they offer at least potential competition.

Still, the distinction was believed in devoutly by the opposition groups. For them the rationalization was convincing. They were convinced of the righteousness of their cause and of the evils of public ownership. And the whole thrust of the American system, which rejected government ownership but enthusiastically sought government aids to private business, was on their side.

[10]However, by the 1940s they were asking for the liquidation of the Home Owners' Loan Corporation. Opposition to this position led to the establishment of the rival National Savings and Loan League, which later supported the Taft-Ellender-Wagner Bill when its position on the Home Loan Bank Board was incorporated in the bill.

[11]Harry Conn, "Housing: A Vanishing Vision," *The New Republic* (July 23, 1951), p. 10; and Tris Coffin, "The Slickest Lobby," *The Nation* (March 23, 1946), p. 340. Richard O. Davies says that HHFA administrator Raymond M. Foley "enjoyed an amicable relationship with the housing industry" and "openly solicited" the friendship of real estate and construction groups. See Richard O. Davies, *Housing Reform During The Truman Administration* (Columbia, Mo.: University of Missouri Press, 1966), p. 60.

[12]Quoted in Bernard Taper, "A Lover of Cities," Pt. I, *The New Yorker* (February 4, 1967), p. 42. Later the phrase was popularized by Michael Harrington.

COMMUNISM

In their warnings against the alien intent of public housing, the opposition did not rest their case with the British example. The specter of the Soviet model was conjured up. At first this was merely an extension of the antisocialist rhetoric. The Taft-Ellender-Wagner Act, it was said, would represent "a sweeping advance on the part of the power planners toward their goal of complete regimentation, Russian style."[13]

But the accusations became more specific and more potent during the early 1950s. Communists, it was alleged, were moving into the public housing projects and organizing them as advance bases for the revolution. "It should be no wonder," said Congressman Ralph Gwinn in 1952, "that the Communists are building cells in the public housing projects across the country since public housing is one of the principles of the Constitution of Soviet Russia."[14] Gwinn cited newspaper reports from Pittsburgh indicating that a man accused by two former FBI agents of being a Communist was living in a housing project, and that the local housing authority refused to do anything about it since "it had no rule under which a Communist may be evicted or barred from a project." On the other hand, Gwinn quoted a Detroit story to the effect that the local housing authority was trying to evict a former *Daily Worker* correspondent and a Communist Party member. This argument became the basis for the 1952 Gwinn amendment, which required public housing tenants to sign a loyalty oath. The bulk of Court decisions went against this requirement, but the amendment was not eliminated until 1956. Even then the Public Housing Administration instructed housing authorities to "exercise administrative authority to prevent occupancy of any low-rent housing project by any person who is subversive."[15]

Further, the opposition claimed that Communists had infiltrated not only the projects, but also the administration of the

[13]Congressman Smith (Ohio), in *The Journal of Housing* (June 1949), p. 178.

[14]*Congressional Record*, XCVIII, Pt. 2, 82d Cong., 2d sess., March 20, 1952, 2681.

[15]"Gwinn Amendment is Dead," *Journal of Housing*, XIII, no. 8 (1956), 279.

program. This charge was particularly effective in Los Angeles. There, Chief of Police William H. Parker delivered a dossier to Mayor Bowron on the alleged subversive activities of Frank Wilkinson, special assistant to the executive director of the housing authority, and nine other officials of the authority. This dossier was used by attorneys for property owners opposing condemnation proceedings in a disputed site area, and they asked Wilkinson, as a chief witness for the housing authority, to list "the names of all organizations, political or otherwise, of which you have been a member, commencing with the dates of your schooling at UCLA from 1932 to 1936." The court accepted the question as relevant and material, and Wilkinson refused to answer beyond listing his qualifications as a "duly qualified expert witness." This refusal became the focus of the State Senate Un-American Activities Committee's investigation. Wilkinson was suspended by the housing authority; then he as well as other management personnel who had been subpoenaed to testify before the committee were discharged.[16] These dismissals, coming after the referendum defeat of public housing, did great harm to the program. Wilkinson especially had been very much in the public eye, for he was a passionate and articulate spokesman for public housing and had represented the program in a series of debates.

Today the accusation that public housing is part of the communist plot is heard only from groups outside the pale of political respectability. But the crucial years of the public housing controversy coincided with the McCarthy era, and it was hardly to be expected that a program of public ownership, designed for the poor, could escape damage in such a period.

GOVERNMENT COMPETITION WITH PRIVATE ENTERPRISE

To the defenders of public housing, the talk of socialism and communism was a smoke screen to cover the basically selfish motives of the private housing industry. On the face of it, indeed, public housing would appear to be inimical to the business associations operating in the field of housing. The natural assumption would be that they would be hurt by the competition offered by a

[16]Frank Wilkinson, "And Now the Bill Comes Due," *Frontier* (October 1965), pp. 10–12.

government program. "Who in the name of high heaven," said a newspaper editorialist, "would expect those in the real estate and building and loan business not to fight federal housing? . . . Maybe one might believe that the federal government—or local government for that matter—should set up grocery stores in every town in the state and operate them in competition with private stores."[17]

Yet the reasoning was fallacious. There was no direct threat to the major private housing associations in public housing. The danger of competition was remote. The legislation required that public housing rents be kept at least 20 percent below the prevailing rents charged in the community for comparable private housing. Public housing was only for the poor.[18] Private home builders did not build for the poor; savings and loan leagues did not lend them money; realtors were rarely involved in sale or rent at the levels available for the poor. If anything, public housing would bring additional business to private companies. The construction itself was contracted to private business concerns, although these were predominately larger builders than those who make up the bulk of the membership of the National Association of Home Builders. While public housing was mostly constructed from fireproof materials rather than wood, a good deal of lumber had to be used, and this would profit the lumber manufacturers and dealers. Many of the building materials firms represented in the Producers Council stood to benefit from public housing.[19] The program even brought business to realtors whenever the building of a housing project involved the dislocation of an existing neighborhood.

[17]*High Point, North Carolina, Enterprise,* April 22, 1948. Reprinted in National Association of Home Builders, "Home Builders' Information Material to Oppose Socialized Public Housing" (Mimeographed kit of materials).

[18]To the extent that public housing represented a net increase in the supply of housing (and this would be true if an equivalent number of slum units were not immediately demolished), it would tend to bring down rents at the lower levels. However, this would have real significance only for owners of very low-priced units, which would usually be slums.

[19]It is true that during periods when building materials were scarce, as after World War II or during the Korean conflict, builders would want to use the available supplies only for high-cost housing. Yet their opposition continued unabated when the conditions of scarcity had passed.

At the local level, it is true, there were some other interests who might be financially threatened by public housing. Chief among these were the slum owners, who included different types of entrepreneurs. Many landlords of substandard housing were persons of modest means, often elderly people living on small, fixed incomes drawn primarily from renting a few run-down apartments or houses. Others were large investors, institutions of various kinds, often of impeccable respectability, who, through trusts and other devices, covered up the record of their holdings. Whether the owners were large or small, the return on their investment tended to be high, often incredibly high.[20] Public housing threatened these profits in two ways. First, it provided alternative housing for the poor, usually at competitive rents. Second, it was connected with slum clearance, even though the provisions of the 1937 and 1949 acts requiring equivalent slum demolition were not enforced immediately or rigorously.

From these facts, and from the analysis of the opposition campaigns around the country, many of the public housing supporters concluded that the slum owners were at the bottom of the trouble. Support for this view could be found in the controversies in Los Angeles, Miami, St. Petersburg, and a few other cities where slum owners were active in the anti-public housing campaigns and contributed heavily to them.[21] There were other places in which their participation was significant, although less obvious, since any

[20]The *Chicago Daily News* gave this account of one slum property in Chicago: "The building once consisted of 70 seven-room apartments. The legal rent for these was $45 a month in 1942. It had risen to $71.50 a month by last year.

Many of these apartments, however, have been converted. Here is what one former seven-room apartment is today:

Two 1-room apartments renting for $41.25 a month each
One 2-room apartment renting for $75.83
One 3-room apartment renting for $60.00.

Total monthly income from an apartment that brought $45 in 1942 is now $218.33." Yet six cases had been filed against this building in five years for hazardous and unhealthy conditions. ("The Road Back," *Chicago Daily News*, 1954, p. 11.)

[21]"City News," *Journal of Housing*, XIV, no. 10 (1957), 391; and "Opposition hits housing program locally through realtors, builders, lenders, property owners," *Journal of Housing*, VII, no. 1 (1950), 9.

publicizing of their contribution would have embarrassed their cause and their allies.

Even so, it is an exaggeration to suggest that slum owners were more than a minor element in the larger number of campaigns. Most realtors, home builders, and mortgage institutions have no direct interest in preserving slum conditions. On the contrary, slum clearance was more likely to be to their advantage, and they have been instrumental in raising building code requirements in some cities to the point at which they have brought about a drastic reduction in the profitability of slum ownership.[22] Thus, in Los Angeles the small property owners, close allies of the realtors in the fight against public housing, were loud in their indignation when the realty board later pressed for vigorous enforcement of the building codes. Clearly, in the local battles slum profits were by no means the universally controlling motive.

However, if public housing represented no obvious, immediate financial threat to most of the parties engaged in the business of housing, they might still worry about what the future might bring. What really concerned them, they said, was the introduction of the "thin end of the wedge" or "the camel's nose under the tent." The camel's nose had been inserted in 1937. Much more of the beast followed in 1949. "The outstanding experience shown by New York City public housing," warned the NAHB, "is that once a full fledged public housing program is adopted, public housing grows, and *grows,* and GROWS. One project leads to another. Every thousand units of public housing completed opens demand for another thousand."[23]

Indeed, the New York City example is impressive, for today the housing authority is landlord to about half a million tenants and owns assets of almost $2 billion.[24] This has been accom-

[22]Charles Abrams suggests, too, that the exodus of middle-income whites from the city centers and their replacement by low-income blacks has inevitably meant a decline in property values and rents, U.S. Congress, Senate, Banking and Currency Subcommittee, *Housing Legislation of 1967, Hearings on Proposed Housing Legislation for 1967,* 90th Cong., 1st sess., Pt. 1, 1967, p. 712; hereinafter referred to as: Senate, *Hearings, Housing Legislation of 1967.*

[23]National Association of Home Builders, "Some Facts About Public Housing in New York City," in "Home Builders' Information Material to Oppose Socialized Public Housing" (Mimeographed kit of materials), p. 1.

[24]Taper, "A Lover of Cities," Pt. II (February 11, 1967), p. 80.

plished by a combination of federal, state, and local aids, which have been provided for the middle-income groups as well as the poor. The housing industry feared that this might be imitated by cities all around the country. It is true that the public housing advocates in 1949 were only asking for a figure of perhaps 10 percent of total construction. But if 810,000 units were completed in six years, could this not lead to pressure from a vastly expanded public housing lobby for a vastly expanded program? The cry was also going up that the housing of the middle-income groups was inadequate and that government should become involved in that area beyond the programs already acceptable to private business. Efforts to pass legislation to this effect were, in fact, made in 1950, though the opposition groups succeeded in aborting them. Where would it all stop? The experience of the inexorable expansion of income tax, of social security, and of many other welfare and redistributive measures provided evidence that the housing industry was describing real political possibilities and not merely imaginary terrors.

In fact, if the danger were real, it was never great. There has not been any tangible prospect that the middle-income groups would want help from government in the housing field other than mortgage insurance and the general underwriting of the industry's credit. Even if there had been more public housing beyond the full Taft-Ellender-Wagner schedule, this would have done little, if any, damage to the private industry, apart from slum owners. No doubt the situation called for watchfulness and resistance to the development of any grandiose plans for expansion, but the private housing interests were sufficiently well organized to be able to handle that. The actual dangers to the private housing industry, even in the long run, simply do not explain the intensity of their opposition to public housing and the expenditures of money, time, and effort they devoted to it.

The explanation must be seen, then, primarily in ideological terms. Customarily, ideology is regarded as the cloak for economic interests. In this case, ideology was largely a substitute for economic interests. The tenuous reality of the long-range danger could only provide an adequate motivation if it were set within the framework of the fight against government power in general. Given the attitudes which are prevalent among the private housing groups, this framework of doctrine was easily provided.

CENTRALIZATION

The antigovernment ideology in America has been aimed especially at the federal level of government. To a considerable extent, the insistence on the virtues of state and local action as against federal intervention has masked efforts to prevent action by *any* level of government. Still, in a country so large and with such a history of antipathy to centralized controls, the appeal to local as against federal government can usually be relied on to stir a sympathetic response in the communities. Consequently, the groups opposing public housing charged repeatedly that the program was an instrument for the imposition of the schemes of the central government upon the reluctant local citizenry. "It would be wonderful," said the *Los Angeles Times* in 1953, "if this victory could be taken as indicating a trend, to believe that the Federal imperialists, despite all their money, are slowly being driven out of the States and the cities."[25]

After the 1937 housing act it might have been thought that the fears of federal "imperialism" had been laid to rest. The intensely personal rule of Harold Ickes gave way to a system that depended on local approval of the program at a number of points. Nonetheless, it must be conceded that the requirement of community endorsement did not build the public housing program into the fabric of local institutions. The Public Housing Administration, largely as a consequence of the need to keep expenditures within reasonable limits, imposed close and continuous controls over many aspects of the local operations. Annual contributions contracts between the PHA and local housing authorities were replete with phrases like "unless PHA otherwise approves," "as the PHA may require," "satisfactory to the PHA."[26] In 1955, one local housing official complained: "It now appears that so many controls and sanctions are to be put into effect that the contract contemplates relegating localities to the status of an agent or a servant of the Federal government."[27] The Public Housing Com-

---

[25]*Los Angeles Times* (August 7, 1953), Pt. II, p. 4.

[26]Robert Moore Fisher, *20 Years of Public Housing—Economic Aspects of the Federal Program* (New York: Harper & Row, Publishers, 1959), p. 148.

[27]Fisher, *20 Years of Public Housing,* p. 149.

missioner denied that PHA controls were excessive; but a later commissioner, Mrs. McGuire, agreed that federal regulations had produced an unhealthy degree of standardization, especially in the field of design, and she encouraged the emergence of much more local variety and creativity.

Of course, where the federal government spends large amounts of money, it cannot escape accountability for how it is used. The law warns sternly against "extravagance" in public housing expenditures. The Comptroller General has issued a number of reports whose titles include phrases such as "installation of unnecessary equipment," "high costs pertaining to sites," "undue increases in maximum federal contributions"[28]—none of which are calculated to encourage a relaxed attitude in Washington agencies toward local initiatives. Nor can the federal government ignore the fact that some local governments are prone to corruption and incompetence.

Clearly the public housing program cries out for an effective federal-local partnership. It was, in fact, among the first programs to establish a relationship between federal and local agencies without much reference to state governments. In some places the formula for central-local cooperation has worked reasonably well. In many small communities, where the program has constituted a mere handful of units which have not stirred up controversy, the arrangement for federal supervision and local approval has been acceptable. However, wherever the potential for vigorous local opposition has existed, the hybrid nature of the housing authorities has left them in an exposed position. Since they were not

[28]Comptroller General of the United States, *High Costs Pertaining to Acquisition of Sites for Selected Low-rent Housing Projects in the Eight-State Area Administered by the New York Regional Office Public Housing Administration Housing and Home Finance Agency,* Report to the Congress of the United States (Washington, D.C.: General Accounting Office, December 12, 1963). Also, Comptroller General of the United States, *High Costs Pertaining to Sites for Selected Low-Rent Housing Projects in the Area Administered by the San Francisco Regional Office Public Housing Administration Housing and Home Finance Agency,* Report to the Congress of the United States (Washington, D.C.: General Accounting Office, December 18, 1963); and, Comptroller General of the United States, *Installation of Unnecessary Equipment for Measuring Consumption of Electricity and Gas in Low-Rent Housing Projects, Public Housing Administration, Housing and Home Finance Agency,* Report to the Congress of the United States (Washington, D.C.: General Accounting Office, June 1963).

purely federal installations, they were not protected by federal guarantees against local political harassment. Since they were not built into the community governmental structure, they lacked powerful local patrons. Under the skillful direction of a Louis Danzig in Newark, it might be possible to steer a local program between the many hazards which constantly threatened its destruction. But the process, even in Newark, was always precarious. In Chicago it became impossible to manage successfully, for the housing authority there had only enough autonomy to deprive it of federalized security and not enough to protect it from the whirlwinds of city politics.

HOME OWNERSHIP

In another of its anti-public housing themes, the opposition successfully grafted its free-enterprise ideology onto the prevailing attitudes toward the poor. Most low-income people cannot afford to purchase homes. They must be tenants, and public housing has confirmed their tenant roles. But most of the private housing organizations—the apartment owners being obvious exceptions— have insisted on the superior virtues of home ownership. "Freedom and civilization," said one NAREB official, "depend upon the widespread ownership of property. . . . We must look to more home ownership as the principle means of attaining the maximum diffusion of property ownership."[29]

In vain, public housing exponents protested that the notion was a dangerous myth, that ownership is much more costly than the real estate advertisements suggest, and that the reality is illusory, since ownership is for many years shared with a mortgage-holding institution.[30] In America, the ethos has been much too powerful to be resisted by the sceptics, and home ownership has become a central political reality.

In the words of a government publication in 1931: "Deep in

---

[29]Charles T. Stewart, "Public Housing—Wrong Way Program," *U.S.A.— The Magazine of American Affairs,* I, no. 4 (June 1952), 91–98. See also, National Association of Home Builders, "American Home Ownership v. Public Housing," Washington, D.C., n.d.

[30]Nathan Straus, *Two-Thirds of a Nation* (New York: Alfred A. Knopf, Inc., 1952), pp. 71–94.

the heart of most American families glows, however faintly, the spark of desire for home ownership."[31] By 1960 this cherished desire was fulfilled in the case of 62 percent of the total number of occupied dwellings. This compares with approximately 40 percent in Britain, a country with an unusually high proportion of homeowners.[32]

And homeowners, who must pay not only their own mortgages, but also high income and property taxes, are unlikely to be enthusiastic about public housing tenants who live in projects that are exempted from having to pay local taxes. It is true that local housing authorities make payments in lieu of taxes to the local governments, and often these are considerably greater than the taxes that came out of the dilapidated dwellings which they replaced.[33] But in-lieu payments do not have the sacred aura of

[31]U.S. Department of Commerce, National Committee on Wood Utilization, *How to Judge a House* (Washington, D.C.: Government Printing Office, 1941), p. 1. Quoted in Glen H. Beyer, *Housing and Society* (New York: Crowell-Collier-Macmillan, 1965), p. 249.

[32]Beyer, *Housing and Society,* pp. 249, 518. However, substantial numbers of middle- and upper-income Americans live in apartments; and given the rise in land costs in urban areas, the future trend may well be toward apartments. The ownership factor can be involved here, too, through cooperative and condominium devices. Yet this is a very different kind of ownership principle than is referred to in the traditional ethic.

[33]The 1949 housing act required that local housing authorities be granted exemption from all real and personal property taxes imposed by local and state authorities. However, it also provided that housing authorities could make payments "in lieu of such taxes in an annual amount not in excess of 10 per centum of the annual shelter rents charged in such project" (Section 10[h]). The HHFA estimated that the contributions made by the local authorities through full tax exemption, less in-lieu payments, would average about 50 percent of the actual federal contributions over the life of a project.

In Los Angeles the housing authority claimed in 1953 that in-lieu taxes were the equivalent of full city taxes and approximately full board of education taxes for the past three years. (See Housing Authority of the City of Los Angeles, "Handbook of General Information," Los Angeles, 1953, p. 7. [Mimeographed].) Similar claims were made by other housing authorities— and at the very least it was argued that in-lieu payments were greater than tax income from a previously dilapidated area. However, the opposition always emphasized the fact of tax exemption, and in some cases there is no doubt but that public housing was built in locations which, in the course of time, would have been developed by private renewal and rehabilitation plans, with or without governmental aid, which would have increased tax payments far beyond public housing in-lieu payments.

authentic property taxes. Most people are unaware of their existence and tend to be responsive to the oppositions' claim that public housing was one more federal depletion of the local tax rolls.

"PRIVATE ENTERPRISE CAN DO THE JOB BETTER"

Whatever the claims for private enterprise as the essential condition of the free society, the credibility of the system depends, in the last analysis on its results. The heart of the case for capitalism is that it is more productive, more efficient, more successful than government ownership and operation. Hence, the case against public housing could not be complete without the proposition that the private housing industry (perhaps with some kind of backing from government) could provide housing for the poor more effectively than a government agency.

This proposition was, in fact, extensively developed by the private housing organizations. It contained several components. First, it was suggested that the poor do not have to have new housing. A high proportion of them own used automobiles, and this does not arouse angry protests that it is the responsibility of government to see that everyone has a new car. By analogy, if the private home-building industry can produce a large number of new dwellings, those who can afford them will move out of their older homes, which will then, by a series of stages, "trickle down" eventually to the very poor. Some of the older units, it is true, have become substandard, but with appropriate housing codes and adequate enforcement of those codes, dilapidated housing can be rehabilitated.

Even where new housing is considered necessary, said the opposition, this can be produced faster and cheaper by private industry than by government. Here figures were cited comparing the average outlays on public housing units with those of low-cost, privately produced housing which, it was contended, was readily available. The private homes were said to be frequently less expensive, and where this could not quite be achieved, it was only because of the tax advantages given to public housing.

In those cases of extreme hardship, where families cannot afford even the lowest rents available on the private market, government should simply extend the principles of welfare aid

and provide them with rent certificates which they can give t
private landlords, who can redeem them for cash from govern
ment.

In contrast with these possibilities, argued the private hous
ing entrepreneurs, public housing is an inflexible and cumbersom
technique, which is inevitably caught up in the red tape an
inefficiency of vast federal agencies.

This was the case presented by the opposition in its testimo
ny against the Taft-Ellender-Wagner proposal from the time i
was introduced, and which was expanded and elaborate
throughout the years of struggle against public housing. From th
outset, however, it was rejected by most of those conducting th
congressional hearings into the housing problem, including Sena
tor Taft.

Taft's seeming apostasy was a source of baffled frustration t
the private housing industry. As the leader of the conservativ
Republicans, he seemed to them to be the least likely of a
spokesmen for the cause of public housing. But they did nc
understand his political philosophy. He wanted the least possibl
government intervention in the economy that was compatible wit
the survival of the economy and with certain basic responsibilitie
toward the poor. His attitude toward the poor had been profound
ly affected by the slums of his own Cincinnati. He became con
vinced that the private housing industry could not cope with th
problem: "Private development and perfectly free enterprise i
the United States . . . have never eliminated those slums and I se
no reason to think that they ever will, because they simply cannc
reach the lowest income group."[34] Erstwhile friends muttered tha
"Taft is becoming a damn Socialist";[35] but he insisted that "with
out it [public housing] I do not think we can solve the prob
lem."[36] His support for the program was qualified. It must b
limited in size, responsive to local interests, and noncompetitiv
with private industry. Nonetheless, he regarded public housing a
indispensable, for he was entirely unconvinced by the argumer
that private business could do the job better. He did not accep
the "trickle-down" theory. The process took too long, and by th

[34]"Legislative History of Public Housing," *Journal of Housing*, XIX, no.
(October 1962), 431.

[35]Davies, *Housing Reform During the Truman Administration*, p. 34.

[36]"Legislative History of Public Housing," *Journal of Housing*, p. 440.

ime housing was accessible to the lowest income group it had
ften reached a stage of dilapidation beyond repair.[37] He rejected
he idea of rent certificates, for these could become a subsidy to
lum landlords. He had no belief that private builders could
roduce housing at prices the very poor could afford.

Subsequently, the industry has done little to refute Taft's
cepticism. There has been almost no new standard housing at
rices even remotely within the reach of the poor. Promises were
1ade in many communities, but they were unfulfilled. During the
ublic housing controversy in Houston, the local builders pur-
hased a whole section in one of the daily newspapers to an-
ounce the formation of a corporation that would immediately
egin construction of 10,000 low-cost homes—2500 for Negroes,
500 for Mexican-Americans, and 5000 for whites. "The first
roup of homes are well under way at this date," said the ad.
Vith the election over, and public housing defeated, a regretful
nnouncement was made: The construction of these homes would
e delayed by materials shortages.[38] Even when "low-cost" hous-
ng was completed in other cities, it required payments well
eyond the rents charged in public housing. It could hardly be
therwise. Building for the poor does not offer the same profit
1argins to be found higher up the income scale. In any field,
roduction for the low-income market only becomes possible
hrough large volume and small per-unit profits. This requires the
echniques of mass production. But the home-building industry is
till made up predominately of small entrepreneurs using an essen-
ially traditional technology.

Rehabilitation of deteriorated housing was the other major
ossibility, and programs to upgrade slum housing have been
ndertaken and sometimes vigorously pursued by private housing

However, the filtering argument should not be dismissed completely. In the
rude form in which it is usually presented by the private housing industry
t is easily refuted. Yet there may well be some relationship between major
ncreases in units available at middle- and upper-income levels and the
upply that becomes available in time at the lower levels—especially where
he filtering process is accelerated by public subsidy. (See Wallace F. Smith,
iltering and Neighborhood Change [Berkeley, Calif.: The Center for Real
*state and Urban Economics, Institute of Urban and Regional Develop-
nent, 1964], pp. 5–9.)

*"Canned Campaign is Both Good and Bad," *Journal of Housing,* VII, no. 8
1950), 265.

associations. But the total results have not been impressive. Th
slums remain, and their scale is still appalling. This has alway
provided the most persuasive argument for public housing. Th
opposition might protest that the "equivalent elimination" provi
sions of the 1949 act had been so loosely interpreted that it wa
not clear that there was any important relationship between pub
lic housing and slum clearance. They could also point to the fac
that over 80 percent of localities participating in the progran
were not big cities but towns with under 25,000 population.
Still, on the slum issue the private housing groups were on th
defensive. In the great cities of the Northeast and Midwest, wher
the squalor was extensive and indisputable, they could be effec
tive only in opposing particular sites for public housing. In th
communities of the West, where slum conditions exist but ar
generally less oppressive and less conspicuous,[40] the oppositio
was better able to overcome the liability of dilapidated housing.[4]

[39]Housing and Home Finance Agency, *17th Annual Report* (Washingtor
D.C.: Government Printing Office, 1963), p. 277.

[40]According to the 1950 Census of Housing, the proportion of substandar
dwelling units in the Pacific region was approximately 10 percent as op
posed to 42 percent in the East-South-Central region. The percentage i
Chicago was more than twice that of Los Angeles. However, the Chicag
figure was not much greater than that of Houston, and in New York th
proportion was actually below that in Seattle and Portland.

Still, there was a qualitative difference between Eastern and Wester
slums. It is true that Charles Abrams reported that in Los Angeles in 195
"shacks made of old crates and little garages on back alleys house thousand
of recent immigrants" (Charles Abrams, "Rats among the Palm Trees," *Th
Nation* [February 25, 1950], p. 177). But this was an exceptional perioc
and even then the degree of dirt and dilapidation was not as great as i
Harlem. Slums in the West are mostly less congested than in the East, an
winter brings greater misery to the tenements of the Eastern and Midwester
cities than to those on the Pacific Coast or in Texas.

Again, the slums of the East and Midwest force themselves more obvious
ly on the awareness of the entire city than is the case in the West. It wa
possible (until recently, at least) for the suburbanite in Los Angeles to b
completely unaware of the presence of a great deal of dilapidated housin
on the other side of his city. The Chicago commuter, on the other hanc
could not escape the dismaying squalor of mile after mile of blight seen fror
the train every weekday morning and evening.

[41]The opposition had another advantage in the Western cities—the tendenc
to have greater recourse to the referendum, resulting from the rejection c
the strong influence of machine politics in the older cities of the East an
Midwest.

ven in the West, however, the housing authorities' case was most
fectively presented by taking politicians and civic leaders on
nducted tours of run-down neighborhoods.[42] Against the grim
idence of the senses, the ideological abstractions and unfulfilled
omises of the realtors and home builders would seem, for the
oment at least, empty and unconvincing. So, Senator Taft's
imary question remained: If the private housing industry could
the job, why hadn't they?

It was not to be expected that the industry would ever quite
ncede that they could not solve the problem. Nonetheless, as
ne went by, their doctrinal refusal to allow any room for direct
vernment action began to lessen. Ideological zeal cannot be
stained indefinitely without at least some distant contact with
ality. The one threat that might possibly be real—the danger of
adual nationalization—was nullified by the House Appropria-
ns Committees, the Eisenhower administration, and the refer-
dum battles. The thin end of the wedge had been inserted in
49—but broken off in 1951. By the mid-1950s it was obvious
at in the foreseeable future there would not be a really large
blic housing program in America. The limited amount that
mained would help take care of families displaced by other
ograms supported by business interests and would thus help
ssen opposition in the communities to those programs. More-
er, from 1956 there was increasing emphasis on rehousing the
derly in public housing to the point at which 32 percent of all
blic housing tenants in 1966 were elderly.[43] It would seem
pecially callous to attack the principle of government assistance
those who were old as well as poor.

Consequently, boredom with the issue began to set in among
e opposition groups. Massive campaigns of grass-roots pressure

his was a technique used with great effectiveness by the housing authority
Los Angeles—until the major attack on the program got under way.

he President's Advisory Committee on Housing in 1954 recommended
re attention to the low-income aged. This was first reflected in the 1956
using act, which included single elderly persons among those eligible for
blic housing. There was further provision for the elderly in the 1959
gislation. Continued emphasis on the elderly under the Kennedy and John-
n administrations resulted in a dramatic increase in the proportion of
derly families from 20 percent of all public housing tenants in 1961 to 32
rcent in 1966 (Senate, *Hearings, Housing Legislation of 1967*, Pt. 1,
116).

can be mounted once, twice, perhaps even four or five times. B
when it became indisputable that public housing was not a su
vival matter for the private housing industry, the membersh
could be aroused no longer, and the leadership turned the
attention to other issues. It was still the official stance of th
housing groups, especially of the realtors, that public housing wa
socialism, that it was an undesirable extension of centralize
power, that it conflicted with the virtues of home ownership, an
that, given the opportunity, they could yet prove their capacity
rehouse the poor more effectively and more cheaply than gover
ment. But, when the dust of battle had settled, public housi
represented about 1 percent of the total housing stock of th
nation; and while the housing industry would prefer comple
ideological purity, conscience and self-interest conspired to allo
them to settle for 99 percent of their goal.

PUBLIC HOUSING AS IDEOLOGY

Ideological drives were not limited to one side in the publ
housing controversy. Many of the protagonists of the progra
were far from being unfailingly empirical. True, the case fc
public housing was based on two pieces of hard data: the mise
able housing conditions of the poor and the inability of priva
industry to improve those conditions. Public housing seemed to l
a sensible response, used almost everywhere else in the world.

Nonetheless, the fact that public housing entailed goverr
ment ownership made it especially appealing to liberals, whos
creed in the twentieth century has included a strong emphas
on the steady expansion of the functions of the federal goverr
ment. In the liberals' doctrine, public housing became a d
vice for demonstrating what could be accomplished by lon
range, imaginative planning in the public interest as against th
sprawling chaos and shoddy construction resulting from the desi
of private developers to make a quick profit. There were, c
course, private economic interests on the public housing sid
too—jobs for the building trades department of the AFL, co
tracts for architects, career advancement for housing officials, an
so on. But economic interest alone could not explain the suppo
for public housing. Deeply held principles, sometimes constitutir

full-blown ideology, were an important motivating factor behind
e program.

By the mid-1950s the zeal of some of public housing's ear-
st proponents began to falter. As has been pointed out, they
iticized its physical appearance, the segregation by class and
ce. But they were ready to concede more than this. They began
argue that public housing ought to be brought into closer
nsonance with prevailing mores and values.

Even the most cherished tenets of their doctrine were reex-
ined. They had insisted that public ownership was immutable.
ow it was recognized that private enterprise might be given a
le not only in construction but also in management and owner-
ip. Even the idea of rent certificates, previously abhorred as a
abolical scheme of greedy landlords, was admitted as a poten-
lly useful technique. New construction had been an article of
gma, but absolution was given to the notion of rehabilitating
apidated dwellings. Home ownership, formerly derided as a
uel delusion for the poor, became a practical possibility.[44]

These concessions, together with the more conciliatory atti-
de of the private housing groups, provided the cues for the
anges in housing policy under the Kennedy and Johnson ad-
inistrations. The time was ripe for a new approach that would
compass an effective combination of public and private pro-
ams without regard to ideological preconceptions.

E NEW EMPIRICISM?

e new, more pragmatic climate has produced three basic con-
pts for rehousing the poor. First, there must be a larger role for
ivate enterprise within a multifaceted public-private partner-
ip. Second, rehabilitation must be applied on a large scale.
ird, more opportunities must be given to the poor to purchase
eir own homes. These concepts are at the heart of a profusion
new program proposals that recently emerged from Congress as
ll as from the Johnson administration.

oyatz Tyler (ed.), *City and Suburban Housing*, The Reference Shelf, Vol.
IX, no. 26 (New York: The H. W. Wilson Company, 1957), pp. 61–64.
arles Abrams, "Public Housing Myths," *The New Leader* (July 25,
55), p. 6.

The Public-Private Partnership

"Shouldn't we find out," asked Mrs. McGuire in a letter local housing authorities in 1961, "whether or not prof motivated management would or would not be compatible wi furthering the sound objective of the program?"[45] It was only question; but the mere mention of the possibility of admitting th profit motive into the very management of public housing w shattering evidence that nothing was sacred, that the old era w gone.

Mrs. McGuire's question related primarily to the manag ment of housing units leased from private landlords. This id was tried out under a provision of the 1961 housing act authori ing housing authorities to undertake demonstration programs experimentation with new methods for rehousing low-incon families.[46] Then the 1965 housing act authorized the short-ter leasing of 10,000 units a year from private owners.[47] This ga the housing authorities a new tool of great flexibility. It w "instant housing,"[48] essentially a rent-certificate program, free many of the restrictions and cumbersome arrangements with loc governing bodies imposed on traditional public housing.[49]

---

[45]Marie C. McGuire, *Newsletter* (Washington, D.C.: Housing and Hor Finance Agency, Public Housing Administration, October 30, 1961), p.

[46]In Washington, D.C., short-term leases were entered into to make roomi houses available for large, low-income families.

[47]Section 23.

[48]Abner D. Silverman, "Low-Rent Housing Program in an Era of Soc Change," an address at the annual meeting of the Carolinas Council Housing and Redevelopment Officials, Asheville, North Carolina, October 1965 (Mimeographed), pp. 2–3.

[49]Leased housing did not require cooperation agreements, workable pr grams, local tax exemption, or the 20 percent rental gap. Within two ye of the introduction of the program, 18,000 units were under contract. (S Senate, *Hearings, Housing Legislation of 1967*, Pt. 1, p. 196.)

Congressman Widnall, author of the rent certificate amendment told NAHRO meeting that "this idea is not new. It was proposed long a by the real estate people and rejected then by your Association—largely would think, because of your mistrust of the source. Years later, one of pillars of your organization, Warren Vinton, proposed the idea anew at c of your national conventions in San Francisco and the unhappy recepti

Then there was experimentation to allow a much greater degree of responsibility to private builders. Usually the housing authorities had controlled every stage of construction. But under the "turnkey" program a builder could contract for an entire housing project on a fixed cost basis.[50] The first of these efforts, in Washington, D.C., was successfully completed, and in 1967 the White House, acting on the advice of a special advisory commission, gave instructions for wider application of the technique.[51] The principle was intended to apply to the management as well as the construction of projects, thus making possible a bypassing of the unwieldy procedures of local housing authorities in getting projects under way. It was also calculated to provide professional management expertise which, the advisory commission had implied, had not been developed by the housing authorities.

Both the leasing and turnkey programs still leave the ultimate control in the hands of local housing authorities. Other approaches place the burden squarely on private industry, offering government support through public credit, tax incentives, and (where these are not sufficient to bring rents down far enough for the very poor) rent subsidies. Thus, the rent-supplement program includes both FHA mortgage insurance to private agencies and direct subsidy to the poor. Then section 221(d)(3) of the 1961 housing act provided help to the income group somewhat above the public housing clientele by making available to nonprofit

---

accorded him at the time, I understand, had him walking the streets of the Bay City" (William B. Widnall, "The Concept and Practice of the 1965 Rent Certificate Housing Amendment," *Critical Urban Housing Issues: 1967* [Washington, D.C.: National Association of Housing and Redevelopment Officials, December, 1967], p. 30).

[50] The turnkey method provided for the contractor to assume responsibility for the whole construction job, from start to finish, within general specifications agreed upon in the contract. The turnkey approach could also be used for rehabilitation projects. (See Joseph Burstein, "New Housing Assistance Methods, Local Housing Authorities and Private Enterprise," in *Critical Urban Housing Issues: 1967*, pp. 27–28).

[51] The commission, under the chairmanship of Edgar F. Kaiser, was appointed to find ways of involving private industry in slum clearance and rehabilitation. Their turnkey recommendation was eagerly seized upon by the Administration for it could be implemented without the necessity of going to Congress for new legislation.

sponsors 100 percent mortgages at below-market-interest rates.[52] Both of these devices could be used in conjunction with the larger Model Cities[53] program and New Towns proposals of the Johnson administration to provide better housing for the poor.

Nor has the stream of suggestions come only from the Administration. Congress, especially the Senate, has been a fertile source of proposals. In July 1967, Senator Robert F. Kennedy introduced an impressively sponsored bill to persuade builders and other businessmen to invest in the slums. His bill offered mortgage loans at 2 percent over fifty years for new housing together with tax incentives, a combination which could return at least 13 to 15 percent after taxes to the investor. The initial authorization was calculated to promote the construction of 300,-000 to 400,000 units of housing.[54] Senators Ribicoff, Mondale, Javits, and Percy[55] have also proposed large-scale programs that would lend government support to the efforts of private enterprise.[56]

Then, the life insurance industry announced in September 1967 that it was ready to lend one billion dollars for the rebuilding of the ghettos. Till now, little private mortgage money has

[52]Both PHA and FHA financing was made available for a project of the New York City Housing Authority and the Lavanburg Foundation to construct a housing project combined with commercial and community facilities, the entire undertaking to be managed by the foundation under contract with the housing authority.

[53]"The Model Cities program not only is dependent upon [rent supplements], but is superdependent on it, because as contrasted to our present public housing, it does not involve the moving of the tenant after he passes beyond the maximum income" (Testimony of Robert C. Weaver, Senate, *Hearings, Housing Legislation of 1967*, Pt. 1, p. 65).

[54]*Congressional Record*, CXIII, No. 108, 90th Cong., 1st sess., July 13, 1967, S9593.

[55]See Senate, *Hearings, Housing Legislation of 1967*, Pt. 2, pp. 1204–1205, for a summary of low-cost housing proposals before the Senate. See also James Ridgeway, "Rebuilding the Slums," *The New Republic* (January 7, 1967), p. 22.

[56]Title IX of the 1968 act was responsive to the congressional interest in a greater role for private enterprise. It creates national housing partnerships, eligible for special income tax benefits, to encourage private investors to put their resources in housing. Several other sections of the act are designed to stimulate the involvement of the private sector in the low-cost housing field.

)een available for poverty neighborhoods since the risk of default
s considered too high. The life insurance companies have de-
:lared themselves willing to venture into this field with the back-
ng of FHA. Since market-interest rates of 6 percent or more
would apply, rent supplements are looked to as the means of
)ringing the payments within reach of the very poor.

Rehabilitation

In her 1961 letter to housing authorities, Mrs. McGuire
suggested that serious consideration be given to the possibilities of
rehabilitating existing substandard structures and pressing them
nto the service of the public housing program. The idea quickly
gained currency and became an important feature of the 1965
housing legislation. There was a rehabilitation provision in the
,hort-term leasing section of the 1965 act, and 15,000 units a
year could be purchased from private owners and brought up to
standard with funds provided for the purpose. Amortization periods of less than the forty years associated with public housing
were authorized to make the new method workable.[57]

These steps are only the beginning of a major effort to clean
up and remodel the slums. HUD sponsored a symposium of
housing experts at Woods Hole, Massachusetts, in 1966, which
produced a proposal for an Urban Development Corporation to
undertake large-scale slum rehabilitation projects and accompanying research in technology.[58] This proposal was not presented to
Congress by President Johnson. However, in 1967 the President
set up a panel under the chairmanship of Edgar F. Kaiser to study
ways of developing a large-scale, efficient rehabilitation industry.[59]
And the 1968 housing act included a number of provisions for rehabilitation assistance in the form of both grants and loans. Robert
Kennedy's proposal, too, suggested rehabilitation as well as new
construction: "In the present state of our technology, many hous-

---

[57]Senate, *Hearings, Housing Legislation of 1967,* Pt. 1, pp. 104–105.

[58]Senate, *Hearings, Housing Legislation of 1967,* Pt. 2, pp. 1629–1630.

[59]See testimony of Edgar F. Kaiser, U.S. Congress, Senate, Banking and Currency Subcommittee, *Housing and Urban Development Legislation of 1968,
Hearings, on Proposed Housing Legislation for 1968,* 90th Cong., 2d sess.,
1968, Pt. 1, pp. 263–286; hereinafter referred to as: Senate, *Hearings, Housing and Urban Development Legislation of 1968.*

ing units in major cities can be rehabilitated for between half and two-thirds of the cost of new construction." Both urban esthetics and cost efficiency thus lead us to prefer rehabilitation.[60]

In many of the big-city ghettos, local campaigns are underway to paint, clean and remodel slum housing. But the Johnson and Kennedy programs went far beyond small-scale patchwork efforts. They sought to promote the massive application of the kind of new technology proposed by Secretary Weaver to Congress in 1966:

> Application of modern technology and science could have a profound effect upon both the cost and quality of urban housing. The long-range possibilities are limitless. Entirely new concepts of structural support and space enclosure could be developed. . . . Improved housing in urban areas is of such critical importance, especially for lower income families, that application of modern technology to both new housing and rehabilitation of existing housing offers perhaps the greatest promise of any of the many areas of urban life to which technology can make a contribution.[61]

This kind of technology offers promise in the field of new construction.[62] Thus far, however, its application has been primarily in the field of rehabilitation, where a number of extremely interesting possibilities have already been opened up. In New York City's 114th Street project, for example, "using city guidance and

[60]Statement of Robert Kennedy, Senate, *Hearings, Housing Legislation of 1967*, Pt. 1, p. 661.

[61]U.S. Congress, Senate, Government Operations Subcommittee, *Federal Role in Urban Affairs, Hearings, 1966*, 89th Cong., 2d sess., 1966, Appendix to Pt. 1, p. 93; hereinafter referred to as: Senate, *Hearings, Federal Role in Urban Affairs,* 1966.

[62]In the post-World War II period, great hopes were placed in the possibility of an inexpensive, assembly-line, prefabricated steel home to be produced by Lustron Company. Despite the estimate of Housing Expediter Woodrow Wyatt that the prefabrication industry would be able to produce 250,000 units by the end of 1946, only 40,000 were delivered. However, the Lustron experiment was bedeviled by the kind of political and financial difficulties that could be avoided today; and the technological possibilities for prefabrication are now considerably greater. (See Davies, *Housing Reform During the Truman Administration,* pp. 52–54.)

lmost $6 million in Federal money, two private foundations are
lpping the insides out of the 36-year old tenements which cover
lmost the entire block, and they are building 458 new apart-
lents."[63] Another experiment on the lower east side of Manhat-
ln, underwritten by foundations and private industry, involved
taking existing tenement structures, gutting them from the roof,
lompletely removing all of the internal structure, and then lower-
lg from the roof whole room units, bathrooms, sitting rooms,
ledrooms, and the works."[64] U.S. Gypsum, Armstrong Cork,
llcoa, U.S. Steel, Westinghouse, and the American Plywood As-
lociation are among the many private companies and groups now
lrying out rehabilitation techniques in New York, Cleveland,
lhiladelphia, Pittsburgh, and other cities.[65]

Rehabilitation offers three important advantages over new
lonstruction. (1) It may be cheaper: In Philadelphia, three-
ledroom units in row housing have been purchased and restored
lor $12,300 apiece.[66] (2) It can be considerably faster. (3) It
lvolves the least amount of disruption of existing neighborhood
latterns, for tenants may be installed in temporary accommoda-
lions while their homes are renovated, then moved back within a
lairly short period. Federal authorities have estimated the poten-
lial number of dwellings that might be rehabilitated at 9 million.[67]

Home Ownership

The poor are no longer considered by the federal govern-
lent to be incapable of assuming the responsibilities of home
lwnership. The 1965 legislation authorized housing authorities to
lell to tenants detached, semidetached, or public row housing

[a]*New York Times* (August 22, 1966), p. L-35.

[b]Testimony of New York Mayor John V. Lindsay, Senate, *Hearings, Federal
Role in Urban Affairs, 1966,* Pt. 3, p. 573. However, the cost of this kind
lf program still appears to be very high, perhaps prohibitively so at this
stage.

[c]Senate, *Hearings, Housing Legislation of 1967,* Pt. 1, pp. 105–111; "Reha-
lilitation," *Journal of Housing,* XXIV, no. 4 (1967), 199–225.

[d]"How to Clean Up the Nation's Slums?" *Newsweek* (August 28, 1967), p.
55.

[e]"How to Clean Up the Nation's Slums?" *Newsweek* (August 28, 1967), p.
55.

units.[68] The 1968 housing act extended this opportunity to an unit which had sufficient individual identity to make it suitable fo sale to public housing tenants. The Administration also moved t encourage home ownership among the poor entirely outside th public housing framework. In 1966, the FHA was authorized t insure below-market-interest mortgages for nonprofit groups tha undertook the purchase and rehabilitation of homes for resale t low-income families.

Then, in its 1968 housing proposals, the Administration too account of the fact that several members of Congress had intro duced home ownership plans for the poor.[69] Senator Charles F Percy, in particular, had made this concept the core of legislatic which he introduced.

It was designed "to advance the opportunities for an enjoy ment of equity housing among the poor" through interest-paymer subsidies which would be reduced as family income increased.[70]

In making his case, Percy was able to cite sources outside c the suburbanite property-owning populace. Some black leader have argued for the superiority of cooperative or individual own ership as opposed to tenancy in either slums or public housing. Percy drew qualified support, too, from Charles Abrams, who i an earlier period disparaged the idea of home ownership for th poor but who now believes that it can serve a useful, though b no means all-inclusive, function.

---

[68]At the time Robert C. Weaver expressed strong reservations about th desirability or feasibility of this idea. (See Senate, *Hearings, Housing Legisl(tion of 1967,* Pt. 1, pp. 72–75.)

[69]Including a proposal by Senator Joseph S. Clark (See, Senate, *Hearing Housing Legislation of 1967,* Pt. 1, pp. 179–180). Senator Robert F. Ker nedy, on the other hand, was skeptical: "We would hope that over a perio of time you are going to get into the concept of ownership in some of th larger cities, but we are going to have to do that, in the beginning, at slower pace" (Senate, *Hearings, Housing Legislation of 1967,* Pt. 1, p. 647)

[70]*Congressional Record,* CXIII, Pt. 1, No. 60, 90th Cong., 1st sess., Apr 20, 1967, S5635-5640. The Senator claimed that his proposal could lead t the production or rehabilitation of two million housing units.

[71]Ted Watkins, founder of the Watts Labor Community Action Committee told *Look* magazine: "We don't want public housing. We want low-interes money so we can buy homes" (T. George Harris, "Is the Race Probler Insoluble?" *Look* [June 27, 1967], p. 36).

The Percy bill ran into difficulties in subcommittee, but a
compromise merger in November 1967 with a bill introduced by
Senator Walter F. Mondale produced general Senate support for
the home ownership principle. This principle was then built into
the 1968 housing act through a subsidy program that would
underwrite interest rates on mortgages for low-income families
down to 1 percent, and through the establishment of a National
Home Ownership Foundation to stimulate private and public
organizations to provide home ownership opportunities for low-
income families.[72]

SOME PERSISTING QUESTIONS

There is obvious validity in these various concepts. Using the
public credit and tax policies to stimulate a much greater involvement of private industry simply extends to the poor practices
which, by and large, have worked well for the middle-income
population. Rehabilitation offers a great potential; a renovated
house may not have all of the desirable facilities of new public
housing, but it can produce fast and significant improvement over
present conditions. Many poor people can, with government help,
become owners of property and thus more inclined to take an
interest in its upkeep and enhancement.

The readiness with which these notions are accepted in
official circles is healthy evidence that the shibboleths of the past
are no longer inhibiting fresh ideas. The watchword in the Department of Housing and Urban Development today is "problem
solving." The old preoccupation with specific programs and the
interests and beliefs which accumulate around them has been
discarded. The incorporation of the Public Housing Agency into a
new Housing Assistance Administration reflects the current emphasis. The housing of the poor can only be improved, it is
suggested, if social, economic, and physical factors are viewed as
parts of an interrelated whole. Total "systems" must be used if
the problem is to be solved. Major elements in the new systems

Authorizations for the interest subsidy program (Title I, Section 235 of the
1968 act) were $300 million over three years. Authorization for the National
Home Ownership Foundation (Title I, Section 107) was $10 million.

must be private-public partnership, rehabilitation, and home ow-
ership.

This is a plausible, indeed impressive, body of reasonin
Nonetheless, there is some danger that the old misplaced hop
and dogmatisms may be replaced by new ones. The current har
empirical style is applied more trenchantly to the assessment
past programs than of new proposals.

Thus great hopes were invested in rent supplements, but th
program ran into early difficulties. Section 221(d)(3) of th
1961 housing act was hailed as a great breakthrough when it wa
inaugurated, but in its first six years, fewer than 60,000 units ha
been started under this rubric. Both of these programs, in othe
words, achieved even less in their early stages than public housir
after 1949.

All of the other proposed programs are still in the exper
mental stage, and big questions hang over them. Thus, many c
them look to nonprofit organizations of various kinds to undertak
sponsorship and management; will we discover the very larg
number of these organizations needed to assume the burdensom
responsibilities of low-cost housing development? Nor is it certai
that private companies will possess the managerial talent neede
to operate housing projects for the poor. The Johnson administra
tion believed that this was available; but the standard principle
of real estate management are not likely to be effective in copin
with the culture of poverty.[73] Home ownership is a much admire
article of faith; but there is little empirical support for the convic
tion of Senator Percy that "a man who owns his own hom
acquires a new dignity. . . . Becoming a homeowner transform
him,"[74] when that man (or husbandless mother of a large family

[73]The Kaiser Commission took note of this problem in its interim report
"The management personnel of major corporations are inexperienced in th
field of low-income housing." The commission proposed the formation c
National Housing Partnerships for the field of low- and moderate-incom
housing, which could spread risks over several ventures, offer higher rate
of return through tax advantages, and "attract top flight management an
technical experts on a competitive career basis." The recommendation wa
accepted on an experimental basis by President Johnson. (U.S. Congress
House of Representatives, *Message from the President of the United State*
Transmitting a Message on Housing and Cities, H.R. 261, 90th Cong., 2
sess., February 22, 1968, pp. 10–12.)

[74]*Congressional Record*, CXIII, Pt. 1, 90th Cong., 1st sess., April 20, 1967
No. 60, S 5640.

ıs been crippled by generations of deprivation and discrimina-
ɔn.[75] Moreover, the most ambitious of the current schemes for
ıilding or rehabilitating vast numbers of dwellings can only be
ɪrried out if new kinds of technology are fully and vigorously
•plied. It is extremely doubtful that the present housing industry
ɪn undertake this, and Glenn H. Beyer has raised the possibility
ɪhat our entire house-building industry, as it exists today, would
: found to be outmoded and in need of replacement by a few
·ge industrial firms."[76] There are indications that some of the
g corporations, with government underwriting, would be very
.erested in entering the field. However, as Beyer points out, we
ɪ still in need of "more facts and more assurance than we have
ɪay concerning the advantages of a truly mass-production ap-
ɔach and other technological advances."[77] Moreover, the labor
ɪons in the construction industry will not easily change the
ɪctices which protect the current ways of operating.[78] And local
ɪilding codes would have to be drastically revised if the new
ɪthods are to be accepted.

Another limitation of the more recent proposals is that, apart
•m rent supplements, they do not help the very poor. Section
1(d)(3) is designed for an income level above the public
ɪusing clientele. Senator Robert Kennedy's plan would have
ɔvided rentals below $100 a month—in some cases as low as
3 or even less. But the median rent in public housing in 1966
ɪs $48,[79] since people who earn less—sometimes much less—
ɪn $3000 a year cannot afford anything close to $100 a month
 shelter. Kennedy was, in fact, admittedly concerned primarily

ıarles Abrams, of course, was not unaware of these difficulties: "Let me
ɪphasize that I do not advocate home-ownership for all families" (Senate,
ɪrings, *Housing Legislation of 1967*, Pt. 1, p. 713). Senator Percy, too,
ɔgnized that many auxiliary aids would have to be provided to make
ɪe ownership feasible for low-income people (Senate, *Hearings, Housing
·islation of 1967*, Pt. 1, p. 71).

·yer, *Housing and Society*, p. 503.

·yer, *Housing and Society*, p. 504.

1969 the Alliance for Labor Action, comprising the United Auto Work-
 and the Teamsters Union, urged the mass production of prefabricated
ɪsing. The AFL-CIO building trades department, however, argued that
ɪses cannot be built on production lines.

ɪnate, *Hearings, Housing Legislation of 1967*, Pt. 1, p. 116.

with families with incomes ranging between $3500 and $6000
year. The home ownership, interest subsidy provisions of th
1968 housing acts are designed for low-income families, but n
the poorest.[80]

None of these reservations is intended to suggest that impo
tant results cannot be obtained from a larger role for priva
industry, from rehabilitation, and from home ownership. But it
important that they not become elements in a new ideology whic
obscures the reality of the problem and raises excessive expect
tions.

It is also important that they not be used to eliminate a
future role for public housing. The program has suffered fro
grave inadequacies, but many of these have been remedied sin
1960. Though there has been a great deal of inefficiency in th
conduct of the program, this will also be the case with a
combination of private and public elements in the future. Certai
ly, the jerry-built tracts which occasioned the great housing sca
dals of the early 1950s testify to the incompetence which can affe
the private industry as well as the public sector.

As Senator Edward W. Brooke has pointed out, public hou
ing is still almost the only truly low-income housing being built
Demand for public housing continues to exceed the supply, a
it is evident that the program which emerged from the 1965 a
could successfully handle a considerably larger number of units.

The 1968 housing act, in authorizing 395,000 additio
public housing units over a three-year period, was recognizi
these realities.[82] Yet, in doing so, it was running counter to t
rhetoric so popular in Congress and, for that matter, in t

[80]Senate, *Hearings, Housing Legislation of 1967*, Pt. 1, pp. 204, 328. On
other hand, Senator Mondale claimed that the Mondale-Percy comprom
proposal would bring home ownership within reach of families with
comes below $3000 (*The New Republic*, [November 11, 1967], p. 45). 80 p
cent of the funds were to go to families with incomes of not more than
percent of public housing admission limits, 20 percent to aid those with
comes less than 90 percent of 221-d-3 limits. The families reached wo
probably be in the $3500–$7000 income range.

[81]Senate, *Hearings, Housing Legislation of 1967*, Pt. 2, p. 1157.

[82]In March 1968 there were 680,000 units of low-rent public housing
operation, with another 55,000 units under construction or soon to be un
construction (Senate, *Hearings, Housing and Urban Development Legis
tion of 1968*, Pt. 1, p. 75).

ministration. That rhetoric, after all, was still expressed in
ms of the American Dream—and it would be difficult to invent
program so antithetical to the American Dream as public hous-
g. The central character in the Dream is the self-reliant individ-
l, rising from poverty to property through his own efforts. This
far different from the larger number of today's public housing
ants, living in projects built by government, trapped in pover-
depending on the public exchequer to pay part or even all of
ir rent. It is not surprising that there should be such a desper-
search for anything that will bring the poor into the main-
eam, that will make home ownership a possibility, and that will
courage private enterprise to work on the problem.

Nonetheless, it is necessary to recognize that there is a gap
tween the individualist dream and reality. For the majority of
people—themselves deeply dependent on government in
ny ways—that gap is already so wide as to strain credulity.
r the very poor, the inheritors of failure, the "underclass," the
may be, for another generation at least, unbridgeable. To
nand, therefore, that nothing be done for the poor unless it is
ught within the prevailing ideological framework may be the
st effective means of "problem solving." We can hardly be sure
t private enterprise, even if underwritten by government to the
nt at which it may be neither private nor enterprising, will be
e to deal effectively with poverty at its hard core. And home
nership may place impossible strains on people whose need is
decent shelter rather than the pride of possessing a mortgage.

No matter what the success, then, of other low-income hous-
programs, the simplest and most direct way to rehouse some
the poor will be through the low-rent public housing program.
program will continue to be something of an anomaly in the
vailing cultural climate. But, after all, the program has been
de more flexible, more in tune with the general ideology.
nversely, that ideology is becoming less rigid and may be able
encompass still another inconsistency—even something as in-
npatible as public housing.

Chapter 6
Prospects

We are still far from achieving the public policy goal set in 194□
of "a decent home and a suitable living environment for eve□
American family." From the point of view of the poor, it is ev□
questionable if any significant progress has been made in t□
direction. While the amount of bad housing appears to ha□
declined considerably since 1949, 5.8 million of the occupi□
dwelling units were classified as substandard in 1966, and millio□
more were deteriorating. Moreover, the substandard classificati□
included a very large amount of really dilapidated housing, a□
in some sections of New York, Chicago, Los Angeles, and oth□
big cities the blight appears to be spreading. Nor are these depl□
able conditions limited to metropolitan areas; many small tow□
and rural areas contain some very bad housing indeed.[1] There

[1] In 1960, urban areas of 2500 or more population contained 54.3 percent □
deteriorated and dilapidated housing, and rural areas 45.7 percent. (U□
Congress, Senate, Banking and Currency Subcommittee, *Housing Legis*□
tion of 1967, Hearings on Proposed Housing Legislation for 1967, 9□
Cong., 1st sess., Pt. 1, p. 198; hereinafter referred to as: Senate, *Hearin*□
Housing Legislation of 1967.)

ttle prospect that the problem will be eased within a reasonable
me as a result of the normal operation of the housing market.
Moreover, the situation calls not only for slum clearance; those
ho are displaced by the removal of the conditions of blight must
e provided with alternative and better housing.

The failure to accomplish this on a large enough scale ap-
ears to be one of the major causes of the violent protests that
ave been erupting in our cities. Obviously, it is not the sole
ctor. Riots break out because of the entire complex of
ievances spawned by poverty and racial discrimination. Cer-
inly, it is not the thesis of this book that, if the Taft-Ellender-
agner program had been completed on schedule, or even if
ere had been very much more public housing than the 1949 act
thorized, the riots would not have occurred. There has been a
od deal of public housing in Harlem. Newark has more public
using per capita than any other city in the country. Perhaps
ey should have had still more, but it is unlikely that this in itself
uld have prevented the violence in those communities. Howev-
, it can be concluded from this study that the attitudes that
oduced the opposition to public housing were essentially the
me as those that helped to create the conditions of revolt. As
e Kerner report makes clear, the white suburbanites and the
ivate housing organizations were instrumental in creating the
ettos. Poverty degrades the quality of life in those ghettos.
nless conditions are changed drastically, the danger of tumult
d turbulence in our central cities will persist.

The problem will have to be attacked from many directions
multaneously. Income maintenance, employment programs, job
aining, education, social services—each of these areas must
ceive much more attention than in the past. But there must also
a massive attack on bad housing.[2] Some—including the au-
or—have argued that this should include more public housing

could be argued that income measures, such as a guaranteed annual
ome or a negative income tax, would obviate the necessity of government
w-cost housing aids, since everyone would have enough money to afford
cent housing. But beneficiaries of any such program would still have dif-
ulty in paying prevailing rents for standard housing. To insure that they
uld do so would mean setting a much higher level for the guaranteed in-
me than anyone is presently proposing. Moreover, a large stock of sub-
ndard and dilapidated housing still exists and would not be disposed of
decades to come in the absence of vigorous government programs.

within the framework established by the 1965 act: that is, con struction on scattered sites rather than high-rise buildings, the fu utilization of social services, sensitive administration, and so o However, public housing alone cannot be looked to as the prin instrument in the campaign against slum conditions, and a num ber of other fiscal and administrative devices must be employe The potential for this appears to be present. A ferment of exper mentation is under way with a remarkable range of interestin proposals. We may be on the verge of significant breakthroughs technology that could drastically reduce costs and constructio time.

We should preserve a certain amount of scepticism abo some of the more extravagant claims for the new techniques a technologies. Nor should we ignore the warnings of Lewis Mur ford and others that crash, mass-production housing progran may produce an antihuman sterility calculated to produce ev further deterioration in the quality of urban life.[3] Yet, this is extraordinarily inventive country, and we are increasingly awa of human as well as technological factors in planning. It shou not be beyond our capacities to contrive intelligent and civiliz ways of offering a better living environment to the poor. T fundamental question is political rather than technical: Can o political system bring into being and then sustain the mechanisi needed to do the job?

THE GOVERNMENTAL SYSTEM

It is the view of some scholars of our governmental structu that the obstructionism of the past is rapidly disappearing. Steph K. Bailey, for years a critic of legislative procrastination, n speaks of "The New Congress,"[4] which has been invigorated presidential leadership, by a greater sophistication among membership, and by a new responsiveness to urban interests. has also been contended that reapportionment will increase Co gress' readiness to tackle city problems with a sense of urgency.

[3]Louise Campbell, "Hearings: The Machine vs. Mr. Mumford," *City,* I (1967), 7–11.

[4]Stephen K. Bailey, *The New Congress* (New York: St. Martin's Pr Inc., 1966).

Certainly there is evidence to support this analysis. The passage of strong open-housing legislation by the 90th Congress surprised most Washington observers. And Bailey's position gains credibility from the impressive scope of the 1968 Housing and Urban Development Act.[5] For this included authorization not only for a substantial increase in the public housing program, but also for new interest subsidy programs for both owners and renters with low incomes, as well as $1.4 billion for urban renewal and $1 billion for model cities in 1970.

Yet, from the vantage point of the poor, the case is not yet proven. The grudging treatment of the antipoverty program and the painfully slow introduction of rent supplements contradict the notion of a radical break with the past.[6] Moreover, the appropriations for some of the key provisions of the 1968 Housing and Urban Development Act fell considerably short of the authorizations. Appropriations for payments under the new home-ownership and rental housing programs were reduced from $11.5 million to $7 million; and the authorization ceiling for each program was cut from $75 million to $25 million. Funds for the National Home Ownership Foundation were completely eliminated from the 1968–1969 budget.[7] And while the Model Cities program received a large increase over the previous year, the amount appropriated was $625 million instead of the $1 billion authorized. Thus the schedule set in the 1968 act has already slipped. Evidently it is still premature to assume that Congress is eager to underwrite urban enterprises on a really ambitious scale.

Public Law 90-448. (Title XVI) The act established a goal of 26 million housing units for the ten-year period from 1969 to 1978; including six million units for low- and moderate-income families. Authorizations to achieve the housing goal were made for three years and comprised $1.2 billion of the act's total authorizations of more than $5.3 billion.

Several Northern, suburban Republican congressmen did vote for the OEO authorization of $1.6 billion in the House in 1967. This may represent a significant shift from earlier Republican attitudes. Still, the amount approved was the same amount as had been appropriated the previous year. Moreover, a considerable number of suburban congressmen voted against antipoverty, Model Cities, rat control, and rent-supplement funds.

A $15 million authorization for grants for tenant services in public housing was also left without appropriations for 1968–1969. And funds to administer the fair housing title of the 1968 Civil Rights Act were reduced from $8 million to $2 million.

It remains the case, in other words, that Congress will only endorse fast and drastic action on behalf of the urban poor if the basic political forces in the country are overwhelmingly favorable to such action.

MONEY

"Do we know," Secretary Weaver has asked, "how to spend 20 times the amount we are now spending? I doubt it. I think we have to get both more money and more know-how."[8] Still, a very large increase in government spending is clearly a requirement if more housing is to be provided for the poor. There are many estimates of how much is needed. After his extensive hearings on urban problems, Senator Ribicoff came to the conclusion that to replace or remodel the 4½ million substandard units of urban housing would cost $50 billion over a period of ten years.[9]

The Kerner Commission's recommendations carried no cost estimates, but called for the provision of 6 million low- and moderate-income housing units over a five-year period. The Johnson administration, as we have noted, accepted the figure of six million units, but proposed a ten-year schedule, with 2.35 million units to be completed in the first five years requiring an outlay of $2.34 billion.[10] In addition, the urban renewal and model cities programs, while not exclusively concerned with low-cost housing, should, if properly conceived, improve immeasurably the living environment of the poor. When these and other programs are taken into account, it is evident that federal expenditures of a least $2 to $3 billion a year for a considerable period will be required. Is this kind of money likely to be available?

[8]Senate, *Hearings, Housing Legislation of 1967,* Pt. 1, p. 68.

[9]For the central cities alone the figure would be $27 billion (*Congressional Record,* CXIII, No. 8, 90th Cong., 1st sess., January 23, 1967, S714). Senator Ribicoff is dealing only with the urban areas. The 1960 Census indicated that a national total of 8.5 million units were substandard, and another four million needed a significant degree of repair or renovation.

[10]U.S. Congress, House of Representatives, *Message from the President of the United States Transmitting a Message on Housing and Cities,* H. R. 261 90th Cong., 2d sess., February 22, 1968, p. 4; and U.S. Congress, Senate Banking and Currency Subcommittee, *Housing and Urban Development Legislation of 1968, Hearings, on Proposed Housing Legislation for 1968* 90th Cong., 2d sess., 1968, Pt. 1, pp. 66–76.

Certainly America is rich enough. The Gross National Product has now moved beyond $900 billion. However, as long as Vietnam and higher taxes continue, it is unlikely that new programs for the poor will be adequately funded. The War on Poverty, after all, was launched soon after a federal income tax cut. It was an opportunity for the majority to be compassionate at no discernible cost. That opportunity is not now available and will not be until the Vietnam war is over. When that happens, and if defense spending is cut sharply, it may be necessary to inaugurate extensive increases in federal spending to prevent a recession. Housing programs could constitute a very convenient field for such spending and offer the advantage of bringing jobs into the ghettos. Furthermore, the Gross National Product will continue to rise: the Joint Economic Committee of Congress has predicted a GNP of $1350 billion by 1975. From $3 to $5 billion (or only an additional half a billion dollars a year if we limit our consideration to public housing, rent supplements, and the new home-ownership programs) would not appear so formidable if the economy were producing well over a trillion dollars a year and there were no major war to drain our resources.

This happy prospect is not assured, however. After Vietnam there will be great pressure to maintain the $80 billion a year defense budget in order to rebuild defense inventories depleted by the Vietnam war and to develop new weapons technologies.[11] Even if defense outlays are cut, greatly increased spending on behalf of the poor is not inevitable. Tax cuts, tax sharing with the states, spending on programs closer to the heart of groups more powerful than the poor (highways, urban renewal, water desalinization, space exploration, and so on) all will be making demands which Administration and Congress will find it difficult to resist. Indeed, in January of 1969, the new Secretary of Housing and Urban Development, George Romney, was already complaining that, given the enormous pressures on the economy, the Johnson administration had been too lavish in its housing plans. "We can't quarrel

In hearings before a joint economic subcommittee of Congress in June 1969, administration officials from the Kennedy-Johnson era noted that there were no effective mechanisms for comparing domestic and military priorities. Thus neither the White House nor the Budget Bureau tried to determine carefully whether the national security and welfare would be better served by building a new aircraft carrier or its monetary equivalent, ,000 low-cost housing units.

with the goals in terms of the need," he said. But, he insisted, "
think the promises have been big, big, big and far beyond th
resources."[12]

Undoubtedly, the continued growth of the economy, com
bined with peace abroad, would improve the chances of obtainin
larger amounts of money to ameliorate the lot of the poor. Bu
there can be no guarantee of the kind of increase needed t
eliminate substandard housing without a significant enhancemen
of the effectiveness of the poor in the total political system.

THE POLITICAL INVOLVEMENT OF THE POOR

If the poor are silent and uninvolved, as they have been tradition
ally, they will not be catered to. Unorganized, inarticulate consti
uencies fare badly in the American political system. This, as w
have seen, contributed to many of the weaknesses in the publ
housing program. It held down its size and built serious defec
into its very fabric. In the communities the controversies rage
around and over the heads of the poor, rarely involving the
directly. Public housing was not an integral part of the loc
structures of power. But then, neither were the poor. Simil
difficulties at the local level have been encountered by oth
antipoverty programs, such as the OEO community action pro
ects. As was the case with public housing, such projects cann
avoid being subjected to the test of community approval. Th
approval will be difficult to obtain until the poor can establi
themselves as an effective force in local politics, with an organiz
tional base that commands respect in place of the prevailin
disdain.

Evidently this necessary condition is beginning to emerg
Primarily because of the Negro movement, the poor are beginni
to stir from their apathy. The War on Poverty is both a result an
a cause of the development of activism among the poor. Th
activism takes many forms: participation in community acti
boards, demonstrations, litigation, and, when the awakened e
pectations cannot be contained by other methods, rebellions.

The potential of an awakened movement of the poor grov
exhilarating to its leadership. Some among them believe th
their strength is so great that they can proceed without alli

[12]*Los Angeles Times,* January 26, 1969, Sec. A, p. 2.

Most of them recognize that the transformation of the ghetto can only come if the federal government provides a vast infusion of new funds. But they believe that the power which comes from controlling the vital center of the cities is sufficient, if properly employed, to force the concessions that they demand.

It is conceivable that this could work, that the majority will become so afraid, or so inconvenienced, that they will buy tranquillity by providing the funds and resources necessary to rebuild the ghettos. Indeed, there is little question but that the riots have directly inspired the current outpouring of bold proposals for transforming the central cities. Beyond a point, however, the strategy of hostile confrontation is unlikely to be productive. If fear becomes the dominant motif among the majority, the response is less likely to be conciliation than vindictiveness. And the majority have not only the advantage of numbers, but also affluence, technological and organizational superiority, and the support of police and army.

This suggests that if the poor stand alone, they are unlikely to achieve their goals. Having established their own sense of identity and purpose, they must, in the perennial fashion of political movements in America, seek allies. Where are these allies to be found?[13]

It will not suffice, as some leaders of the radical left have argued, to build a coalition of the poor. For one thing the poor—no matter how broadly defined—constitute not only a minority, but also a diminishing minority. There has been a significant reduction in recent years in the proportion of the population below the poverty line. One official estimate indicates a decline from 24 percent of the total population in 1959 to 19 percent in 1965, with further substantial reductions since. Herman Miller and others believe that this trend will continue, and that there are good prospects for a virtual solution to the problem within a generation—with the exception of the Negro.

Moreover, within this dwindling minority there are few beyond the militant members of the black community who are likely to engage in a sustained, organized effort to advance their interests as a class. For all the recent activity among the poor, they are still the least politically effective segment of the population.

Hence the necessary coalition will have to include people who have direct access to the decision-making process nationally, as well as in the communities. It is difficult for the militant leaders of the poor to accept this, for in the coalitions of the past the minority groups and the poor were dominated by articulate, experienced, and affluent liberals. However, given the growing maturity and self-confidence of the new leadership of the poor, they should be in a position to avoid being subordinate members of future coalitions.

ELEMENTS OF A NEW COALITION

The liberal and "public interest" groups who have always fought for the poor can still be relied upon for support in the future. Some of them will be resentful of having their preeminence in the reform movement challenged by younger militants. But, in the last analysis, the traditional aggregation of church, welfare, labor, minority group, civic, professional and political leaders will work for the cause of low-cost housing.

However, these will not be enough. They were not able to provide the sustained sources of strength needed by public housing, and the ambitious programs of the future must be backed by powerful men and groups whose interests are directly served by those programs.

These will include, in the first place, a new generation of urban-oriented, national politicians. It is significant that Robert Kennedy and Charles Percy should both have selected low-cost housing as an issue on which to build their claims to national attention. It was an attractive issue for them because it enabled them to project themselves as men of fresh vision, energy, and compassion. In their talk of harnessing science and technology for a major onslaught on the problem, they appealed to a technologically oriented society. By emphasizing the role of private enterprise, they neutralized the fears that they were challenging the fundamentals of the system. In working for the central cities they garnered votes of critical importance in Presidential campaign strategies.

Next there are the growing numbers of local political and business leaders who are concerned about the decline of the central cities. They are disturbed by the threat to the stability of their communities posed by actual or potential riots. They are unwilling to write off the enormous investment in civic, cultural and business facilities that has been made in the downtown areas. Their concern is not yet widely shared among the populace of the suburbs. Still, as decision makers and opinion leaders move more actively to halt the deterioration within the core cities, suburban apathy or hostility may be changed into at least grudging acquiescence. The local leaders know that they cannot bring about the transformation of the central cities with local resources alone and that consequently they must have help from the federal government. And, as grants are requested and approved for urban enewal,[14] Model Cities, and so on, the pressure for yet more ederal support will grow. Mayors and city officials, as well as ocal business, labor, and civic leaders will be increasingly heard rom in Washington on this issue.

Finally, there is prospective support from industry. It is true hat Chapter 5 expressed some concern that excessive hopes night have been raised about the capabilities of private industry o provide housing for the poor, and it was suggested that the free nterprise rhetoric being used by Democratic as well as Republi-:an leaders tended to undermine the role of public housing. In >olitical terms, however, there are important practical advantages o be gained from a greater emphasis on private industry. When a eader of the National Association of Home Builders is the con- ractor for one of the first turnkey projects, his organization is ikely to discover new virtues in public housing.[15] The right to ease or buy existing housing gives local housing authorities un- •recedented opportunities to make friends among landlords, small >roperty owners and realtors, especially in periods when the 10using market is depressed. Rent supplements, too, will encour- •ge more business support for low-cost housing.

Of much greater significance politically is the prospect of >ringing big corporations into the field. Already the pledge of $1 >illion in mortgage funds from the life insurance industry has .tepped up the pressure on Congress to provide the rent supple- nents that would put this money to work for the poor. Then there ire the possibilities suggested by the involvement of the big ndustrial corporations. In the fields of defense and aerospace, •ompanies have been able to use their sponsorship by the federal ;overnment to exert immense influence on government for their >wn preservation and enlargement. If some of these same corpo- ations were given large contracts by government to produce or ehabilitate low-priced housing, the cause of the poor might be ;iven some very persuasive advocates in Washington.[16]

'HUD officials have indicated that there will be more emphasis in future ırban-renewal programs on low-cost housing.

'Senate, *Hearings, Housing Legislation of 1967,* Pt. 2, p. 1135.

'The interest of private corporations is seeking government contracts for he solution of social problems has already given rise to talk about a "social- ıdustrial complex." Michael Harrington sees this as an ominous prospect,

It would be naïve to suggest that consensus is about to replace conflict in this field. The bitterness that pervades the black movement and the conservatism of the white suburbanites make continued unrest and friction inevitable. Nonetheless, if the business and political elements mentioned do, in fact, develop a vested interest in the provision of housing for the poor, this could help replace the politics of confrontation with the politics of coalition.[17]

HOUSING AND THE AMERICAN SYSTEM

As we look back on the struggle over public housing in the 1950s the effect is somewhat crude and primitive and absurd. The unreasoning hostilities, the harsh slogan, "Do You Want To Pay Somebody Else's Rent?" at the heart of the opposition's case, the prejudice and status fears, the irrelevant ideologies, the tedious repetitiveness of argument and maneuver, the inertia of the legislative process and the inflexibility of bureaucracies—all add up to

---

for he believes that business methods and priorities, even when sincerely and honestly applied, are at cross-purposes with social needs. He insists that "new institutions of democratic planning" must be built to get the job done *(Harper's Magazine* [November 1967], pp. 58, 60). Undoubtedly Harrington points to a real danger. However, corporation-government collaboration offers a prospect of action in the foreseeable future; and if the kind of action is questionable, it may still be preferable to waiting for the "new institutions of democratic planning" that are unlikely to eventuate in America for some time to come.

[17]The Urban Coalition is designed to serve precisely this purpose. The coalition comprises some of the top leaders of business, finance, labor, city government and minority groups, and operates both nationally and in a number of cities. It has called for a massive attack on poverty in the cities including the provision of 1,000,000 housing units a year. The setting of such a high target figure for housing inevitably provokes the charge that this is a pious, grandiose proposal that is not based on realistic possibilities. After all, total national housing production has been generally below 1,500,000 units a year.

Nonetheless, in the past the unrealistic demands came from housing officials and welfare and labor groups. Now the names of David Rockefeller and Henry Ford II and other business leaders are associated with the more extravagant proposals, so that it is not as easy to dismiss the demands as the product of impractical visionaries.

one of the least attractive episodes in the American political experience. True, it was not entirely wasted. A number of people of very low income moved out of dreadful slum conditions into soundly built housing equipped with the necessary contemporary amenities. The public housing program, as it emerged after the sound and the fury, was much improved by the traumatic encounter, and several other promising programs are evolving. Yet, if the outcome was acceptable to the majority of the people—as it probably was—it left a significant minority still living in conditions that constitute a national disgrace.

Perhaps in the circumstances of the time we could not have expected more. We were already a rich people, but not yet rich enough. We were urbanized, but still thinking about our rural and small-town past. Our technology was unparalleled, but the breakthroughs in the housing field were still some way off. Now there is the prospect that these obstacles will be removed. We are on the threshold of true economic abundance, of commitment to urbanism, of technological mastery.

Other obstacles, however, persist. The cautious pace of the legislative process, the vulnerability of the system to obstructive groups, the general mistrust of government action, the reluctance to approve the spending of large amounts of tax monies, racial antagonisms, the disdain of the majority for the poor—none of these has been eliminated. It is still possible that one or more of these difficulties will prevent our dealing effectively with the housing problem of the poor. If this should prove to be the case, if at the end of yet another decade millions of people continue to live without hope amidst dilapidation and decay, it would constitute a most profound and dangerous failure of the American political system.

Select Bibliography

This bibliography does not attempt to encompass the enormous literature on housing, urban problems, poverty, government, and politics in America which relate to this study. I am listing here only those written sources most directly pertinent to the concept developed in this book. A large number of additional references are to be found in the footnotes.

GOVERNMENT PUBLICATIONS

For reasons of space the various hearings and reports on housing legislation by the Banking and Currency Committees of the Senate and House of Representatives from 1945 through 1968 are not listed here. The most significant of these, however, have been cited in footnotes throughout the book, as was also done with the congressional debates on housing reproduced in the *Congressional Record*.

Unless otherwise stated, the government documents noted below have been published by the Government Printing Office in Washington, D.C.

U.S. Commission on Civil Rights. *Report,* 1959.

Housing Report, Book 4, 1961.

U.S. Congress, House of Representatives, Select Committee on Lobbying Activities. *Housing Lobby, Hearings Pursuant to H. Res. 298,* 81st Cong., 2d sess., 1950.

————. *General Interim Report on H.R. Rept. 3138,* 81st Cong., 2d sess., 1950.

————. *United States Savings and Loan League, H.R. Rept. 3139,* Pursuant to H. Res. 298, 81st Cong., 2d sess., 1950.

U.S. Congress, Senate, Government Operations Subcommittee. *Federal Role in Urban Affairs, Hearings,* 89th Cong., 2d sess., 1966.

U.S. Department of Health, Education, and Welfare, Social Security Administration, Division of Research Statistics. *Slums and Social Insecurity,* by Alvin L. Schorr, Research Report no. 1 (1963).

————, and U.S. Housing and Home Finance Agency. *Services for Families Living in Public Housing* (1963).

U.S. Department of Labor and U.S. Department of Commerce, Bureau of Labor Statistics and Bureau of the Census. *Social and Economic Conditions of Negroes in the United States,* BLS Report no. 332, Current Population Reports, Series P-23, no. 24 (October 1967).

U.S. Housing and Home Finance Agency. Annual Reports from 1947.

————. *Our Nonwhite Population and Its Housing* (July 1963).

————. *A Study of Housing Programs and Policies,* by Ernest M. Fisher (January 1960).

————, Public Housing Administration. *Selected Aspects of Administration of Publicly Owned Housing,* by Abner D. Silverman (January 1, 1961).

————. *Low Rent Public Housing:* The United States Housing Act of 1937 as amended through October 15, 1964 (1964).

U.S. National Advisory Commission on Civil Disorders. *Report of the National Advisory Commission on Civil Disorders* (New York: Bantam Books, Inc. 1968).

U.S. President's Advisory Committee on Government Housing Policies and Programs. *Recommendations on Government Housing Policies and Programs* (1953).

BOOKS, ARTICLES, DISSERTATIONS, PAMPHLETS

Abrams, Charles. *The Future of Housing* (New York: Harper & Row, Publishers, 1946).

———. "Public Housing Myths," *The New Leader* (July 25, 1955), pp. 3–6.

———. "Rats Among the Palm Trees," *The Nation* (February 25, 1950), pp. 177–178.

———. "Slums, Ghettos and The G.O.P.'s 'Remedy,'" *The Reporter* (May 11, 1954), pp. 27–30.

Anderson, Martin. *The Federal Bulldozer: A Critical Analysis of Urban Renewal* (Cambridge, Mass.: The M.I.T. Press, 1965).

Baisden, Richard Norman. "Labor Unions in Los Angeles Politics," unpublished Ph.D. dissertation, Department of Political Science, University of Chicago, 1958.

Baldwin, James. *Nobody Knows My Name* (New York: The Dial Press, Inc., 1961).

Bauer, Catherine. "The Dreary Deadlock of Public Housing," *Architectural Forum,* CVI (May 1957), 140–142, 219, 221.

Bellush, Jewel, and Murray Hausknecht., eds. *Urban Renewal: People, Politics, and Planning (New York: Doubleday-Anchor, 1967).*

Beyer, Glenn H. *Housing and Society* (New York: Crowell-Collier and Macmillan, Inc., 1965).

Bouma, Donald H. "The Social Power Position of a Real Estate Board," Supplemented paper delivered at the Sociology Section, Annual Meeting, Michigan Academy of Science, Arts, and Letters, Wayne State University, March 24, 1961.

Brown, Robert K. *Public Housing in Action: The Record of Pittsburgh* (Ann Arbor, Mich.: University of Pittsburgh Press, 1959).

Bryant, Drayton S. "The Next Twenty Years in Public Housing," *Social Work,* IV, no. 2 (April 1959), 46–54.

Clark, Kenneth. *Dark Ghetto: Dilemmas of Social Power* (New York: Harper & Row, Publishers, 1965).

Coffin, Tris. "The Slickest Lobby," *The Nation* (March 23, 1946), pp. 340–342.

Congressional Quarterly. *Housing a Nation* (Washington, D.C.: Congressional Quarterly Service, 1966).

Conn, Harry. "Housing: A Vanishing Vision," *The New Republic* (July 16, 1951), pp. 12–14; (July 23, 1951), pp. 10–12; (July 30, 1951), pp. 12–13; (August 13, 1951), pp. 15–16.

Davies, Richard O. *Housing Reform During the Truman Administration* (Columbia, Mo.: University of Missouri Press, 1966).

Dean, John P. "The Myths of Housing Reform," *American Sociological Review,* XIV, no. 2 (April 1949), 281–288.

Deutsch, Morton, and Mary Evans Collins. *Interracial Housing* (Minneapolis: University of Minnesota Press, 1951).

Eckardt, Wolf von. "Black Neck in the White Noose," *The New Republic* (October 19, 1963), pp. 14–17.

Fisher, Robert Moore. *20 Years of Public Housing—Economic Aspects of the Federal Program* (New York: Harper & Row, Publishers, 1959).

Friedman, Lawrence M. *Government and Slum Housing* (Chicago: Rand McNally & Company, 1968).

———. "Public Housing and the Poor: An Overview," *California Law Review,* LIV (May 1966), 642–669.

Friedman, Rose D. *Poverty: Definition and Perspective* (Washington, D.C.: American Enterprise Institute for Public Policy Research, 1965).

Frost, Richard T., and Janet McLennan. "The Northwest Tower Dispute," Rocco J. Tressolini and Richard T. Frost, eds. *Cases in American National Government and Politics* (Englewood Cliffs, N.J.: Prentice-Hall, Inc., 1966), pp. 216–226.

Glazer, Nathan. "Housing Problems and Housing Policies," *The Public Interest,* no. 7 (Spring 1967), pp. 21–51.

Harrington, Michael. *The Other America* (Baltimore: Penguin Books, Inc. 1962).

Hartman, Chester. "The Limitations of Public Housing," *Journal of the American Institute of Planners,* XXIX, no. 4 (November 1963), 283–296.

Hill, Herbert. "Demographic Change and Racial Ghettos: The Crisis of American Cities," *Journal of Urban Law 231,* XLIV (Winter 1966), 231–285.

Kaplan, Harold. *Urban Renewal Politics: Slum Clearance in Newark* (New York: Columbia University Press, 1963).

Lewis, Oscar. *La Vida* (New York: Random House, Inc., 1966).

McDonnell, Timothy L. *The Wagner Housing Act* (Chicago: Loyola University Press, 1957).

McEntire, Weldon Davis. *Residence and Race* (Berkeley, Calif.: University of California Press, 1960).

McGuire, Marie C. *Newsletter.* Washington, D.C.: Housing and Home Finance Agency, Public Housing Administration October 30, 1961 (Mimeographed).

Mayer, Albert. "Public Housing Architecture," *Journal of Housing,* XIX, no. 8 (1962), 446–456.

———. "Public Housing as Community," *Architectural Record* (April 1964), pp. 169–178.

Meyerson, Martin, and Edward C. Banfield. *Politics, Planning, and the Public Interest* (New York: The Free Press, 1955).

Meyerson, Martin, Barbara Terrett, and William L.C. Wheaton. *Housing, People, and Cities* (New York: McGraw-Hill, Inc., 1962).

Miller, Herman. *Poverty American Style* (Belmont, Calif.: Wadsworth, 1966).

National Association of Home Builders. "Home Builders' Information Material to Oppose Socialized Public Housing" (Mimeographed kit of materials).

———. "American Home Ownership vs. Public Housing" (Washington, D.C., n.d.).

National Association of Housing and Redevelopment Officials. *Critical Urban Housing Issues: 1967* (Washington, D.C.: National Association of Housing and Redevelopment Officials, December 1967).

———. *Journal of Housing* (Washington, D.C.: National Association of Housing and Redevelopment Officials, 1944 to present, a monthly publication).

National Association of Real Estate Boards. *Realtor's Headlines,* a weekly newsletter (Washington, D.C.: National Association of Real Estate Boards).

————. "Some Examples of Successful Opposition to Socialized Public Housing," 1965 (Mimeographed).

National Community Relations Advisory Council. *Equality of Opportunity in Housing* (New York: National Community Relations Advisory Council, June 1952).

The National Housing Conference. *The Housing Yearbook* (Washington, D.C.: The National Housing Conference).

Piven, Frances Fox, and Richard A. Cloward. "Desegregated Housing: Who Pays for the Reformers' Ideal?" *The New Republic* (December 17, 1966), pp. 17–22.

Rainwater, Lee. "Poverty and Deprivation in the Crisis of the American City," a statement presented to U.S. Congress, Senate Subcommittee on Executive Reorganization. Occasional Paper No. 9 (Washington, D.C. December 6, 1966) (Mimeographed).

Realtors' Washington Committee. "Federal Expenditures and Commitments Under Public Housing Act" (Washington, D.C.: July 20, 1949) (Mimeographed).

Ridgeway, James. "Rebuilding the Slums," *The New Republic* (January 7, 1967), pp. 22–25.

Roshco, Bernard. "The Integration Problem and Public Housing," *The New Leader* (July 4–11, 1960), pp. 10–13.

Salisbury, Harrison. *The Shook-Up Generation* (New York: Harper & Row, Publishers, 1958).

Schriftgiesser, Karl. *The Lobbyists* (Boston: Little, Brown, 1951).

Silverman, Abner D. "Low-Rent Housing Program in an Era of Social Change," an address at the annual meeting of the Carolinas Council of Housing and Redevelopment Officials. Asheville, North Carolina (October 7, 1965) (Mimeographed).

Stewart, Charles T. "Public Housing—Wrong Way Program," *U.S.A.—The Magazine of American Affairs,* I, no. 4 (June 1952), 91–98.

Straus, Nathan. *The Seven Myths of Housing* (New York: Alfred A. Knopf, Inc., 1944).

————. *Two-Thirds of a Nation* (New York: Alfred A. Knopf, Inc., 1952).

Taper, Bernard. "A Lover of Cities," *The New Yorker* (February 4, 1967), pp. 39–91; (February 11, 1967), pp. 45–115.

Tyler, Poyatz, ed. *City and Suburban Housing*, The Reference

Shelf, XXIX, no. 26 (New York: The H. Wilson Company, 1957), 61–64.

Vinton, Warren Jay. "Representative Smith's Roadblock," *The Housing Yearbook, 1959* (Washington, D.C.: The National Housing Conference, 1959), pp. 13–16.

Wendt, Paul F. *The Role of the Federal Government in Housing* (Washington, D.C.: American Enterprise Association, 1956).

Wilkinson, Frank. "And Now the Bill Comes Due," *Frontier* (October 1965), pp. 10–12.

Worshop, Richard L. *Public Housing in War on Poverty* (Washington, D.C.: Editorial Research Reports, July 22, 1964).

Index